Just React!

Learn React the React Way

Hari Narayn

Apress®

Just React!: Learn React the React Way

Hari Narayn
Melbourne, VIC, Australia

ISBN-13 (pbk): 978-1-4842-8293-9   ISBN-13 (electronic): 978-1-4842-8294-6
https://doi.org/10.1007/978-1-4842-8294-6

Managing Director, Apress Media LLC: Welmoed Spahr
Acquisitions Editor: Aditee Mirashi
Development Editor: James Markham
Coordinating Editor: Aditee Mirashi

Cover designed by eStudioCalamar

Cover image designed by Freepik (www.freepik.com)

Distributed to the book trade worldwide by Springer Science+Business Media New York, 1 New York Plaza, Suite 4600, New York, NY 10004-1562, USA. Phone 1-800-SPRINGER, fax (201) 348-4505, e-mail orders-ny@ springer-sbm.com, or visit www.springeronline.com. Apress Media, LLC is a California LLC and the sole member (owner) is Springer Science + Business Media Finance Inc (SSBM Finance Inc). SSBM Finance Inc is a **Delaware** corporation.

For information on translations, please e-mail booktranslations@springernature.com; for reprint, paperback, or audio rights, please e-mail bookpermissions@springernature.com.

Apress titles may be purchased in bulk for academic, corporate, or promotional use. eBook versions and licenses are also available for most titles. For more information, reference our Print and eBook Bulk Sales web page at http://www.apress.com/bulk-sales.

Any source code or other supplementary material referenced by the author in this book is available to readers on GitHub via the book's product page, located at https://github.com/Apress/Just-React. For more detailed information, please visit http://www.apress.com/source-code.

Printed on acid-free paper

Dedicated to my precious daughter, Ithal,
and all her hilarious reactions

Table of Contents

About the Author ix

About the Technical Reviewer xi

Acknowledgments xiii

Introduction xv

Chapter 1: Time to React 1

Think (HTML and JavaScript) Before You React 1

How React Reacts Compared with JavaScript 7

React vs. Angular 13

Where to React? 13

Summary 16

Chapter 2: JavaScript Before You React 17

Get Started 17

Variables 20

Reference Types 23

Conditionals and Loops 27

Functions 29

Events 33

Arrow Functions 34

Modules 38

Subclassing 41

Async/await 43

Template Literals 48

Summary 50

Chapter 3: Start Reacting **51**

Set Up an Environment to "React" 51

How to React? 52

create-react-app 66

Introduction to Components 70

JSX 71

Reacting to Inputs 72

Styling Your Component 75

State in React 77

Virtual DOM 82

Props 85

Just React to Child 90

Props and State 96

React on a Condition 97

Summary 101

Chapter 4: Think React **103**

VS Code Extensions 103

Restructuring the React Form 104

Combining Reactions 116

Sibling Reactions 122

Component Chat Continues… 127

Reacting to Edits 135

More Reactions to the Parent 142

Summary 146

Chapter 5: Rethink React **149**

React Lazy and Suspense 150

Props Drilling Issue 154

Multi-view React App 161

React Context 185

Summary 189

Chapter 6: React to Bugs **191**

Chrome Reacts 191

Don't React, Debug First 195

Console Reactions 197

React to Errors 200

React Developer Tools 205

React to Bugs Within VS Code 209

Summary 214

Chapter 7: Reacting in Style **215**

CSS-in-JS 216

Styled Components 217

CSS 219

Sassy CSS (SCSS) 222

CSS Modules 226

CodeSandbox 231

Material UI 233

Responsive React 234

Summary 241

Chapter 8: Hook into React **243**

Life of a Class 243

Life of a Function and the Birth of Hooks 250

useState 253

useEffect 256

useRef 262

useReducer 266

useContext 273

Remember to React.. 278

useMemo.. 285

useCallback... 289

Few More "Hookies" 294

Custom "Hookies" 295

Summary.. 298

Chapter 9: React Back **299**

React to Routes.. 299

Manage Access Before We React.. 304

HTTP Reactions 330

Redux 334

Summary.. 341

Chapter 10: New Reactions **343**

New Root and the New Way to Render.. 343

React Concurrently... 346

React Slowly for Faster Response... 347

Server on Suspense 351

Automatic Batching.. 354

"Too Strict" Mode... 359

New "Hookies" 360

Summary.. 361

Index.. **363**

About the Author

 **Hari Narayn** is a passionate techie with 12 years of experience in architecting and building web and mobile applications. He has worked with React, Microsoft 365, SharePoint, Azure, Teams, Power Platform, .Net, Angular, and JavaScript (JS). He has built web and mobile solutions for various clients across the world. He is a Microsoft Certified Power Platform Solutions Architect, Microsoft Certified M365 Developer Associate, and a Microsoft Certified Azure Solutions Architect Expert. He is also the author of the Apress book 'Building the Modern Workplace with SharePoint Online.' He is a native of Kerala, India, and is currently based in Melbourne, Victoria, Australia. He works as a senior technical specialist in the Victorian Public Service.

About the Technical Reviewer

Frank W. Zammetti is a lead architect/developer for one of the largest financial firms in the world by day and an author/musician/techie/husband/father by night. He is the author of 13 books for Apress on various topics in software development, as well as several independent articles for various publications. He has served as a technical reviewer on several other books and has been a speaker at various technical conferences and meetups. Frank is a contributor to several open source projects and founder of a few as well. In addition to technical writing, his first novel, *The Darkness Beyond the Light*, is now available for free online. And if all that isn't enough, Frank is also exceptionally good at finding the corner of furniture with his toes in the middle of the night. Like, seriously, why does this keep happening to Frank?!

Acknowledgments

First, I'd like to say thanks to my wonderful wife, Divya, for keeping me motivated and helping me through this writing process. Without her constant support, this book would not have been possible. Thanks to my adorable daughter, Ithal, for all her cute interruptions. Thanks to my mom for her endless support and care.

I'd like to thank my coordinating editor, Aditee Mirashi, for making my job easy by providing continuous support. My sincere thanks go out to the development editor, James Markham, the production editor Dulcy Chellappa, the production coordinator Krishnan R S, and the entire team at Apress and Springer Nature who worked on this book.

Frank W. Zammetti, the technical reviewer, deserves a big thank you for reviewing this book with such care and expertise. I was fortunate to have Frank review this book.

Introduction

React is a JavaScript library for building user interfaces in a simple and efficient way. We stay close to this concept of React in this book. Basically, this book explains React in its simplest form. It's designed to be digestible, with straightforward examples so that you can learn React by mastering it slowly. Using the most recommended and latest techniques, this book will teach you how to design React components the React way.

We'll begin by gaining a basic understanding of the Web. Then we'll see how React fits into the picture. The second chapter goes over modern JavaScript concepts to make sure you're padded for learning React.

Reacting starts in Chapter 3, and we'll talk about the ingredients behind React and make sure the basics are sound. During this chapter, you will learn about components, JSX, props, state, the Virtual Document Object Model (DOM), conditional rendering, and building a React app.

Chapter 4 shifts our attention to thinking in the React way and how to design React components. You will learn more about component design and interaction. You will see how a parent component interacts with a child and how sibling components interact. Based on all these concepts, you will build a multicomponent app. In Chapter 5, the book asks you to rethink. You will learn about potential design flaws in React and learn how to tackle them. Then, you will build a multi-view React app and learn about React Context.

As we move forward into Chapter 6, we will examine different ways to debug React apps. The Chrome DevTools, Visual Studio (VS) Code tools, and React DevTools will be discussed in depth. Throughout Chapter 7, you will learn how to style React apps. We will discuss SCSS, Cascading Style Sheets (CSS) modules, etc.

Hooks await you in Chapter 8. Here, we will explore the component lifecycle in detail. Each React Hook will be explained with examples. When you finish this chapter, I promise you'll be a Hook master. The penultimate chapter will look at how React interacts with backend services. It will cover routing, API communication, authentication, and Redux. After discussing the impressive features of React 18 in the final chapter, we will draw a conclusion.

While reading this book, if you have any questions, you can contact me by leaving a comment at Just React Q&A (`https://jrhn22.wordpress.com`).

In terms of career opportunities, React is certainly one of the most in demand technology. According to most surveys, React is the most popular web framework/library in 2022. So what are you waiting for? Let us *Just React!* and enjoy this responsive ride with "React" together! Enjoy the read! Enjoy the learning! Just enjoy React!

CHAPTER 1

Time to React

As you browse the Web regularly, do you consider how reactive it is? How does it respond to you? Do you get reactions without refreshing your page? React is a JavaScript library that focuses on these reactions. This may explain its name, "React."

In React, you can build individual user interface (UI) components. The concept of components is central to React. A component is a JavaScript class or function that can accept inputs and output a React element that describes how a section of the UI should appear. All the components you build together can make a complex UI. React renders this UI. We will discuss components throughout this book. This chapter will provide a solid foundation on the concept of the Web and how React fits in. By the end of this chapter, you will learn what React is, where you can use it, and the advantages of using it.

Think (HTML and JavaScript) Before You React

Before we get started with React, let's look at how HyperText Markup Language (HTML) and JavaScript (JS) work together. HTML, Cascading Style Sheets (CSS), and JS are the three technologies that make up a web page. HTML forms the structure of the web page. CSS focuses on appearance. JS enables the interactions between the user and the page. If we take an example of a Facebook post, the Like button you see is made of HTML with CSS. When you click "Like," it updates your like. Here you received a response from the web page. JS is the crazy guy behind the scenes who looked at your click and let you know that you already clicked this, by changing the "Like" icon to blue.

I will show you how HTML and JS work together in the client browser using Google Chrome as the browser. When you learn React, we will build on top of this basics. This is to ensure that you understand the basics well and how React works internally before you learn it's features. This will help you make the right decisions while developing a React application.

© Hari Narayn 2022
H. Narayn, *Just React!*, https://doi.org/10.1007/978-1-4842-8294-6_1

First, let's examine what HTML is. HTML is a language used to define the structure of content. It comprises a set of codes in a text file called tags. Each tag will have a start and an end. For example, a basic HTML file looks like Listing 1-1.

Listing 1-1. HTML

```
<!DOCTYPE html>
<html>

<head>
  <title>My first html page</title>
</head>

<body>
  <div id="app">
    <p id="p1" style="color:red">Just React</p>
    <p id="p2" style="color:green">2022</p>
    <button>Change Content</button>
  </div>
</body>

</html>
```

Let us first check what is inside the body tag; div and p elements are examples of HTML tags.

An HTML element can have attributes, which include a name and a value. The name identifies what information a user wants to add, and the value defines what it means.

In the preceding code, for div we defined the value app for the attribute id. Using the style attribute, we defined the style of the element p. As you move through this book, you will see examples for different tags and attributes.

A content is the part that appears between a start and an end tag. In the preceding example, Just React is a content. An HTML element comprises the start tag, its attributes, the content, and the end tag. In the preceding example, the <p id="p1" style="color:red">Just React</p> is an element. The div element contains this p element as well. Therefore, p is the child element of the div element. The div contains two more child elements, which are the p element with id p2 and a button element.

Let us now look at the other wrapper elements we defined. The `<!DOCTYPE html>` tag tells the browser what version of HTML we are using. For older versions, we need to add a declaration to this tag. For HTML 5, we can just declare it like this. The `<head>` element defines data about the file. The `<title>` element defines the title of the document. You can see the title in the browser tab when you run the HTML on your browser. As the `title` is a data about the document, that is, a metadata, you need to put it inside `<head>`. The `<body>` element contains all the contents of the HTML document.

Put the code in Listing 1-1 into a notepad and save as `Listing1-1.html`. Go to the saved location, right-click, and open it in the browser. You can see the page displays the text `Just React` in red and the text `2022` in green. Whenever you open an HTML file saved on your local drive, the browser reads it but does not understand it. Then, how does the content get displayed eventually in the browser?

Every browser has an engine that constructs a Document Object Model (DOM) tree from the HTML content it reads. The DOM views an HTML document as a tree of nodes. Each node represents an HTML element. For example, refer to Figure 1-1 to see how the DOM tree of Listing 1-1 will look like.

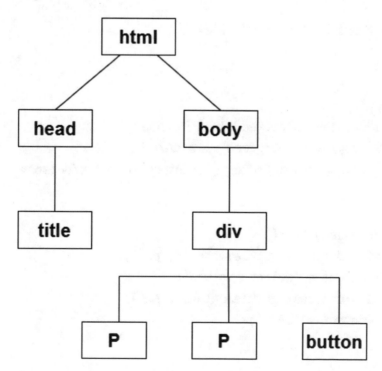

Figure 1-1. *DOM tree*

Next, the browser determines what styles need to apply to elements and creates another tree, called the CSS Object Model (CSSOM) tree. Then it combines the DOM and CSSOM trees to produce the render tree. The difference between a DOM tree and a render tree is that the render tree knows about the styles.

In contrast to the DOM tree, the render tree has information about the styles. Afterward, the browser computes the width, height, location, size, and position of each node in the render tree. Finally, it paints the elements on the screen. This allows us to view the content on the screen.

Next, let's see how we can use JavaScript to add an extra element to this HTML we created. Change Listing 1-1 to include a script tag just below the div element. Refer to Listing 1-2.

Listing 1-2. HTML with JavaScript

```
<!DOCTYPE html>
<html>

<head>
  <title> My first html page </title>
</head>

<body>
  <div id="app">
    <p id="p1" style="color:red">Just React</p>
    <p id="p2" style="color:green">2022</p>
    <button onClick="changeContent()">Change Content</button>
  </div>
  <script>
    function changeContent() {
      const p1 = document.getElementById('p1');
      p1.textContent = 'Welcome to Web';
      const p2 = document.getElementById('p2');
      p2.textContent = '1991';
    }
  </script>
</body>

</html>
```

In an HTML file, we can add a reference to a JS code by using a script tag. If you refresh the browser screen and click the button, you see that the content has been changed to `Welcome to Web and 1991`. What exactly happened here? When the browser engine interpreted the HTML file, it also noticed the `script` tag and executed it.

Inside the `script` tag, we defined a function `changeContent`. A function is a set of code that performs a specific task. The function is invoked during the button click. We added a property `onClick` to the button element. The `onClick` is a JavaScript event. We will explore events in more detail in the next chapter, but for now, understand that when we add `onClick=" changeContent()"` to a button, the `changeContent` function gets executed when the button is clicked. In this function, we access both the p elements and change their content. Hence, the content is changed. The JavaScript here manipulated the DOM tree by accessing the p elements and changing their content. When parts of the DOM tree change, the browser recalculates the CSS, revalidates parts of the render tree, does a reflow (redoing the layout), and then repaints the screen. We made changes to the DOM tree twice in this function, to update content of each of the p elements.

On the browser screen, open the developer tools by pressing F12 on the keyboard. You can see the HTML under the `Elements` tab. Refer to Figure 1-2.

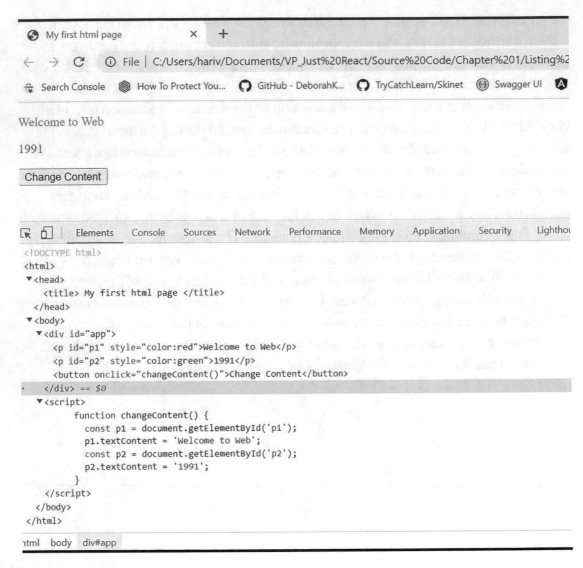

Figure 1-2. *HTML and JavaScript*

The purpose of this section was to show you how HTML and JavaScript work together on a web page and how JS does DOM manipulation. In the next section, we will look at how plain JS compares to React.

How React Reacts Compared with JavaScript

In this section, we'll compare how plain JavaScript (vanilla JS) and React work and what the major differences are.

If you look at Listing 1-2, we're using the following code to access the p element:

```
const p1 = document.getElementById('p1');
```

Here document represents the root node of the DOM tree. The getElementById searches the DOM tree and returns the p element whose id attribute matches with the specified string. Hence, we have the first p element object assigned to the variable p1. In the next line, we update its content:

```
p1.textContent = 'Welcome to Web';
```

Likewise, we update the content of the next p element as well:

```
const p2 = document.getElementById('p2');
p2.textContent = '1991';
```

So each time, the script traverses the DOM tree to find the specific node and updates the respective p element. After updating, the browser performs a reflow and repaints the updated parts, as explained in the last section. For every DOM update, the process repeats. For large-size applications with a huge DOM tree and more DOM updates, this can have a negative impact on performance.

React uses a concept called the Virtual DOM to work a bit differently. It creates two copies of the DOM in memory. When we change the DOM, it changes one copy of the DOM. Then, it compares that copy with the other copy to determine what has changed. This process is called diffing.

React then batches these changes and applies them to the real DOM in one shot. This way, it minimizes the reflow and repaint. This is how React improves performance.

Let's look at the difference between the UI render processes in plain JavaScript and React next.

As we have seen in the previous section, we created the initial UI using HTML, and the browser displayed it. Then, the JavaScript got executed, and the browser repainted the screen with the updated UI.

If you look at Listing 1-1, before we added a script, the HTML we sent to the browser is the following:

```
<div id="app">
  <p>Just React</p>
</div>
```

So we defined the UI in our local drive file, and the browser built the UI based on these definitions. That's how it displayed the content Just React in red color.

Consider we are creating this as a React app. In React, we won't define the UI initially like we did with plain JS. Instead, we define only the root element with no contents inside:

```
<div id="app"></div>
```

The UI then gets defined on the browser based on the instructions we create. These instructions are defined inside components. Each section of the UI is created as a component. Each component we define is actually a JavaScript function. For example, we can define the UI for Listing 1-1 in React like this:

```
function App() {
    return
    (

        <>
        <p>Just React</p>
        <p>2022</p>
        <button onClick={changeContent}>Change Content</button>
        </>

    )
    }
```

This component, App, returns JavaScript XML (JSX). JSX looks like HTML, but it is not. You will learn about JSX in detail in Chapter 3. For now, just understand it is an easy way of describing the UI you want to create. The syntax is like that of the HTML. JSX internally creates React elements.

In the browser, this described component is finally rendered to the root div element, which was initially loaded into the browser.

This is the current state of the component now. If we want to update the content of the p elements like we did in Listing 1-2 using JS, we need to update the state of the component.

Let me write the complete App component definition to make the same update with React. Refer to Listing 1-3.

Listing 1-3. DOM Update Using React

```
import { useState } from "react";
function App() {
  const [statep1, setStatep1] = useState("Just React");
  const [statep2, setStatep2] = useState("2022");

  function changeContent() {
    setStatep1("Welcome to Web");
    setStatep2("1991");
  }

  return (

    <>
      <p>{statep1}</p>
      <p>{statep2}</p>
      <button onClick={changeContent}>Change Content</button>
    </>

  );
}
export default App;
```

Note   Don't worry about the code at this stage. Instead, just focus on what we are trying to achieve. All of the technical terms will be explained in greater detail when we go through each concept from Chapter 3 onward. The code will make sense when we get there.

The UI elements and the JavaScript code are encapsulated in a single component here. We defined an initial value for the content of p elements, which are Just React and 2022. These values are assigned to the variables statep1 and statep2. This variable values are then set as the content of the respective the p element. This is the current state of the p elements.

Next, look at the content inside the changeContent function. Inside the function, we set a new state to each of the p elements. This means, during button click, the content of the first p element changes to Welcome to Web and the second p element content changes to 1991. So here the state of the component changes. When the state is changed, React updates the Virtual DOM and applies the changes to the real DOM after the diffing process. If there are multiple state changes happening at once, React batches these state changes together before updating the DOM.

Figures 1-3 and 1-4 show how the DOM update works in this example in plain JavaScript.

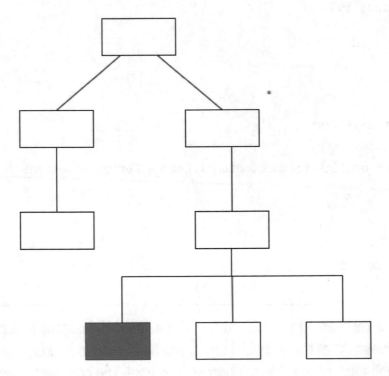

Figure 1-3. *Plain JS – DOM update 1*

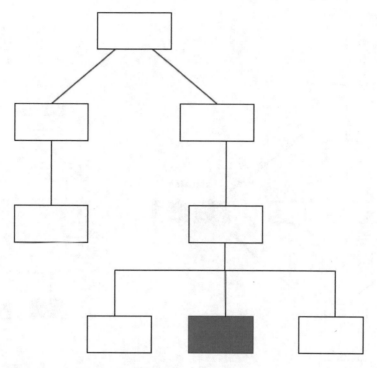

Figure 1-4. *Plain JS – DOM update 2*

As you can see, the DOM updated twice. So the browser repeated the reflow and repaint process for the updated sections. Figure 1-5 shows how the same update works if this is a React application.

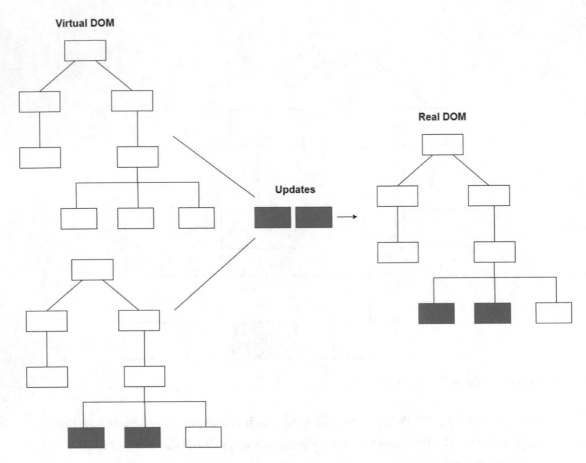

Figure 1-5. *React – batch update to the real DOM via the Virtual DOM*

So, in summary, React encapsulates UI sections as components. It controls the components using their state. React batches the state changes and applies them to the DOM after the diffing process. React manipulates the DOM much less, allowing it to improve performance. As a developer, all you have to worry about is building components and managing state. You don't have to concern about how the UI gets applied to the browser. React loves to do that behind the scenes for you.

Note   There is a common misconception that each DOM change by plain JS causes the browser to repaint the entire page. That's not true. Modern browsers are smart enough to only update what needs to be updated. With plain JS, the browser is forced to recreate only parts of the DOM (the updated element and its children) during each update. And the reflow and repaint process follows for those parts. Here is where React brings in performance improvements by making use of the Virtual DOM and batching changes together.

React vs. Angular

There are many libraries and frameworks available that are built on top of JavaScript. A JavaScript library is a library of pre-written JavaScript code that allows for easier development of JavaScript-based applications. React is a JavaScript library, whereas Angular is a JavaScript framework. A framework comes with a structure and more features.

React focuses on the user interface (UI). React updates the real DOM only after the diffing process. This reduces direct manipulation and helps in improved performance. Even though Angular is a complete frontend framework, its DOM-based system can cause its apps to run slowly when dealing with many data requests. Angular provides more features and may be an overkill for smaller projects.

So, to keep things simple, Angular is a great framework and suitable for some applications. React may be well suitable for some other projects. As I mentioned earlier, React is much simpler to learn, and it is the most suitable tool for developing highly reactive web pages, like Facebook or Instagram. React is smaller in its size, faster and more popular among developers. Companies like Facebook, Instagram, PayPal, Netflix, Airbnb, etc. are making use of React as their core frontend technology. In the next section, let us go a little deeper into some use cases of React and how React fits into those.

Where to React?

When you go to a website, there will be three dominant entities involved in the content display: you, the browser, and the server. You make a request to the browser; the browser sends the request to the server and comes back with a response. There are two kinds of applications: single-page and multi-page. In a single-page application (SPA), the browser gets only one page from the server. So, when you as the user make a request to the browser again and again, the browser responds to you by changing certain parts of the single page. In this process, the browser does not reload any new page from the server. The browser takes only updated instructions from the server and does the rendering by itself. A single-page application interacts with the user by dynamically rewriting the current web page with new data from the web server, instead of the default method of a web browser loading entire new pages.

For example, Airbnb.com is an SPA. If you go to Airbnb.com and navigate to various options, notice that the page does not reload. In contrast, if you go to Amazon.com for shopping, you notice the page gets reloaded when you click various links on the site. You may notice the "X" button appears on the left of the browser bar when you navigate between the pages. This will not happen on single-page websites like Airbnb or Twitter. Refer to Figures 1-6 (MPA) and 1-7 (SPA) to have a visual understanding of the two kinds of applications.

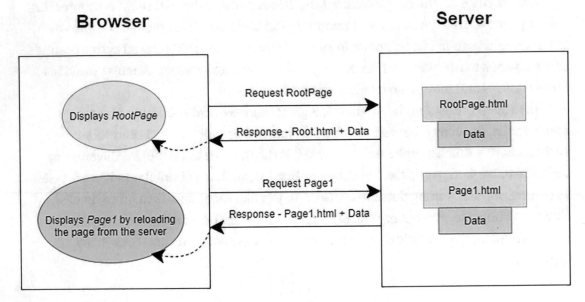

Figure 1-6. *Multi-page application*

Browser   **Server**

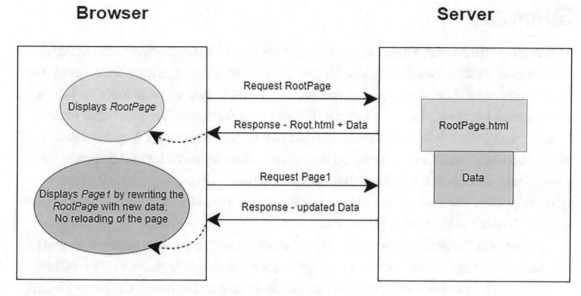

Figure 1-7. *Single-page application*

An SPA reacts much faster. It is the JavaScript that is doing the entire job. There are no round trips to the server. It loads a single HTML page from the server and then responds to the user by rewriting the current page. Have a go on websites like Airbnb, Twitter, Netflix, etc. and see how they respond to you.

Do only SPAs use React? Not necessarily. You can even use React in MPAs. Basically, you can use React for two purposes. One is to build SPAs, where React controls the entire UI after the browser loaded the single page from the server. The other purpose is to control parts or widgets of a page in MPAs. In SPAs, when you switch between pages, React can control that behavior. Even though you may feel you are navigating to a different page, only one page gets updated behind the scenes.

This section aimed to give you an understanding of where to use React on a high level. You also learned the difference between SPAs and MPAs. We will develop both types of applications in this book.

Note   The final code at the end of each chapter is available in the respective chapter section in the repository. You can access the repository via the book's product page, `https://github.com/Apress/Just_React`. All the listings mentioned in this chapter are located under Chapter 1 ➤ Listings.

Summary

This chapter threw some light on where React fits into web development. We started with understanding how HTML and JavaScript work together to display a web page. We discussed the DOM and how JS manipulates the DOM to make a page reactive. I did a comparison between plain JavaScript and React to make you understand what exactly React is and what it is built for. Then we went to compare React with Angular, again to make you understand where React stands against other frameworks and libraries. To conclude, I described the difference between SPAs and MPAs and how each of these types of applications works in a browser. Again, this was to illustrate how React can work with each of these kinds of applications.

To sum up, the goal of this small chapter was to make you understand where you can use React and why to use it. In the next chapter, we will go a little deeper into modern JavaScript. This is essential to provide you the base on learning React. Chapters 1 and 2 give you the basics so you know what happens internally when you type in React code. If you are already much familiar with JavaScript and its modern features, then feel free not to react to Chapter 2 and just go straight into Chapter 3. I would recommend that you master plain JS before you start "React"! The goal of Chapter 2 is to help you with that.

CHAPTER 2

JavaScript Before You React

Once upon a time, programmers used JavaScript (JS) only to add interactive features to web pages. Those days are long gone. Today, JavaScript is even used to develop games. JavaScript is without a doubt the most popular programming language in the world.

In our first chapter, I emphasized the importance of learning JS before working on React. In a few pages, this chapter will help you gain a basic understanding of JS. I do not mean this chapter to cover every JS concept but to equip you with the knowledge before you move on to React.

This chapter introduces Visual Studio Code (VS Code) as a code editor. The chapter focuses on the basics and ECMAScript 2015 (ES6) and above features of JS. ECMAScript is a specification, and JavaScript is a programming language that adheres to this specification. ECMA is an organization responsible for defining standards and maintaining these specifications. ES6 and above versions are the latest of these specifications.

In this chapter, we'll cover most JavaScript concepts to familiarize you with the language before we move on to React. You may skip the sections you already familiar with.

Get Started

We need a code editor to work on JavaScript. Let us use Visual Studio Code. VS Code is a lightweight code editor that works well with JavaScript and React. You can download VS Code from https://code.visualstudio.com/ and install it on your machine. After installation is complete, go to Extensions on the left-hand side and install an extension called "Live Server." Refer to Figure 2-1.

© Hari Narayn 2022
H. Narayn, *Just React!*, https://doi.org/10.1007/978-1-4842-8294-6_2

Figure 2-1. *Installing an extension in VS Code*

By using this extension, you will view your code in the browser without having to copy and paste the link into the browser. You will see the changes automatically in the browser without having to refresh the page.

Click File ➤ New File. VS Code will show you a message to select a language to get started. Click it, search for HTML, and select it. Copy and paste the code in Listing 2-1 and save as Listing 2-1.html.

Listing 2-1. HTML with JavaScript

```
<!DOCTYPE html>
<html>
<body>
    <div id="app"></div>
    <script>
        const childDiv = document.createElement("div");
        childDiv.textContent = new Date();
        document.getElementById("app").append(childDiv);
```

```
    </script>
</body>
</html>
```

Once you saved the file, click the "Open Folder" button on the left-hand side of Explorer. Open the folder in which you saved the preceding HTML file. A prompt will open, and it will ask you, "Do you trust the authors of the file in this folder?" Click the checkbox to trust all files and then click "Yes, I trust the authors." Now, you can view all the files of the folder on the left-hand side of Explorer.

Next, right-click the Listing 2-1.html file and then select "Open with Live Server." Refer to Figure 2-2.

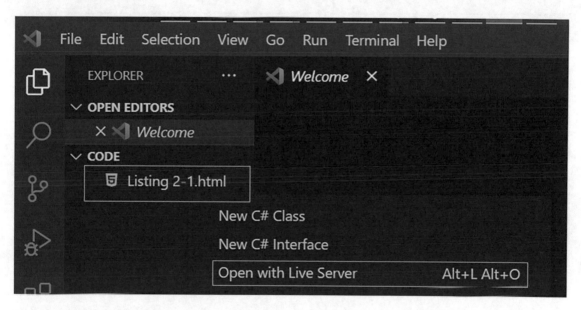

Figure 2-2. *View HTML in the browser*

The HTML file opens in the browser with a URL similar to http://127.0.0.1:5500/ Listing%202-1.html. You can view the current date and time in the browser.

In this simple script, we created a div element and assigned a content to it. We accessed the root div using its id attribute and appended the div to the root div.

As you may have observed, we added the script tag below the HTML element. This is to ensure that the browser loads the parent div first before we do the append operation in JS. If we place the script tag above, the browser will wait for the JS to load before it displays the existing HTML content. You should know the loading of JS depends on where you place the `script` tag. Usually, it would be best to put the `script` tag below the current HTML. However, there are scenarios where we put the script tag above or inside the `<head>` tag.

In the preceding example, we updated the contents of the HTML using JS. We executed the HTML in the browser. This was a simple example to show how JS interacts with HTML elements. In the next section, let us look at some basic JS concepts.

Note   Each of the code blocks mentioned throughout this chapter is available in the Chapter 2 folder in the GitHub repository. You can refer to it via the book's product page, `https://github.com/Apress/Just_React`.

Variables

In Listing 2-1, you used the `const` keyword to declare the `childDiv` variable. What does this mean? You created an element and stored its value in a variable called `childDiv`. You used this value in the second and third lines. So a variable is a container where you can store values to be used later. For instance, in our example, the variable `childDiv` is holding the reference to an HTML element object. Then, you used that variable to set a text content to it and then to append it to the parent element.

We must create a variable before we can use it. The `const` keyword does that, and this is what we call the declaration of a variable. In modern JS, we use `let` and `const` to declare a variable. Let us identify the difference between these two keywords.

Note   You can run the code samples in this chapter using jsfiddle.net.

The following is an example where you assign a string value to a variable. Let us see how `let` and `const` differ in handling this:

```
let bookname = "Just React";
bookname = "No, it is JavaScript";
```

This code works fine. The second line overrides the value you assigned in the first line. In the first line, we are initializing the variable bookname along with its declaration. Declaring a variable means we are creating a variable. Initialization means you are assigning an initial value to a variable at the time of its declaration. In the second line, we are assigning a new value to the variable bookname.

If you use const instead of let, what happens?

```
const bookname = "Just React";
bookname = "No, it is JavaScript";
```

You will get an error in the second line, saying that we already declared the variable bookname. You must assign a value to a const variable at the time of declaration, and you cannot change it afterward like you did with let.

In JavaScript, variable values can be of different data types based on the value we assign. For example, the variable bookname holds a value of type string. If you assign a number value to bookname, the variable now holds the value of type number. See the following:

```
const bookname = 8;
```

Let us examine one of the JavaScript data types, object. An object is a complex data type that can hold collections of data. We can initialize an object as follows:

```
const book = { bookname: "Just React", publisher: "Apress", year: 2022}
```

An object contains properties. Each property has a key and a value. In the preceding example, the object book has three properties. We define each property as a key-value pair. For example, bookname: "Just React" is a property of the object. bookname is the key, and Just React is the value of the specified property. An object can contain properties of any type. The properties of the object in this example are of both string and number types.

You can access a property of an object like this:

```
book.publisher
```

This will give you the value Apress.

Imagine you want to change one of the property values of an object. Say you want to assign a new value to the bookname of the object book. We can do it like this:

```
book.bookname = "No, it is JavaScript";
```

21

You may think this will throw an error because we declare the object as `const`. However, for an object, you can change its properties even if we declare the object as `const`. So the preceding code works just fine. This is because you are not updating the object, only updating its properties. If you attempt to change the object itself, as shown in the following, it will throw a duplicate declaration error. Here, you are attempting to change the object itself, not its properties:

```
book = { bookname: "No, it is JavaScript", publisher: "Apress"}
```

Note   `const` always is the better choice if you will not need to change the value of the variable later. Use `let` only if necessary.

There are various data types available in JavaScript, such as number, string, Boolean, array, and object. In JS, you can't specify the type while declaring or initializing a variable. For instance, you can initialize a variable as follows:

```
let bookname = "Just React";
```

From the preceding line, the browser identifies the bookname as a string. If you declare a variable with the initial value of a string, the browser identifies it as a string variable. Similarly, if you declare a variable with the initial value as a number, the browser identifies it as a number variable. In this way, the browser automatically identifies the data type from the assigned value. So we call JavaScript a dynamically typed language. If the value is a string, always provide it with quotes. If the value is a number or Boolean, do not provide it with quotes. See the following example:

```
let currentYear = 2022; //This variable holds a value  of type number
let isPandemicOver = true; //This variable holds a value of type boolean.
let vaccines= ['Pfizer', 'Moderna', 'AstraZeneca']; /*This variable holds a
value of type string array. */
let book = { bookname: "Just React", publisher: "Apress", year: 2022};
/*This variable holds a value of type object.*/
```

> **Note**   To comment on a single line or multiple lines of code in JS, we can enclose the comment text with /* and */. Alternatively, we can comment on a single line by using two slashes. Comments are not an executable code; they just enable you to recall code later and help others understand your code.

Reference Types

In the previous sections, you learned about different data types in JS such as number, string, Boolean, object, and array. We call objects and arrays as reference types, while we call other data types as primitive types.

A primitive type stores the value of a variable. When you assign a variable that stores a primitive value to another, the value stored in the variable is copied into the new variable. We can see the following example:

```
let bookName = "Just React";
let newBookName = bookName;
```

Here, the JS engine copies the value stored in the variable bookName to the variable newBookName. Add another line as shown in the following:

```
bookName = "Just JS";
```

Now the bookName variable has a new value, Just JS. However, this will not have any effect on the variable newBookName. newBookName will still have the value Just React. It means that the variable newBookName just copies a value from the variable bookName and its existence is independent of bookName. Let us check this in jsfiddle. We will make use of jsfiddle in this section to test JS code.

Go to https://jsfiddle.net/. You don't have to sign up. You can just start coding straight away. However, if you sign up and log in, you can save the work too.

Copy the following code to the JS box:

```
console.log(bookName);
console.log(newBookName);
```

You can see Just JS and Just React are logged into the console, respectively. This proves that the value of newBookName hasn't changed. Refer to Figure 2-3 for steps.

23

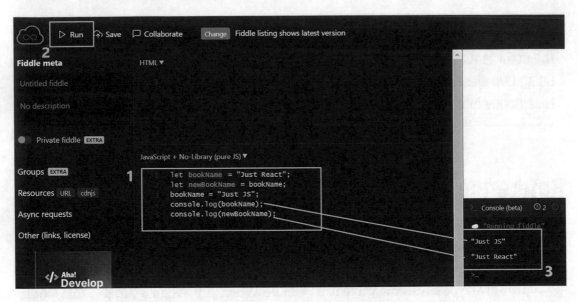

Figure 2-3. *Value types (Steps: 1, copy code to the JS box; 2, run the code; 3, see the console logs)*

Let's look at reference types next. The reference type stores a reference to the memory where the value is stored. When you assign a variable that stores a reference value to another, it copies only the reference into the new variable. Let's look at an example:

```
const book = {
name: "Just React",
year:2022
}
const nextBook = book;
book.year = 2023;
console.log(nextBook);
```

Check the output in the console by running this code in jsfiddle. You will see the following (refer to Figure 2-4):

```
{
  name: "Just React",
  year: 2023
}
```

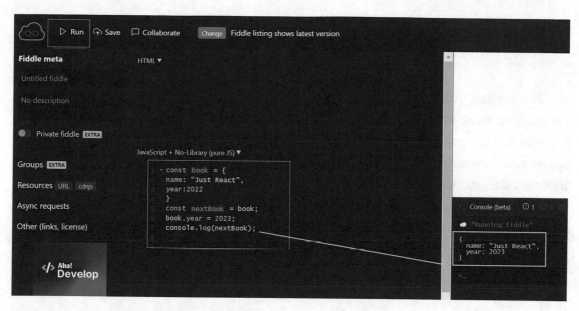

Figure 2-4. *Reference types*

Note that the value of year has been updated to 2023. You updated the year property of the book object, and the year property of the nextBook object was also updated. This confirms that just the reference was copied when you copied the book object. Whenever you update a property value, it updates the value in memory. It does not matter from where the value is referenced; the updated value always appears from memory. This also holds true for array elements.

Let's see how we can copy the value instead of the reference from reference-type variables, such as objects and arrays. To copy the value, you must copy the object's properties. Update your code as follows:

```
const book = {
name: "Just React",
year:2022
}
const nextBook = {...book};
book.year = 2023;
console.log(nextBook);
```

Check out the result in jsfiddle. It looks like this:

```
{
```

```
  name: "Just React",
  year: 2022
}
```

The update to the book object had no effect on the `nextBook` object. In the code line `const nextBook = {...book}`, we copied the properties of the object. So, the object reference is not copied here like in the preceding example. This example used the spread(`...`) operator. The spread operator takes an array or object and spreads it into individual elements. Here, using the spread operator, we spread the properties of the book object into the `nextBook` object. You can also add additional elements to an array or new properties to an object, using the spread operator. See the following example:

```
const book = {
name: "Just React",
year:2022
}
const nextBook = {...book, publisher: "Apress" };
console.log(nextBook);
```

In this example, you created the `nextBook` object by using the spread operator (`...`) as before. Then, we added a new property, `publisher`, to it.

Try executing this code in jsfiddle, and you will get the output like this:

```
{
  name: "Just React",
  year: 2022,
  publisher: "Apress"
}
```

This also works for arrays. Here's an example:

```
const yearArray = [2019, 2020, 2021];
const newYearsArray = [...yearArray, 2022, 2023];
console.log(newYearsArray);
```

The output will be like this:

```
[2019, 2020, 2021, 2022, 2023];
```

While you work on React projects, you may find the spread operator very useful.

Conditionals and Loops

Using `if/else` statements, you can decide based on a condition. For example, the following code checks whether a Boolean variable is true or false. If true, it sets the value of a second variable to 3500 and otherwise 200:

```
let isNormalTravelResumed = false;
let ticketsAvailable;
if(isTravelResumed === true)
{
 ticketsAvailable = 3500;
}
else
{
ticketsAvailable = 200;
}
```

There are few values considered as falsy in JavaScript. When these values evaluate, they evaluate to the Boolean value `false`. The values `false`, `0`, `-0`, `""`, `null`, `undefined`, and `NaN` are considered falsy. All other values will evaluate to `true`. These are called truthy.

So, in the preceding code, instead of specifying `if(isTravelResumed === true)`, you can simplify the if statement like this:

```
if(isTravelResumed)
```

Similarly, `if(!isTravelResumed)` is equivalent to `if(isTravelResumed === false)`. Let's look at loops next.

Loops are used to perform repeated operations. There are different loops available in JS. Let us see how we can transform the following code using a `for` loop:

```
let yearArray = [2018, 2019, 2020, 2021, 2022];
console.log(yearArray[0]);
console.log(yearArray[1]);
console.log(yearArray[2]);
console.log(yearArray[3]);
console.log(yearArray[4]);
```

This code logs out each year in the array into the console. We can rewrite the code using a for loop as follows:

```
for(let i=0; i< yearArray.length;i++)
{
 console.log(yearArray[i]);
}
```

In this for loop, we initialize the variable i with a value of 0. In the next line, the exit condition i< yearArray.length is evaluated. The console log inside the loop is executed because 0 is less than the length of the array. Next, the update expression i++ is executed, and it will increase the value of i to 1. Then, the process repeats until the value of i is not less than the array length. The loop ends the execution there.

The for loop simplifies the code when you want to run a line of code repeatedly. Let us see how we can rewrite the same code by using for/in and for/of loops:

```
for (let i in yearArray)
{
  console.log(yearArray[i]);
}
```

The for/in loop is similar to the for loop. The difference is that it does not have the counting logic (i++) and the exit condition (i< yearArray.length). The for/in loop does not guarantee you the order in which the data is accessed. In this example, 2018 may get logged before 2021.

The for/of loop is your best choice for the iteration. The for/of loop respects the order. It iterates over the value of the objects like the for loop:

```
for (let i of yearArray)
{
  console.log(yearArray[i]);
}
```

while is another type of JS loop where a statement gets executed unless a specified condition is true. See the following example:

```
let count = 0;
while(count < 5)
{
```

```
console.log('hello JS');
  count++;
}
```

Here, `hello JS` gets logged into the console five times.

There are many other ways in JS to loop over a collection, such as an array or an object. We will get into use cases of this while doing projects in React in the upcoming chapters. This section was just an overview of conditionals and loops in JS.

Functions

As with most programming languages, JS has functions. A function is a set of code that performs a specific task. You can call a function as many times as necessary within your code using a single line of code. This avoids having to write the same set of code in multiple places.

In JS, you can use built-in browser functions or create your own custom functions. As the name shows, built-in functions are pre-built, and all you need to do is call them when you need them. You build custom functions from scratch in your code.

For this exercise, let us create an HTML file with JS code to illustrate how functions work. Copy the following code into VS Code and save as functions.html. Refer to Listing 2-2.

Listing 2-2. Swap Case Function

```
<!DOCTYPE html>
<html>
<body>
    <input type="text" id="inputName" />
    <button onclick="swapCase()">Swap Case</button>
    <span id="outputName"></span>
    <script>
        function swapCase() {
            const name = document.getElementById("inputName").value;
            const characters = name.split("");
            const changedCharacters = characters.map(
                function(c){
```

```
                if (c == c.toLowerCase()) {
                    return c.toUpperCase();
                }
                else {
                    return c.toLowerCase();
                }
            });
        const changedName = changedCharacters.join("");

        document.getElementById("outputName").textContent =
        changedName;
        }
    </script>
</body>
</html>
```

When you open the file with Live Server, you will see a text box with a button next to it. If you enter any text in the text box and click the button, the function will switch the case of each character, and it will display the output next to the button. Refer to Figure 2-5 for an example.

Figure 2-5. *Swap case function*

Here, the swapCase function converts the case of each character to its opposite case. Let's examine each element of the code line by line. Here we have three elements: an input element, a button, and a span element. You can enter a text value in the input element. The button element calls the function swapCase. We added a property onClick to the button element. The onClick is a JavaScript event. We will explore events in the following section, but for now, understand that if we add onClick="swapCase()" to a button, the swapCase function gets executed during the button click.

Finally, the span element displays the converted text.

Our swapCase function is a custom function we created. Within this custom function, we are calling several built-in functions. Let's review the function line by line. We will note down the output in each step based on the example in Figure 2-5. Assume you entered React into the input box. In the first line, we are reading the value entered in the input box and putting it into the variable name:

```
const name = document.getElementById("inputName").value;
```

The variable name will have the value React stored into it now. In the next line, we are calling a built-in function called split. This function accepts a parameter and splits the string using the parameter as the delimiter. The split function splits the string into individual characters as we pass a blank parameter to it. We then store these characters into an array variable called characters:

```
const characters = name.split("");
```

Now the array variable characters will have the value ['R','e','a','c','t']. In the next line, we use two built-in functions, toLowerCase and toUpperCase. toLowerCase converts the character to lowercase, and toUpperCase converts it to uppercase. We iterate over each character using a method called map(). map() is a built-in JS method that allows you to iterate over an array and change its elements using a function. A JS method is a property of an object that contains a function definition.

The map() method calls a function on every element of an array and returns a new array that contains the results. As you can see, we are passing a function to the map() method. Look at the following line:

```
const changedCharacters = characters.map(
            function(c){
                if (c == c.toLowerCase()) {
                    return c.toUpperCase();
                }
                else {
                    return c.toLowerCase();
                }
            });
```

The function checks the case of the character and returns its opposite case. This happens for each character from the array. This is the capability of the map() method. The result of one execution is passed to the same function again and again.

By now, the variable changedCharacters will have the value ['r','E','A','C','T'].
The function will initially return ['r','e','a','c','t'] by changing the first
character, and the function will get called again with the result as the parameter. In the
second execution, the result will be ['r','E','a','c','t']. Finally, the result will be
['r','E','A','C','T'] after all the characters are swapped.

In the next line, the characters in the array are joined together with the help of the
built-in function join:

```
const changedName = changedCharacters.join("");
```

Now the variable changedName has the value rEACT. The next line puts this value to
the element span, which has the id outPutName:

```
document.getElementById("outputName").textContent= changedName;
```

This explains the complete code. This gives you an understanding of custom
functions, built-in functions, and methods. We will go deeper into some methods and
features of JS in the following sections.

Prior to that, let me explain how we swapped characters using the map() function in
little more detail. For that, we need to know a few more things about functions.

A variable can hold a reference to a function. For example, in the following the
variable swap holds a reference to a function:

```
const swap = function (c) {
            if (c == c.toLowerCase()) {
                return c.toUpperCase();
            }
            else {
                return c.toLowerCase();
            }
```

And then we can pass this reference for other functions to use. This way, we can pass
the variable reference of the preceding function to the map() function in the preceding
example:

```
    const changedCharacters = characters.map(swap);
```

So we can declare a variable to hold the function and then pass that reference variable to another function. In the preceding example (Listing 2-2), we went one more step ahead. We just bypassed the variable in the middle by directly passing the function to another function, which is the map() function here:

```
const changedCharacters = characters.map(
        function (c) {
            if (c == c.toLowerCase()) {
                return c.toUpperCase();
            }
            else {
                return c.toLowerCase();
            }
        });
```

Events

In Listing 2-2, we added an event listener. What exactly are these events? In this section, we will dig into that.

Events are actions that get fired inside the browser, most commonly through user interactions, though not always. We can attach an event to a specific element, like an HTML element, or to the entire browser window. In Listing 2-2, we attached an event to a button element. The event gets fired once the user clicks the button. In the same way, you can attach events to various actions, such as when a user closes their browser window, when a user loads a web page, or when a user submits an HTML form.

The onClick event in JS allows you to execute a function when you click an element. Refer to Listing 2-2, under the function section, where you called the swapCase function at the onClick event.

addEventListener() is a method to add an event to an element. To remove the event, you can use removeEventListener(). You can add or remove the click event from the button with id btnCase using the following code:

```
document.getElementById("btnCase").addEventListener ("click", swapCase);
 document.getElementById("btnCase").removeEventListener ("click",
swapCase);
```

The `setTimeout` function can attach an event to a browser window. The `setTimeout` creates a timing event that gets fired after a specified number of milliseconds. This timing event is attached to the browser window.

Arrow Functions

Earlier, you learned about functions. How does the syntax of a function look like? As you can see in Listing 2-2, a function syntax looks like this:

```
Function swapCase() {
//code inside.
}
```

You can change the preceding function into an arrow function like this:

```
const swithCase = () => {
//code inside.
}
```

Arrow functions are functions having this kind of syntax. Arrow functions represent regular functions differently.

Listing 2-2 illustrated the use of a `map()`. Here the `map()` method calls a function on every element of the characters array. The function is called again and again by passing the previous function result as an argument. So, the function here inside `map()` is called a callback function. The arrow function simplifies the callback function and makes it less verbose. By "less verbose," I mean it does not have the "function" keyword compared with a regular function. Let us update the `map()` method using arrow function syntax:

```
const changedCharacters = characters.map((c) => {
    if (c === c.toLowerCase()) {
      return c.toUpperCase();
    } else {
      return c.toLowerCase();
    }
  });
```

You can run Listing 2-2 now with the replaced line. It will work just like before. So this is another way of creating functions in modern JavaScript.

The major advantage with arrow functions is related to the use of the this keyword in callback functions, when we use map(), setTimeout(), etc.

When you use the this keyword, it usually gets you a value based on the context in which the function is called. this in a regular function always refers to the context of the function being called. However, in the arrow function, this has nothing to do with the caller of the function. It refers to the scope where the function (the enclosing context) is present. Let me explain this with the help of the following example. Refer to Listing 2-3.

Go to https://jsfiddle.net/ and copy the code in Listing 2-3 into the JavaScript box.

Listing 2-3. Regular Function and the this Keyword

```
let yearData = {
      year: 2022,
      printYear: function() {
        console.log(this.year);
        setTimeout(function() {
            console.log("After 2 seconds");
          console.log(this.year);
        }, 1000)
      }
    }
    yearData.printYear();
```

Let us investigate the code. We declared an object yearData. This contains a variable year with the value of 2022. Next, it contains a function printYear. This function logs the year value to the console. Again, after 2 seconds, it logs the year value. We did this using the setTimeout function. Execute the code in jsfiddle, and you see that initially it logs the year value as 2022. But, after 2 seconds, the year value is logged in the console as undefined. Refer to Figure 2-6.

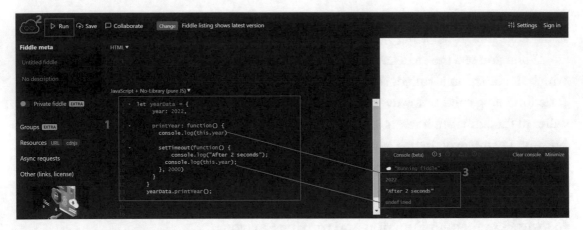

Figure 2-6. *this keyword in a regular callback function (Steps: 1, copy code to the JS box; 2, run the code; 3, see the console logs)*

Let us see why this happened. We defined the `year` inside the `printYear` function. Initially logging to the console was done within the function `printYear`. So it can access the value of year using the `this` keyword.

The second time, logging was done inside the `setTimeout` function, not the `printYear` function. That means console log is not called within the context of where the year is defined. Therefore, `this.year` logged as `undefined`.

Let us now rewrite the `setTimeout` as an arrow function like this:

```
setTimeout(() => {
  console.log("After 2 seconds");
  console.log(this.year);
}, 2000);
```

Now, replace the function `setTimeout` from Listing 2-3. Refer to Listing 2-4.

Listing 2-4. Arrow Function and the this Keyword

```
let yearData = {
    year: 2022,
    printYear: function () {
      console.log(this.year);
      setTimeout(() => {
        console.log("After 2 seconds");
        console.log(this.year);
```

```
    }, 2000);
  },
};
yearData.printYear();
```

Copy the code in Listing 2-4 to jsfiddle and execute. Refer to Figure 2-7.

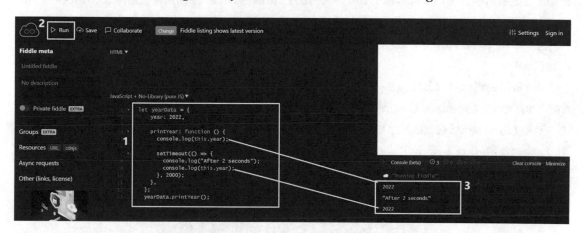

Figure 2-7. *this keyword in an arrow function (Steps: 1, copy code to the JS box; 2, run the code; 3, see the console logs)*

It logs the year value as **2022** both times now. Refer to Figure 2-7. What does the arrow function do differently here?

The arrow function only cares about where it is defined, not where it is called from. The setTimeout function calls the console log where we accessed this.year. We defined this function within the printYear function. We also declared the variable year within the same function where the setTimeout function was declared. Therefore, the setTimeout function can access the variable year. This is known as lexical scoping in JS.

Arrow functions are only concerned with the lexical scope, not with the context from which they are called. As a result, when we declare setTimeOut as an arrow function, it can access the year through this.year.

This behavior makes arrow functions very useful for callback functions such as when we use map(). This will be handy while learning React, where we will use a lot of callback functions.

Modules

In simple terms, a JS module is a file. We have seen HTML with JS embedded in it using a `script` tag. Instead, we can separate the JS into a file. HTML pages can refer to the saved JS through a directive called `import.` In the same way, if you have a complex JS application, you can break it up into several JS files. We can import content from one file to another by importing the module from file 1 to file 2. To import a module, say `A.js` to `B.js`, the `A.js` should contain the `export` keyword, and the `B.js` should use the `import` directive.

We will split our Listing 2-1.html into one HTML file and two JS files and see how they can work together. Create a JS folder in the Code folder that we created earlier.

You can use VS Code Explorer to create a new folder and a new file such as HTML or JS. Refer to Figure 2-8.

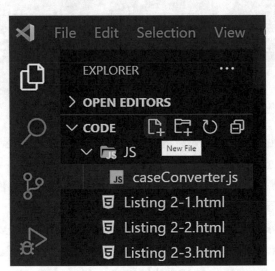

Figure 2-8. *VS Code Explorer*

Create two JS files "caseConverter.js" and "swapCase.js". Copy the code from Listings 2-5 and 2-6, respectively. The code follows.

Listing 2-5. caseConverter.js

```
export const convertCase = (chars) =>{

  const changedCharacters = chars.map((c) => {
      if (c === c.toLowerCase()) {
        return c.toUpperCase();
      } else {
        return c.toLowerCase();
      }
    });    return changedCharacters;
}
```

The preceding file contains a function that accepts a sequence of characters and returns an array of the characters in the opposite case. We export this module by using the export keyword in front of the function. See Listing 2-6.

Listing 2-6. swapCase.js

```
import {convertCase} from "./caseConverter.js";
export function swapCase() {
    const name =  document.getElementById("inputName").value;
    let characters = name.split("");
    let changedCharacters = convertCase(characters);
    let changedName = changedCharacters.join("");
    document.getElementById("outputName").textContent =  changedName;
}
```

In swapCase.js, the function swapCase gets the value of the input field. It splits it into characters and calls the convertCase function from the convertCase module. Note that we imported the convertCase module using the import keyword.

We then join the converted characters in the array in the next step and then place them into the output element. By splitting JS into two modules, we achieve the same functionality. Now, let's see how we can refer to the modules in the HTML file.

Create a new file, Listing 2-7.html. Copy the code from Listing 2-7.

Listing 2-7. HTML with an Imported Module

```
<!DOCTYPE html>
<html>
<body>
    <input type="text" id="inputName" />
    <button id="btnCase">Swap Case</button>
    <span id="outputName"></span>
    <script type="module">
        import {swapCase} from '/JS/swapCase.js';
        document.getElementById("btnCase").addEventListener("click",
        swapCase);
    </script>
</body>
</html>
```

Here, we introduced a script tag and referenced an external JS module. Before moving on to the details of referencing an external JS module, let us look at how we can reference a plain JS file in an HTML.

We use the script tag to include an external JS file in an HTML file. The script tag inserts an executable code into HTML. We can make use of the two properties of the script tag: the type, which specifies the type of the file, and the src attribute, which specifies the path to the JS file. For example, we can include a reference to an external JS file in HTML like this:

```
<script type="text/javascript" src="/JS/yourjs.js"></script>
```

In this example, we are referencing a JS module. Here we specify the type as module:

```
<script type="module"></script>
```

To import the function swapCase from the swapCase module JS file, we use the import keyword:

```
import {swapCase} from '/JS/swapCase.js';
```

Compared with the Listing 2-2.html, we add an id property to the button and remove the onclick event from the button:

```
 <button id="btnCase">Swap Case</button>
```

Instead, we add an event listener, click, to the button inside the script tag:

```
document.getElementById("btnCase").addEventListener("click", swapCase);
```

So, whenever you click the button, it will invoke the swapCase function. Note that the script tag must have the property type with the value module. This is essential for the browser to load the module. Because the swapCase module imports the convertCase module in it, we don't need to include that module in the HTML file.

Note   Most of the modern browsers support JS modules. However, note that some browsers or older browser versions may not support this.

By executing the HTML in a browser, you will see the same functionality we achieved with the code in Listing 2-2.html. Our code is much cleaner now compared with Listing 2-2.html. We arranged the code into one HTML file and two JS modules. The module-based system is vital when working on JS projects as it will also assist you when coding with React, using components.

Subclassing

In the programming world, object-oriented programming (OOP) is a very common term. We did not initially associate JS with object-oriented programming. We heard the term OOP associated more with server-side programming with languages such as C# and Java at first. Certainly, you know now the JS is no longer the JS we have known before. In this section, we will look at a key OOP concept called subclassing.

Note   This section aims to familiarize you with JS classes and subclassing before you work with React. This scope of OOJS is much broader than this section.

We already talked about what an object is, what a property is, etc. In this section, let me explain to you the concept of a class. We create a class with the class keyword, and it can have properties and methods. Properties are variables attached to classes, while methods are functions attached to classes. We have already discussed variables and functions.

Using jsfiddle again here, we will describe this concept using an example. Visit jsfiddle.net and enter the JS code in the box marked JS. Refer to Listing 2-8.

Listing 2-8. Subclassing

```
class Book {
  author = "Hari";
  publisher = "Apress";
  getPublisher = () => {
    console.log(this.publisher);
  };
}
class ReactBook extends Book {
  name = "Just React";
  publishedYear = 2022;
}
const reactBook = new ReactBook();
console.log(reactBook.name);
reactBook.getPublisher();
```

Our code defines two classes, Book and ReactBook. Both classes have properties and methods. For example, name is a property of the class ReactBook, and publisher is a property of the class Book. getPublisher is a method of the Book class. The class ReactBook inherits from the Book class using the extends keyword. This means the properties and methods of the Book class will be available to the objects of the ReactBook class as well.

Using the object of the ReactBook class, we access the getPublisher method of the class Book. If you run the code in jsfiddle, you can see Just React and Apress as outputs. Refer to Figure 2-9.

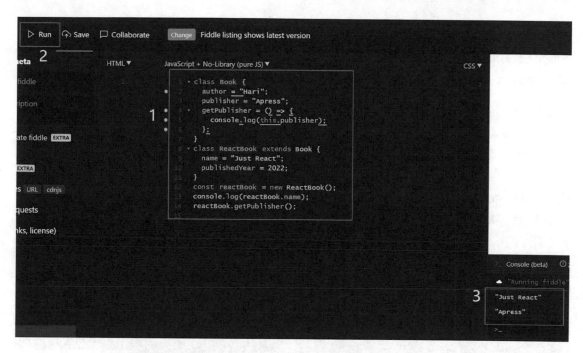

Figure 2-9. *Subclassing with JS*

This concept is called subclassing. Here in this example, ReactBook is a subclass. A subclass inherits the properties and methods of a class. Also, it can modify the properties of the parent class. A real-world example is a tree and a branch. A branch inherits the features of a tree, but it can have additional features, such as additional fruits or leaves. It can change the property of a tree as well. For example, a tree has a total of 1000 leaves; a new branch can increase the total leaves to 1100.

Async/await

JavaScript is a single-threaded programming language. This language can only process one line of code at a time. Let me show you an example of synchronous and asynchronous programming. In this example, we are trying to display the strings Learning and React in the console. Refer to Listing 2-9 to see how the execution would be in synchronous mode.

Listing 2-9. Synchronous JavaScript

```javascript
console.log("Learning");
display();

function display() {
  const what = getContent();
  console.log(what);
}
function getContent() {
  return "React";
}
```

You can see the output of the code by copying it into jsfiddle and then running it. Refer to Figure 2-10.

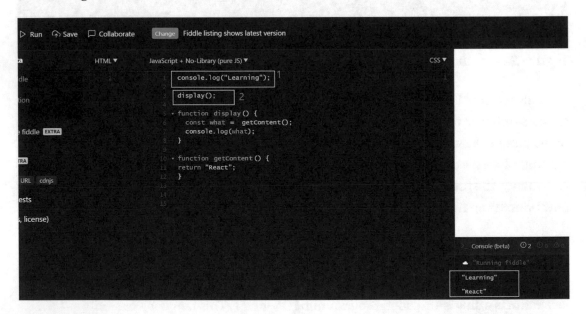

Figure 2-10. *Synchronous execution in JS*

We printed both strings out on the console with no issues. As you can see, in synchronous execution, the code is executed line by line. The script logged Learning into the console first. Then it called the display function. The function display called another function getContent that returned the value React. Both strings therefore ended up logged to the console.

Let's rewrite the same program by delaying the return of the string React by 2 seconds. We will delay the execution by using the setTimeOut() function. Refer to Listing 2-10.

Listing 2-10. Asynchronous JavaScript

```
console.log("Learning");

display();

function display() {
  const what = getContent();
  console.log(what);
}

function getContent() {
  setTimeout(() => {
    return "React";
  }, 2000);
}
```

Just copy the code into jsfiddle to see the output as illustrated in Figure 2-11.

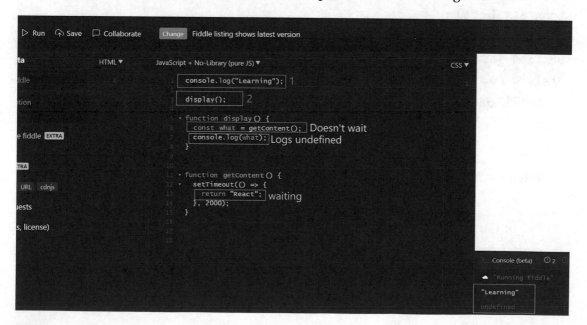

Figure 2-11. *Asynchronous execution in JS*

The second line logged undefined instead of React. The display function did not wait for the getContent function to return anything. Instead, it continued to execute. We call this asynchronous execution.

It may be necessary to use web Application Programming Interface (API) calls to get some information in real-time projects. An API call is a call to the server, and it may take a few seconds or more to receive the information from the server. In the preceding example, setTimeout() was used to simulate the delay that can occur when calling a server-based API. It executes and creates a timer in the browser's web API component.

Asynchronous programming creates issues in our code since JS does not wait for a line to finish and moves on to the next line of code. Async/await solve this problem by making the code appear to be synchronous. However, the code is asynchronous behind the scenes. To understand this better, let us rewrite the code in Listing 2-9. Refer to Listing 2-11.

Listing 2-11. Async/await/a

```
console.log("Learning");
display();
async function display() {
  const what = await getContent();
  console.log(what);
}
function getContent() {
  return new Promise((resolve, reject) => {
    setTimeout(() => resolve("React"), 1000);
  });
}
```

Run the code in jsfiddle, and the output will look like Figure 2-12.

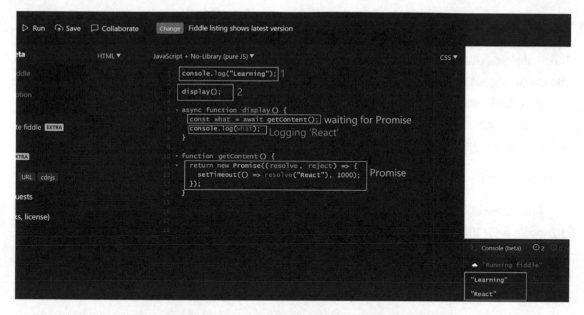

Figure 2-12. *Asynchronous execution with Async/await in JS*

So now we have the desired result. The second line logged React, not undefined like before. The display function waited for the getContent function to complete its execution.

Let us look at the changes we did in the functions display and getContent. First, let me explain the changes to getContent. We wrapped the setTimeOut() method with a Promise:

```
return new Promise((resolve, reject) => {
  setTimeout(() => resolve("React"), 1000);
});
```

A Promise is an object that represents a proxy for a value that may become available at a later point in time. When we wrap a function inside a Promise object, the function will not return a value initially. Instead, the function will return a promise to provide the value in the future. So, initially, the value of the Promise object will be in the pending state.

When the function gets executed successfully, the Promise object's state becomes fulfilled. If the function fails, the Promise object's state becomes rejected. So the state of the Promise can go from pending to fulfilled or rejected.

When the state of the `Promise` object becomes `fulfilled`, `resolve()` will get called, and the value will be returned to the caller function, which is the `display` function here. If the state of the `Promise` becomes `rejected`, the `reject()` method will get called, and the error object will be returned to the caller. We didn't define `reject()` in this example as there is almost no chance of an error since it returns just a string.

Let us look at changes we did to the function `display`. We added an `await` keyword in front of the getContent function call:

```
const what = await getContent();
```

When we add an `await` keyword in front of the function call, it makes the rest of the code wait until a value is returned. So here, the second line `console.log(what)` waits until the variable what gets a value. Once the `Promise` is resolved, the `getContent` function returns the value, and the variable what will have the value `React`.

Note that we marked the function `display` with an `async` keyword. If we want to use `await,` the execution context must be marked as `async`. Since we use `await` inside the display function, we need to mark that function as `async`. Basically, `async` makes a function capable of using `await`.

Template Literals

Previously, in JS, if we wanted to concatenate a string and a keyword, we used quotes and the plus operator. See the following example:

```
let bookName = "Just React";
console.log("The book name is "+bookName);
```

In modern JS, we can make use of template literals. Template literals are literals delimited with backticks (`` ` ``). Template literals are enclosed by backticks (`` ` ` ``) instead of double or single quotes.

In template literals, placeholders are indicated by the dollar sign and curly braces like this:

```
${expression}.
```

Using backticks, that is, by using `` ` ``, we can write the preceding lines of code as follows:

```
const bookName = "Just React";
console.log(`The book name is ${bookName}`);
```

If we take an example of an object, let us see how we can write using template literals:

```
const book = { bookname: "Just React", publisher: "Apress", year: 2022};
console.log(`The book ${book.bookname}, is published in  ${book.year} `);
```

See the following, where we call a function inside the template literal:

```
function multiply(a, b)
{
return a*b;
}
console.log(`If you multiply 5 with 6, you get ${multiply(5,6)} `);
```

Let us execute in https://jsfiddle.net and see the results. Refer to Figure 2-13.

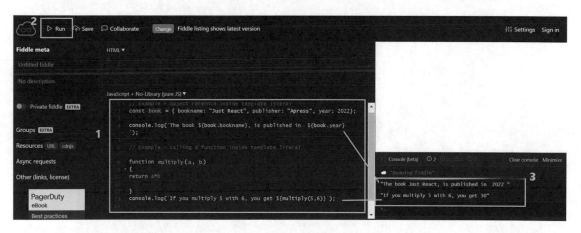

Figure 2-13. *Template literals(Steps: 1, copy code to the JS box; 2, run the code; 3, see the console logs)*

Template literals are a very helpful feature while building React projects.

Summary

The aim of this chapter was to make you familiar with JavaScript. We started with basics and learned how to use JS in an HTML page. You learned about variables, functions, and arrow functions. We discussed conditionals, loops, and events. You learned how to import and export JS files using modules. We dealt with reference types and the spread operator. Last but not least, you learned one of the most important aspects of modern JS, asynchronous programming. We talked about promises and the Async/await syntax. Finally, we concluded the chapter with an overview of template literals.

The chapter focused to help you learn or refresh your knowledge on modern JavaScript and made you comfortable with the language before moving on to React. However, mastering JS is much beyond this chapter. You will need to do real-world projects and do more practice to master JS. But you are all set to start Reacting by refreshing/learning concepts discussed in this chapter. We will start with React in the next chapter. Get ready to React!

CHAPTER 3

Start Reacting

The focus of this chapter is to get you started with the React journey. The primary goal of this chapter is to teach you about the setup of React projects and the fundamental concepts of React.

Our first step will be to set up a development environment for React. Next, you will create your first project by setting up all the configurations yourself. We will build a React application from scratch to learn how React works behind the scenes. During this process, I will introduce you to Babel and Webpack. Following that, we will proceed to create a React application using a tool, `create-react-app.`

We will discuss components and JavaScript Extensible Markup Language (JSX). You will learn about the concepts of the Virtual DOM, props, and state. I will explain these concepts with the help of an example application. You will create a simple student enrolment form. You will learn about how components can interact with each other.

The chapter will take you the exciting world of Components, JSX, prop, state, etc. by using an example project and will serve as a foundation for learning React. Be sure to grasp the concepts and basics before leaving each section. At the end of this chapter, you will be in a good position to experiment and learn distinct features of React. Let us start by building a software environment.

Set Up an Environment to "React"

As a first step, install Visual Studio Code (VS Code), which you might have already done during Chapter 1. The next step is to install Node. Node is a runtime environment for JavaScript (JS). Go to `https://nodejs.org/` and install the latest LTS version. Restart VS Code after you have finished installing Node. By clicking Terminal ➤ New Terminal, you will run commands within VS Code. The command `node -v` displays the current Node version. See Figure 3-1 for an example.

© Hari Narayn 2022
H. Narayn, *Just React!*, https://doi.org/10.1007/978-1-4842-8294-6_3

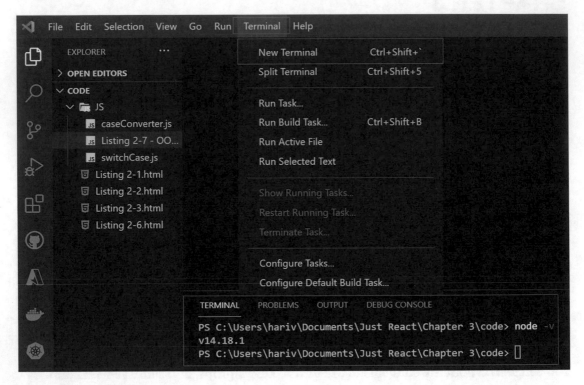

Figure 3-1. *VS Code terminal*

Note   In this book, I am using Node 16.13.0. I would recommend using the same version to avoid any issue while running the code. However, you are free to use the latest LTS version that is available while you are building new projects. The direct link to the page for downloading the version 16.13.0 is `https://nodejs.org/dist/v16.13.0/`. On this page, click the file link according to your operating system. For example, for a Windows x64 machine, click node-v16.13.0-x64. msi and it will get downloaded.

How to React?

You can now start creating your first React project. The easiest way to create a React project is to use the command `create-react-app`. With this command, you can set up a frontend build pipeline without having to know how Babel or Webpack works. However, we will not use this command to create the first project. This is because we need to understand how React internally works. Hence, let's tackle the hard path first. Afterward, we can create React projects using the amazing tool `create-react-app`.

As we move through the project creation process, it's crucial that you understand each concept. Spend time understanding each step before moving on to the next one. You are doing all the setup yourself, and this enables you to comprehend how React works internally.

Note   Each of the listings and projects used in this chapter is available in the Chapter 3 folder in the GitHub repository. You can refer to it via the book's product page, `https://github.com/Apress/Just_React`.

Here we go. Open VS Code, click View from the top, and then select Terminal. This will open the terminal. Alternatively, you can press Ctrl+` to open the terminal. Then, set the directory on the location of your local drive where you would like the project to be. Then, follow the following steps.

Step 1: Initialize the project.

Run the `npm init` command. Just keep pressing Enter until the command stops executing. This will create the file `package.json` in your directory. Refer to Figure 3-2.

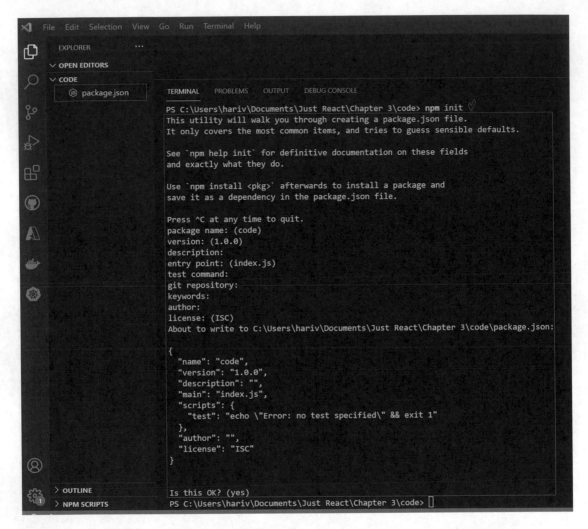

Figure 3-2. *Create package.json*

So we created a file called package.json using the command npm init. You might ask, What is Node Package Manager (npm)? What is npm init? And what is package.json?

npm is a package management tool that contains code packages. You have learned about modules in Chapter 2. A code package is similar to that. You can package a project and publish it to npm as a Node.js module. Other projects can then reference this package by installing it as a dependency. We can install these via the command line. You need to install Node.js to use npm. We already installed Node.js during the environment setup. NPM got installed as part of this Node installation process. A package.json contains information about a project, such as its name, version, description, etc. With the package.json you just created, you can see all this information. The information is in JSON format, with key/value pairs. The values are all set to default for now. Refer to Listing 3-1.

Note   There is a different process to package and publish a project. We are not discussing that here. Here, we are talking about how to install an NPM package to our project.

Listing 3-1. package.json

```
{
  "name": "code",
  "version": "1.0.0",
  "description": "",
  "main": "index.js",
  "scripts": {
    "test": "echo \"Error: no test specified\" && exit 1"
  },
  "author": "",
  "license": "ISC"
}
```

The init command is a short-hand way of saying to initialize. So what we did here is to initialize the project using npm. The result is the package.json file, which contains the information about our project.

Let us keep the project folder open. In VS Code, click Open Folder on the left-hand side of Explorer and open the folder location in which you ran the command and created package.json. I created it inside the folder code.

Step 2: Install react and react-dom.

The next step is to install two dependency packages, which are react and react-dom. The react and react-dom are npm packages that you will need for your React app. The react package is the React library itself. It is the library your code will depend on to produce the HTML, CSS, and JS that will run in a browser. It is the actual React library that helps you build amazing user interfaces.

You use ReactDOM as the middleman that renders your React elements in the browser. The react-dom package helps you put your root HTML file into the browser using root.render(). First, we use the createRoot() method of ReactDOM to access the root node, and we call render(). Apart from createRoot() and render(), you won't interact with ReactDOM directly from your code very much. Why do we need two packages? A loose coupling between React packages and the browser makes sense. We don't use ReactDOM in mobile devices. We use React-Native for mobile development with React. React-Native acts as the middleman there. We use ReactDOM only in web apps.

Now let's install these two packages. Type npm install react react-dom in the terminal. Refer to Figure 3-3. npm install is an npm command that installs one or more npm packages.

Figure 3-3. *Installing react and react-dom*

As shown in Figure 3-3, the command successfully installed the packages. A folder node_modules got created with react and react-dom folders. Also, it created a JSON file, package-lock.json. The packages are now linked to the project.

During npm install, it autogenerated package-lock.json. It keeps track of the exact versions of all packages that are installed so that a product is 100% reproducible, even if the maintainers update the packages. package-lock.json contains information regarding the version of the React package and its dependencies. You can see that the React package depends on three packages: js-tokens, loose-envify, and scheduler. These packages were also installed when you ran the command. You can find the corresponding folders to these packages in the node_modules folder. The node_modules folder contains all the libraries downloaded via npm.

So far, we have initialized the project and installed npm packages that are required for running React code. If you look at package.json, you can see that it has react and react-dom also as dependencies.

Step 3: Create your index files.

We need to create an HTML and a JS file that will serve as the entry point of our project. You can see the New Folder and New File icons next to the CODE folder. Click New Folder and create a new folder and name it src. Then select the src folder and click New File. Name it index.html. Copy the code in Listing 3-2 into index.html.

Listing 3-2. index.html

```html
<html>
<body>
    <div id="root"></div>
    <script src="index.js"></script>
</body>
</html>
```

As you can see from Listing 3-2, this HTML file has a div element with id root. Also, it refers to the index.js file, which we are yet to create. Create a new file under the same src folder and name it index.js. Copy Listing 3-3 into index.js.

Listing 3-3. index.js

```js
import React from 'react';
import ReactDOM from "react-dom/client";
```

```
const root = ReactDOM.createRoot(document.getElementById("root"));
root.render(
  <React.StrictMode>
    <h1>Just React</h1>
  </React.StrictMode>
);
```

In the `index.js` file, we imported `react` and `react-dom` packages. We used the `createRoot` and `render` methods of `ReactDOM` to render an `h1` element inside the root `div` element.

Will the code work now? No, the browser cannot understand our code at this stage. Let's continue on to the next step.

Step 4: Set up Webpack.

It is time to set up Webpack. As discussed before, in a React application, we will have a lot of code modules that we are referring to. So the total application package size can become huge. Webpack is a bundler that bundles all the JS files. It goes through the application package and creates a dependency graph to map all your modules. Depending on the graph, it creates a `bundle.js` file, which can then be inserted into an HTML file.

Let's install Webpack packages and create a Webpack configuration file. We will further explore Webpack after that.

To install Webpack packages, return to the VS Code terminal and enter the following command:

```
npm install webpack webpack-cli webpack-dev-server html-webpack-plugin
--save-dev
```

We use the `webpack` package to bundle all our code. The `webpack-dev-server` package allows us to execute the application in a local server during development. The webpack-cli package provides a set of commands we can use while setting up the project. The `html-webpack-plugin` is a Webpack plugin that is used to inject the bundled JS file into the HTML file. Using the `--save-dev` option ensures that it only added these packages as development dependencies. We do not require the preceding packages to run the application in production but for development.

Figure 3-4 shows the command execution. Also, you can see the current folder structure with HTML and JS files.

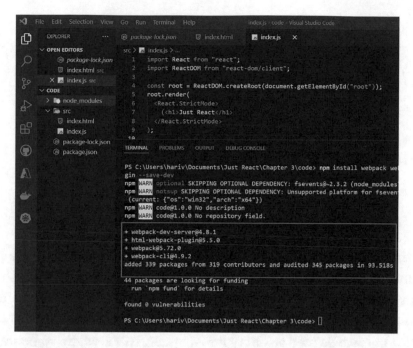

Figure 3-4. *Installing Webpack dependencies*

Once we installed the Webpack packages, we need to set up a Webpack configuration file. Create a file called `webpack.config.js` under the root folder, which is the same directory where the `package.json` sits. Then, copy the code from Listing 3-4.

Note   You can run a command, `touch webpack.config.js`, from the root directory to create this file. If you create by clicking the icon, from VS Code explorer, it may be created inside any child folders. If that happens, drag it on to the root.

Listing 3-4. webpack.config.js

```
const path = require('path');
const HtmlWebpackPlugin = require('html-webpack-plugin');
module.exports = {
  mode: "development",
  entry: path.join(__dirname, "src", "index.js"),
  output: {
    path:path.resolve(__dirname, "dist"),
```

```
  },
devServer: {
   open: true
  },

  plugins: [
    new HtmlWebpackPlugin({
      template: path.join(__dirname, "src", "index.html"),
    }),
  ],
};
```

During the first step, we defined two variables, `path` and `HtmlWebpackPlugin`. The requires function mapped the modules to the respective variables. The `path` variable holds the `path` module, and `HtmlWebpackPlugin` holds the `html-webpack-plugin` module. The `path` is a native Node JS module that allows us to concatenate file paths.

In the next line, we defined an `entry` for Webpack. This is where Webpack bundles and creates the dependency graph. We pointed the entry at the `index.js` file. We also defined `mode` as `development`. This is important as it tells Webpack to use its built-in optimizations. Next, we defined an `output`. This tells Webpack where to bundle the application. We specified it as a new folder `dist` under the root folder. The `devServer` key launches your local server by default without typing the URL. Having the key `plugins` ensures that the bundled JS gets injected into the `index.html`.

We now have set up bundling for your application so that we send only a single JS file to the browser. However, the browser will not understand your code because Webpack bundled it with JSX code plus ECMAScript 2015 (ES6) and above code. Before you bundle and send to a browser, you need to convert your code into something that a browser can understand. Let's do that in the next step.

Step 5: Set up Babel.

This step is about setting up Babel. Babel is a JavaScript compiler. Babel converts ES6 and above code into a version of JS that runs in any browser, as well as JSX code. JSX is what we use for writing HTML in React. Your browser would not understand modern JS or JSX. You write your code in JSX and modern JS. Babel makes sure that the browser understands it.

We call Babel a transpiler. Transpiling is a special type of compiling where source code written in one language is transformed into another language that has a similar level of abstraction.

Go back to the VS Code terminal and run the following command to install the Babel packages:

```
npm install @babel/core babel-loader @babel/preset-env @babel/preset-react
--save-dev
```

babel/core is the core Babel library, which does the transpiling. The babel/preset-env package is a preset that allows you to use modern JS without worrying about browser compatibility issues. The babel/preset-react package exactly does the same thing but for JSX code. And the babel-loader is a package that tells Webpack how to interpret and translate files before it does the bundling. The transformation occurs on a per-file basis before Webpack constructs the dependency graph.

Refer to Figure 3-5, where we install all the required Babel packages.

Figure 3-5. *Installing Babel*

We currently have all the required packages. One thing is still missing, which is to add the Babel loader into the Webpack configuration. Let's do that in the next step.

Step 6: Update Webpack to enable transpiling.

As I mentioned earlier, in the Webpack configuration, we need to use the Babel loader to make sure that the code is transpiled before bundling. For that, let us add the following code to `webpack.config.js`. We have created this file under the root directory during step 4:

```
module: {
  rules: [
    {
      test: /\.?js$/,
      exclude: /node_modules/,
      use: {
        loader: "babel-loader",
        options: {
          presets: ["@babel/preset-env", "@babel/preset-react"],
        },
      },
    },
  ];
}
```

This code section sets a rule to use babel-loader. Also, we specify only JS files be transpiled, using the `/\.?js$/` expression. We only need our code to be transpiled, not the `node_modules` folder. So we specify `node_modules` under the `exclude` section. In addition, we add the presets `babel/preset-env` and `babel/preset-react,` so that Babel transpiles both ES6+ syntax and JSX code.

Update `webpack.config.js` to include the preceding code. Now, the file should look like Listing 3-5.

Listing 3-5. webpack.config.js

```
const path = require("path");
const HtmlWebpackPlugin = require("html-webpack-plugin");
module.exports = {
  mode: "development",
```

```
    entry: path.join(__dirname, "src", "index.js"),
    output: {
      path: path.resolve(__dirname, "dist"),
    },
    module: {
      rules: [
        {
          test: /\.?js$/,
          exclude: /node_modules/,
          use: {
            loader: "babel-loader",
            options: {
              presets: ["@babel/preset-env", "@babel/preset-react"],
            },
          },
        },
      ],
    },
    devServer: {
      open: true,
    },
    plugins: [
      new HtmlWebpackPlugin({
        template: path.join(__dirname, "src", "index.html"),
      }),
    ],
};
```

Step 7: Build and run!

We are now at the last step of building and running the app. To do so, locate the scripts tag in package.json and update as in the following:

```
"scripts": {
    "start": "webpack serve",
    "build": "webpack"
}
```

The script `start` will use the Webpack server and run the application locally. The `build` will create a bundle.

Launch the VS Code terminal and run the command `npm start`. See Figure 3-6.

Figure 3-6. *Running your app*

This will open the localhost, and you can see the heading `Just React` in the browser. Refer to Figure 3-7.

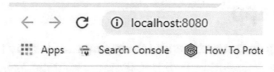

Just React

Figure 3-7. *React code executed on the local server*

Remember, we have provided only one h1 element with this content. We can change the index.html or index.js code while the application is running, to include more content. The browser page will update automatically and display our updated content without needing to refresh.

Note   The code in the index.js may look a bit odd at this stage, especially the <h1>Just React</h1> part, as you are yet to learn how to code in React. For now, just understand that it is a way of adding a header to display in the browser. This will make sense when I explain components and JSX in the upcoming sections.

Congratulations! You have just developed your first React application, the hard way. And you did it all by yourself! As mentioned earlier, the whole point of this exercise was to help you understand how a React application works internally.

From now on, you can just use the create-react-app command to create everything for you. We discuss that next.

Note   To stop execution from the VS Code terminal, just press Ctrl+C on the keyboard and press Y for the prompt in the terminal. You can use the cls command to clean up the console. To create a folder, use the md command. To navigate to the folder, use the cd command.

---

create-react-app

The `create-react-app` command is a toolchain that enables you to create a React app without worrying about the configuration. Let's create a React project using this tool.

In the VS Code terminal, stop execution if you didn't already. Let us create a new folder (`Projects`). Remember to create this outside of the previous project folder you created in the previous section, to avoid any conflicts. Open the folder in VS Code Explorer using File ➤ Open Folder. Run the following command:

```
npx create-react-app just-react
```

The Node Package Execute (`npx`) is an `npm` package runner you can use to run any package from the NPM registry without even installing it. The `npx` comes with the `npm` when you install Node.js. The last parameter `just-react` is the name of our project.

It will take a few minutes for the command to finish executing. It will install quite a few packages. Figure 3-8 illustrates how the VS Code Explorer screen will look like after the command completes its execution.

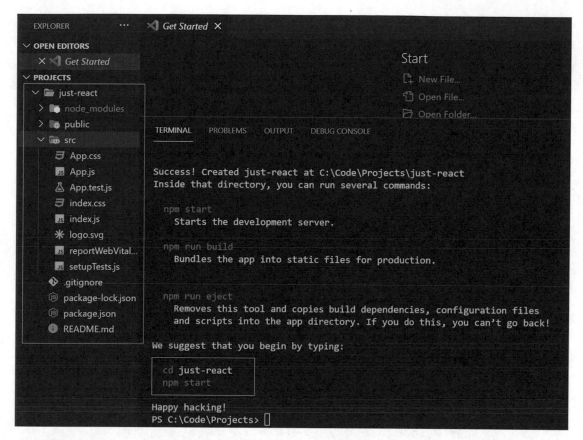

Figure 3-8. *create-react-app*

As you can see, several JS files got created for you, such as package.json, package-lock.json, node_modules, etc. Move to your project folder using the cd just-react command. If the files are not opened on the VS Code Explorer (left-hand side), click File from the top and then select Open Folder and then open the project folder that way. Next, run the command npm start. This will open the localhost page in your browser. It will display the React logo along with the text "Edit src/App.js and save to reload".

Note   To run the commands, if the terminal is not visible in VS Code, you can click "View" from the top and then select Terminal.

Go to src ➤ App.js file. Update some contents inside the file. Say you can update the "Learn React" text to "Just React". Keep the browser open side by side. You can see the browser refreshes automatically with the new content.

Refer to Listing 3-6 where I just updated "Learn React" to "Just React". You can edit any tags or content.

Listing 3-6. App.js

```
import React, { Component } from "react";
class App extends Component {
  render() {
    return (
      <div className="App">
        <header className="App-header">
          <p>
            Edit <code>src/App.js</code> and save to reload.
          </p>
          <a
            className="App-link"
            href="https://reactjs.org"
            target="_blank"
            rel="noopener noreferrer"
          >
            Just React
          </a>
        </header>
      </div>
    );
  }
}
export default App;
```

Let's see how this rendering worked.

The index.html is the entry point of our application. In public ➤ index.html, you can see the div element with the id root. In src ➤ index.js, you can see the following code, where the ReactDOM renders the App component into the div:

```
const root = ReactDOM.createRoot(document.getElementById('root'));
root.render(
  <React.StrictMode>
```

```
  <App />
 </React.StrictMode>
);
```

You can see that the index.js renders the App component, which subsequently loads the content in App.js in the browser. As you can see, it already imported all the required packages in the components. Everything is pre-built for you by the create-react-app tool. You just need to build your own components on top of this.

As a summary, the following are the points we learned:

1. How to create a new React project with create-react-app.

2. The tool create-react-app configured everything for you, including project initialization, file creation, package import, Webpack setup, Babel setup, etc.

3. index.html is the entry point of the application.

4. index.js loads the App component into the root element of index.html.

5. We defined the App component in the App.js file.

6. By modifying the App.js (App component), you can change the application content, and the browser automatically updates the page based on the changes.

Note   To view the React version you are using, run the command npm ls react from the VS Code terminal. I am using React 18.1.0 for the examples in this book. When you run create-react-app, it will create the app by default in the latest version.

Let us continue by learning about components and JSX in the next section. We will build on top of the project we created in this section.

Introduction to Components

Components are building blocks of any React app. A React application's user interface (UI) is a component, and it can comprise multiple components. A brick wall is a real-life example. Each brick here is a component that goes into the final component, the wall.

A component is a JavaScript class or function that takes an input optionally and returns a React element. That element describes how a portion of the UI should appear. The following example will help clarify this.

Go to the project you created in the previous section. Go to the src folder of your project and replace the entire code in App.js with the following. Refer to Listing 3-7.

Listing 3-7. App.js

```
import './App.css';
function App() {
  const handleClick = () => {
    alert("Start Reacting");
  };  return (
    <div className="App">
      <button onClick={handleClick}>Just React</button>
    </div>
  );
}
export default App;
```

You will see that the browser page gets updated and the button Just React appears. When you click it, you will get the alert Start Reacting. This component, App, is an example of a functional component. In this example, the component has no input parameters. The component returns the following element, which describes how the UI section should look:

```
<div className="App">
  <button onClick={handleClick}>Just React</button>
</div>
```

Within a div element, we added a button element with the value Just React. The App function returns this element. The button click invokes a function handleClick. This function is also a part of the App component:

```
const handleClick = () => {
    alert("Start Reacting!");
};
```

Last, there is an export keyword that exports this component so other components can refer to it:

```
export default App;
```

A component contains both UI elements and their associated functionality. Here, the App component combined the content of the div and button elements with the handleClick function.

In React, components enable reusability and modularity. Every component has a task, and it focuses on that. We have two types of components in React, class components, and function components (you can either use the term function component or functional component. Both denotes the same). When you progress through the chapter, you will learn about components in detail.

We learned in this section that a React app is built from components. Components are fundamental to a React app. It is important to break the app into components, each of which focuses on completing a single task. Components can optionally accept inputs and return React elements. Each component represents a part of the UI.

JSX

In the previous section, you saw that we returned the div and button elements in the App component. It looks like HTML, but it is not. It's known as JavaScript XML (JSX). JSX is used by React to describe how the UI looks like. We can write the component code in plain JS, including the creation of HTML elements. JSX makes it easier by providing a visual feel like HTML.

JSX appears to be HTML, but it is a syntax coating on top of JavaScript. JSX allows you to write HTML in React and helps you create user interfaces easily.

We discussed a tool Babel in the section "How to React," Step 5. Babel makes your browser understand your JSX.

Let us see how JSX appears in the browser. Go to the browser page where you opened the App component earlier. Then, press F12 to open the developer tools. If you have already stopped execution, simply enter the command npm start, to restart the app.

Next, click Sources and examine the page tree and locate the bundle.js and search for function App() inside that. Refer to Figure 3-9.

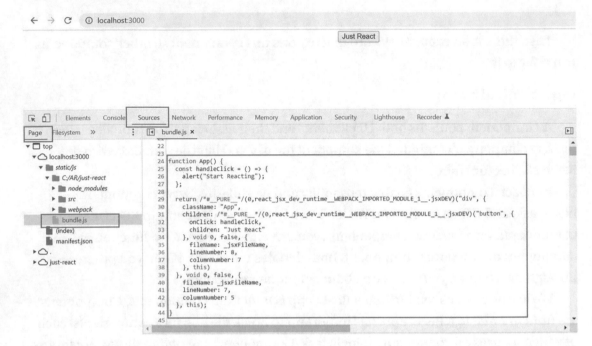

Figure 3-9. *Inspecting the component*

As you can see, behind the scenes, Babel already converted our code into JavaScript code the browser understands. Instead of using JSX, if we have written your code like this, it would be harder to both write and maintain. JSX makes our React life easier.

In short, JSX is your visual-friendly coding option to construct the DOM in React. You will learn to write more complex JSX as and when we advance through sections and chapters. Next, let's build a small app in React so that you can learn more about components, JSX, and the rendering process in React.

Reacting to Inputs

In this section, we will create an input form inside a component and then display it in the browser. We will accomplish this by adding on to the just-react app we created earlier.

Let's create a component named EnrolmentForm and create a form for the users to provide student details.

Right-click the src folder and click New File. Name it EnrolmentForm.js. Copy Listing 3-8 into EnrolmentForm.js.

Listing 3-8. EnrolmentForm.js

```
import "./App.css";
function EnrolmentForm() {
  return (
    <div>
    <form>
      <h1>Student Details</h1>
      <label>First name:</label>
      <input type="text" name="fname" />
      <br />
      <label>Last name:</label>
      <input type="text" name="lname"   />
      <br />
      <br />
      <input type="submit" value="Submit" />
    </form>
  </div>
  );
}
export default EnrolmentForm;
```

Let's go over the code line by line. As you can see, this is just a simple form with two inputs and a button. There is a reference to App.css on the top. Ignore it for now. We will add some code inside that for styling, at a later point in time.

The index.js already contains the logic to render the App component. But, if we need to see the contents of the enrolment form in the browser, we should update the App component to render the EnrolmentForm component. So let's update the App.js, from where we left at Listing 3-7 in the previous section.

Refer to Listing 3-9 for the updated App.js.

Listing 3-9. App.js

```
import './App.css';
import EnrolmentForm from './EnrolmentForm';
function App() {
```

```
  return (
    <div className="App">
      <EnrolmentForm>Just React</EnrolmentForm>
    </div>
  );
}
export default App;
```

Let's go over the code line by line. First, we imported EnrolmentForm using the following statement:

```
import EnrolmentForm from './EnrolmentForm';
```

This makes it available to use in the current component, which is App. The ./ EnrolmentForm is the path to EnrolmentForm.js.

Inside the div element, now we replaced the previous button element with the EnrolmentForm tag. Also, we removed the handleClick function, which we don't require at this stage.

In the browser, you can see that the form is now displayed. Refer to Figure 3-10.

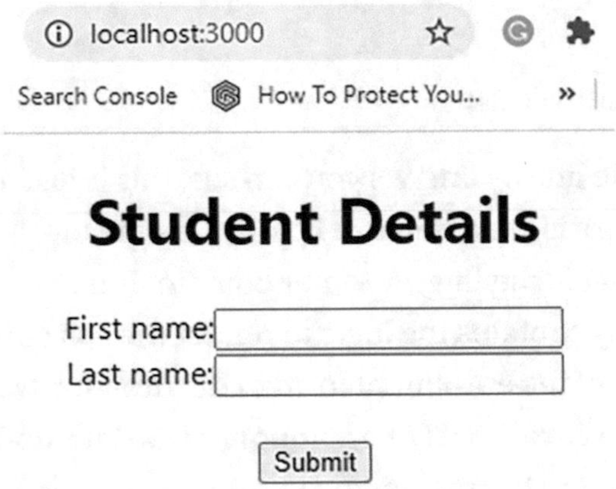

Figure 3-10. *Form in a React component*

We added the EnrolmentForm component to the root component, the App component. We have seen how the form looks in the browser. Note that the form elements we added inside the EnrolmentForm component are written in JSX. The JSX here describes how the form should look like. In the next section, let us add some styles to the form and learn how to implement some basic styling in React components.

Styling Your Component

We can style HTML elements by using Cascading Style Sheets (CSS) classes or by using inline styles. We can do the same with React elements. In this section, we will examine the basic styling of a component.

If you look at `EnrolmentForm.js`, you can see that we added a reference to `App.css`. The `App.css` is created by default when we created the application. Let's remove the existing code there and add some new classes to it. Copy the following CSS code into `App.css` and replace the existing code there (Listing 3-10).

Listing 3-10. App.css

```css
.enrolForm {
   font-family:sans-serif;
   font-size: 26px;
   text-align: center;
   width: 500px;
   padding:100px;
}

.enrolForm input[type=text] {
  margin :20px;
  padding:20px;
  border:0;
  box-shadow:0 0 25px 4px rgba(0,0,0,0.06);
  border: 2px solid #eee;
  width: 250px;
  font-family: inherit;
  font-size: inherit;
}

.enrolForm input[type=submit]
{
  background: #4691A4;
 font-family: inherit;
  font-size: inherit;
  cursor: pointer;
```

```
  color: white;
}
```

The preceding CSS code defines three classes. One is the enrolForm class. The other two are based on the input type. The second class enrolForm input[type=text] applies to all text fields inside a form that has the class enrolForm. Finally, the third class enrolForm input[type=submit] is the class used for all button elements inside a form if the form has the class enrolForm. As you may already know, CSS classes begin with the . symbol.

Now we need to apply the class enrolForm to our form so that the input elements get these styles. Update the form element in the EnrolmentForm.js. Replace the <form> tag with the following code. Refer to Listing 3-8 in the previous section for the EnrolmentForm.js code:

```
<form className="enrolForm">
```

The className keyword in JSX is used to describe a class to an element. Now the form and the child input elements are styled as per the defined classes. View the app now in the browser. It will look as in Figure 3-11.

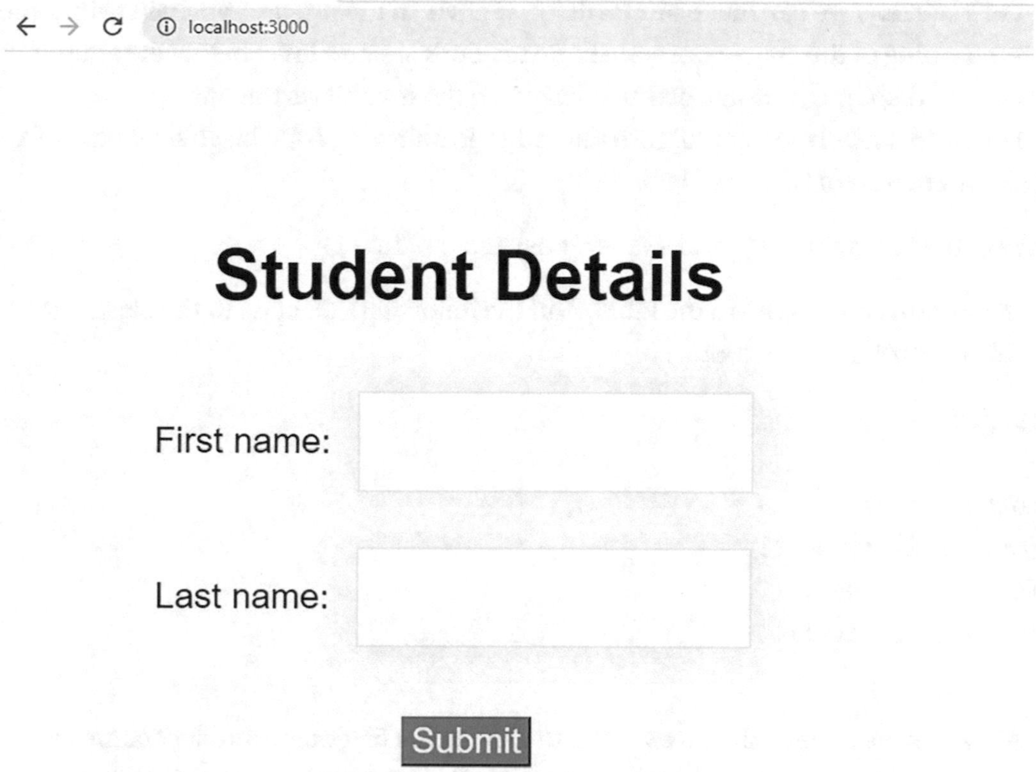

Figure 3-11. *Styles in a React component*

Now the form looks better since we applied all the styles defined in `App.css`.

With this section, you learned how to apply basic styling to a component by importing a CSS file and using the `className` keyword. In Chapter 6, we will dive deeper into styling in React and introduce you to dynamic styles, modules, etc.

We now have a simple form with some basic styling. You can enter data into both the input boxes and also click the button. In the next section, we'll see how to capture and display your data after you click the button.

State in React

State is a plain JavaScript object used by React to represent information about the component's current situation. A normal variable's value will vanish when we exit the function, provided that we declared it in the function's scope. However, in React, it preserves the state variable's value.

Let's see how we can make our form interactive. In the process, you will gain some understanding of the concept of state in React. Let's create a label below the submit button and display a message on the label when the user clicks the button.

Let's add a label element to the form. Add the following code just below the `</form>` tag in the `EnrolmentForm.js` file:

```
<label id="studentMsg" className="message"></label>
```

Let us add some styles to the label. Add the following CSS class to the classes that you added earlier in `App.css`:

```
.message
{
  color:green;
  font-family: inherit;
  font-size: 30px;
  font-style: italic;
}
```

Now that we have a label, we want it to display the first name and last name as soon as the user enters those into the text boxes and clicks the submit button. To display these names, let's add some logic to `App.js`.

For this scenario, what we would have done in plain JavaScript would be to get the values of the first name and last name from the input fields. We can achieve this by querying the elements by their id or another attribute. With React, we achieve this by managing the state.

In this example, we will use a React Hook called `useState()` to handle state. We will learn more about Hooks in Chapter 8. For now, just understand that the `useState` Hook is a function that allows you to declare state variables in the functional components.

When you pass the initial state to this function, it returns a variable with the current state value and another function to update that value. The first element holds the value, and the second element is the function, which can update the value of the first variable.

For example, let us declare a state variable for the first name as in the following using the `useState` Hook:

```
const [firstName, setFirstName] = useState("");
```

As shown by the empty quotes parameter on useState(), firstName is a variable that has an empty initial value. The function setFirstName can set the value of firstName. For example, with the following code, you can set firstName to John:

```
setFirstName("John");
```

Refer to Listing 3-11 and update EnrolmentForm.js to store the first name and last name to the label. We will go into detail about the code in the following.

Listing 3-11. EnrolmentForm.js with State

```
import { useState } from "react";
import "./App.css";

function EnrolmentForm() {
  const [firstName, setFirstName] = useState("");
  const [lastName, setLastName] = useState("");
  const [welcomeMessage, setWelcomeMessage] = useState("");

  const handleSubmit = (event) => {
    setWelcomeMessage(`Welcome ${firstName} ${lastName}`);
    event.preventDefault();
  };

  return (
    <div>
      <form className="enrolForm" onSubmit={handleSubmit}>
        <h1>Student Details</h1>
        <label>First name:</label>
        <input type="text" name="fname" onBlur={(event) =>
        setFirstName(event.target.value)} />
        <br />
        <label>Last name:</label>
        <input type="text" name="lname" onBlur={(event) =>
        setLastName(event.target.value)} />
        <br />
        <br />
        <input type="submit" value="Submit" />
        <br />
```

```
        <label id="studentMsg" className="message">
          {welcomeMessage}
        </label>
      </form>
    </div>
  );
}
export default EnrolmentForm;
```

Let's examine the code line by line. First, we imported useState from react, so that we can use it to create state variables:

```
import { useState } from "react";
```

Then, we added three state variables: one for the first name, one for the last name, and one for the welcome message. The welcome message will be set to the label once the user clicks the submit button:

```
const [firstName, setFirstName] = useState("");
const [lastName, setLastName] = useState("");
const [welcomeMessage, setWelcomeMessage] = useState("");
```

In the following JSX code, you can see that the setFirstName method is called on the onBlur event of the input field where the user enters their first name:

```
<input type="text" name="fname" onBlur={(event) => setFirstName(event.
target.value)} />
```

When a user enters the value and clicks outside of the first name input field, the setFirstName method called with event.target.value sets the entered value to the firstName variable. The event.target returns the element that triggered the event, which is the input field for the first name in this case. The event.target.value thus gives us the value, which is entered in the first name input box. So the setFirstName method sets the entered value to the firstName variable.

A similar thing happens for the input field for the last name when the user enters a value and clicks outside:

```
<input type="text" name="lname" onBlur={(event) => setLastName(event.
target.value)} />
```

The setLastName method sets the entered value in the last name input field to the lastName variable. Therefore, the first and last name values will be saved to the respective state variables once the user has finished entering them in their respective input fields.

During the onSubmit event of the form, we set it to invoke the handleSubmit function. This form submit occurs when the user clicks the submit button:

```
<form className="enrolForm" onSubmit={handleSubmit}>
```

Now, we set the first name and last name values in the output label inside the handleSubmit function:

```
const handleSubmit = (event) => {
    setWelcomeMessage(`Welcome ${firstName} ${lastName}`);
    event.preventDefault();
};
```

The function handleSubmit sets the message Welcome first name last name to the state variable welcomeMessage.

Note   We use event.preventDefault() in order to avoid additional browser loads. A form submit event will invoke browser refresh, which is a native behavior of the submit button. We cancel this default behavior by adding event.preventDefault(). Whenever you use a submit button, add this line at the end of the event function.

In JSX, we set the welcomeMessage variable value to the output label, so that the label will print out the value of the welcomeMessage variable:

```
<label id="studentMsg" className="message">
        {welcomeMessage}
      </label>
```

When the user enters their first name and last name and clicks the button, the function handleSubmit gets called. Then it sets the value to the welcomeMessage variable. The label appears with the message that contains the name.

Now, let's view the app in the browser. Enter values for the first name and last name. Click the button, and you'll see the values printed out below it. Refer to Figure 3-12. I highlighted the user steps with the red tick marks and numbers.

Student Details

First name: John

Last name: Smith

Submit

Welcome John Smith

Figure 3-12. *State handling in a React component(Steps: 1, enter first and last names; 2, click the button; 3, the message appears)*

In this example, we have seen how we can make an input form interactive by handling the state of the elements. It is noticeable that React and JavaScript differ significantly in how they handle input values and produce output.

Next, let's examine how React code is being executed in the browser behind the scenes.

Virtual DOM

In the first chapter, we discussed the Document Object Model (DOM) and Virtual DOM. Let us see how the Virtual DOM works with respect to the app just-react, which we created in an earlier section. In the DOM, HTML elements are represented as a tree of objects. For example, in our student enrolment form component, we consider each input field as a node in the object tree. Refer to Figure 3-13 for a pictorial representation of the DOM in relation to the enrolment form. We considered only the input fields and the output label here.

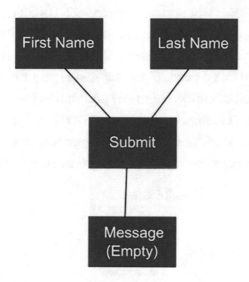

Figure 3-13. *DOM tree of a React component*

When parts of the DOM change, the browser recalculates the CSS, revalidates parts of the render tree, does a reflow (redoing the layout), and then repaints the screen.

The following shows how we can update the output label in the enrolment form with plain JavaScript code:

```
const fieldLabel = document.getElementById("studentMsg");
fieldLabel.textContent = "Welcome John Smith";
```

We are accessing the DOM from our code in the preceding JS example to retrieve a label by its id and then write to it.

The JSX code we have written inside the return statement in the enrolment form component does not create any HTML elements or insert anything into the DOM. The JSX code is just a description of what we want the browser to display. We just described how the enrolment form should look through our JSX code. React then constructs a Virtual DOM tree of elements as per our JSX description. The Virtual DOM tree is a blueprint that exists in memory but is never rendered.

In the Virtual DOM, React builds an in-memory DOM tree, which is then rendered to the real DOM. During our school days, we might have written notes in a quick and dirty form during the lectures. Later, we merge these notes into a more readable form, after making all the required corrections. The Virtual DOM is something similar to these quick notes.

Let's continue with our enrolment form as an example. When the content of the output label is updated, React will update the Virtual DOM. It compares this to the previous Virtual DOM where the label content was blank. Finally, it will patch the real DOM with the difference. Here, the browser will not repaint the entire DOM; rather, it repaints only the changed DOM parts. If you are making multiple changes, React will find the minimum amount of modifications by comparing the previous and current copies of the Virtual DOM. Comparing the Virtual DOM and pre-updated Virtual DOM is called diffing. As the result of diffing, it creates a patch and updates the DOM. Refer to Figure 3-14, which shows how the Virtual DOM updates the DOM.

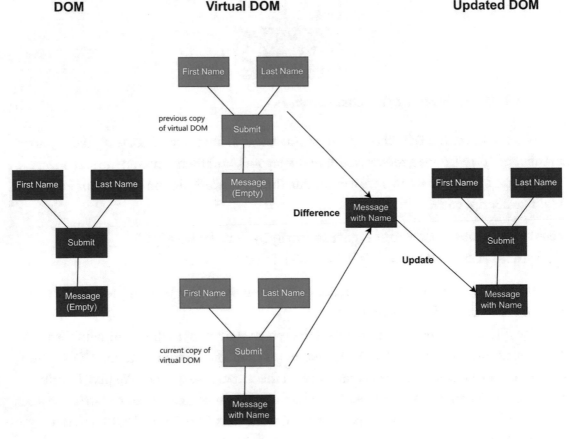

Figure 3-14. *Virtual DOM*

Props

Props to React elements are like attributes to HTML elements. In React, props allow components to communicate. For example, we can send data from the App component to the EnrolmentForm component by using props.

Let us continue with the example of our EnrolmentForm component. As of now, we are displaying the form title as Student Details. Imagine the following scenario: We need a separate form title for undergraduates and postgraduates. The title should be UG Student Details for undergraduates and PG Student Details for postgraduates. To accomplish this, we need to pass a prop from the App component to the EnrolmentForm component.

As you know, we are calling the EnrolmentForm component from the App component. The App component is the parent component here, and EnrolmentForm is the child component. Let us see if we can pass a parameter from the parent to the child. To start with, let us add a drop-down element to the App component so that the user can choose Undergraduate or Postgraduate. Then, we can display the form title accordingly. Update App.js as shown in Listing 3-12. We will discuss the code changes after the listing.

Listing 3-12. App.js with Passing Props

```
import "./App.css";
import EnrolmentForm from "./EnrolmentForm";
import { useState } from "react";

function App() {
  const [program, setProgram] = useState("UG");
  const handleChange = (event) => {
    setProgram(event.target.value);
  };

  return (
    <div className="App">
      <div className="programs">
        <label>Choose Program:</label>
        <select className="appDropDowns"
          onChange={handleChange}
          value={program} >
```

```
            <option value="UG">Undergraduate</option>
            <option value="PG">Postgraduate</option>
          </select>
        </div>
        <EnrolmentForm chosenProgram={program} />
      </div>
    );
}
export default App;
```

Let's examine the code in detail. After the required import statements, we initialized a state variable `program` with a default value `UG`. `const [program, setProgram] = useState("UG");`.

If we look at the JSX section, we added a `div` element on top of the `EnrolmentForm` tag. Within the `div` element, we have a `label` and a `select` element. The label is just to display `Choose Program:`. Using the drop-down (the `select` element), the user can select either Undergraduate or Postgraduate. We set the values for the `select` options, UG for undergraduate and PG for postgraduate:

```
<select className="appDropDowns"
          onChange={handleChange}
          value={program} >
          <option value="UG">Undergraduate</option>
          <option value="PG">Postgraduate</option>
    </select>
```

We set the onChange event of the `select` element to invoke a function handleChange. Whenever the user selects a value, the handleChange method gets called, and it sets the value of the state variable `program` according to the selection:

```
const handleChange = (event) => {
    setProgram(event.target.value);
  };
```

The `event.target.value` is UG if Undergraduate is selected and PG if Postgraduate is selected. So the value for `program` gets set accordingly.

Last, we added a prop to the `EnrolmentForm` tag called `chosenProgram`. We set it to the state variable `program`. The variable will have the value either UG or PG depending on the user selection. By default, the drop-down will have the value Undergraduate. This is because, when we initialized the variable program, we have set its default value to UG:

```
<EnrolmentForm selectedProgram={program} />
```

We added some styles to the new elements. Update App.css with the following additional CSS classes as shown in Listing 3-13. You can add your own styles as well if you like.

Listing 3-13. Additional Classes in App.css

```css
.App {
  font-family: sans-serif;
  font-size: 26px;
  text-align: left;
  width: 100%;
  padding-top: 50px;
  float: left;
}
.programs {
  padding-left: 100px;
  width: 100%;
  float: left;
}
.appDropDowns {
  color: black;
  font-family: inherit;
  font-size: inherit;
  margin-left: 10px;
}
```

If you see the app in the browser now, you will see the drop-down to select Undergraduate or Postgraduate. But the title will still say Student Details without specifying the default Undergraduate. Changing the drop-down also will not have any effect on the form title at this stage.

This is because we do not set the EnrolmentForm component to receive the prop, even though the App component passes the selected program as a prop. If you look at EnrolmentForm.js, the EnrolmentForm function has no parameters.

We must pass the props as a parameter to this component. The props parameter will return an object, from which we can get the value of the passed prop. Update the EnrolmentForm component by adding props as a parameter. You must also add the value of the chosenProgram prop to the h1 tag to display it in the title. Refer to Listing 3-14 for the updated code for EnrolmentForm.js. Let me go through each change after the listing.

Listing 3-14. EnrolmentForm.js with Receiving Props

```
import { useState } from "react";
import "./App.css";

function EnrolmentForm(props) {
  const [firstName, setFirstName] = useState("");
  const [lastName, setLastName] = useState("");
  const [welcomeMessage, setWelcomeMessage] = useState("");

  const handleSubmit = (event) => {
    setWelcomeMessage(`Welcome ${firstName} ${lastName}`);
    event.preventDefault();
  };

  return (
    <div>
      <form className="enrolForm" onSubmit={handleSubmit}>
        <h1>{props.selectedProgram} Student Details</h1>
        <label>First name:</label>
        <input
          type="text"
          name="fname"
          onBlur={(event) => setFirstName(event.target.value)}
        />
        <br />
        <label>Last name:</label>
        <input
          type="text"
          name="lname"
          onBlur={(event) => setLastName(event.target.value)}
        />
```

```
      <br />
      <br />
      <input type="submit" value="Submit" />
      <br />
      <label id="studentMsg" className="message">
        {welcomeMessage}
      </label>
    </form>
  </div>
);
}

export default EnrolmentForm;
```

As you can see, we made two changes to the EnrolmentForm component. First, we added props as a parameter to the component:

```
function EnrolmentForm(props)
```

Next, we added {props.selectedProgram} in front of Student Details in the heading:

```
<h1>{props.selectedProgram} Student Details</h1>
```

Now, if you look at the form in the browser, by default you will see UG Student Details as the form title. And it changes based on the program you select. Refer to Figure 3-15.

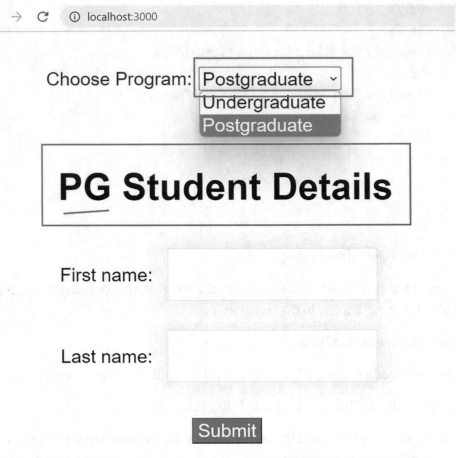

Figure 3-15. *Components communicate using props*

This simple example explained what a prop is and how components communicate using props.

Just React to Child

In our example in the preceding section, we have seen how we passed data from the parent component (App) to the child component (EnrolmentForm). The parent component passed the prop down the tree. Because of this, the child component could access the information from the parent. What if we want to pass information up the tree, that is, from the child component (EnrolmentForm) to the parent App component? Let us look at that next.

The child component cannot directly pass props to the parent component. However, there is a way we can achieve this. We can create a function in our parent component and then pass this function as a prop. For example, we create a function `parentFunction` in the App component, with `dataFromChild` as a parameter:

```
const parentFunction = (dataFromChild) => {
      console.log(dataFromChild);
};
```

Next, we can pass this function as a prop like this:

```
<EnrolmentForm parentFunction={ parentFunction } />
```

So here the function `parentFunction` is passed as a prop. Now this function is accessible for the child component from the props object. The EnrolmentForm component can invoke the function and pass arguments like this:

```
props.ParentFunction("I am passing this data");
```

This makes the data available in the parent component.

This way, the parent component can pass one or more functions to the child component. The child component can then use these functions to pass data and update the parent component's state. Let's see this in detail with our enrolment form project.

Assume that we have 100 seats for each program. Consider that the form we created is for internal use, where the staff users enter the students' information. As soon as the staff submits a new student's information, we need to subtract one seat from the total seats and display the remaining seats to the staff user.

The App component needs to display the remaining seats. This means whenever the user clicks the submit button on the `EnrolmentForm` component, we need to update the state in the parent component (`App`), so that it can display the correct number of seats.

Update `App.js` with the following code. Refer to Listing 3-15. We will discuss each change in the following.

Listing 3-15. App.js with a Function Passed as a Prop

```
import "./App.css";
import EnrolmentForm from "./EnrolmentForm";
import { useState } from "react";

function App() {
```

```
  const [program, setProgram] = useState("UG");
  const [seats, setSeats] = useState(100);
  const handleChange = (event) => {
    setProgram(event.target.value);
  };
  const setUpdatedSeats = (updatedSeats) => {
    setSeats(updatedSeats);
  };  return (
    <div className="App">
      <div className="programs">
        <label>Remaining Seats - {seats}</label>
        <br/>
        <br/>
        <label>Choose Program:</label>
        <select
          className="appDropDowns"
          onChange={handleChange}
          value={program}
        >
          <option value="UG">Undergraduate</option>
          <option value="PG">Postgraduate</option>
        </select>
      </div>
<EnrolmentForm
        chosenProgram={program}
        setUpdatedSeats={setUpdatedSeats}
        currentSeats={seats}
      />
    </div>
  );
}
export default App;
```

In comparison to the previous code, that is, Listing 3-12, we made only four changes to App.js.

First, we've created a state variable for seats, with an initial value of 100:

```
const [seats, setSeats] = useState(100);
```

Then, we defined a function that receives a parameter and sets seats with that:

```
const setUpdatedSeats = (updatedSeats) => {
    setSeats(updatedSeats);
};
```

Next, look at the JSX code where we added a label above the Choose Program label showing the number of remaining seats. The label displays the text Remaining seats - 100 initially:

```
<label>Remaining Seats - {seats}</label>
```

Finally, we added two more properties to the EnrolmentForm tag. We passed the variable seats and the function setUpdatedSeats to the EnrolmentForm component as props along with the previous prop program:

```
<EnrolmentForm
    chosenProgram={program}
    setUpdatedSeats={setUpdatedSeats}
    currentSeats={seats}
/>
```

We have the seats displayed in the app with an initial value of 100, which you can see in the browser now. However, the number of seats will not update if we add a new student. In order to make that work, we need to update the state of seats in the App component when the user clicks the submit button on the EnrolmentForm component.

We just need to make one change in EnrolmentForm.js to implement this. Update the handleSubmit function in EnrolmentForm.js as in the following:

```
const handleSubmit = (event) => {
    setWelcomeMessage(`Welcome ${firstName} ${lastName}`);
    props. setUpdatedSeats(props.currentSeats-1);
    event.preventDefault();
};
```

We added one line of code, props.setUpdatedSeats (props.currentSeats-1), to the handleSubmit function.

This invokes setUpdatedSeats in the App component by passing the remaining seats as the argument. The remaining seats are calculated by reducing one from the current number of seats. The setUpdatedSeats function receives this parameter and sets the value of seats accordingly:

```
const setUpdatedSeats = (updatedSeats) => {
    setSeats(updatedSeats);
  };
```

Now, try entering and submitting student details. You'll see the number of seats gets updated. Refer to Figure 3-16.

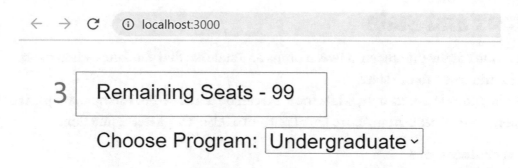

Figure 3-16. *Updating the parent state using props(Steps: 1, enter first and last names; 2, click the button; 3, the seats are updated)*

Here, we illustrated how to use props to update the state of the parent component by passing a function from the parent component and then invoking it from the child component. This example illustrated the two-way communication between components using props and state. Next, let's discuss the difference between props and state.

Props and State

Let us look at the difference between props and state, so that you know when to use props and when to use state.

The props are read-only, while the state can be updated. For example, we passed the current state of seats from App to EnrolmentForm. Also, we passed a function:

```
<EnrolmentForm
    setUpdatedSeats={setUpdatedSeats}
    currentSeats={seats}
/>
```

The EnrolmentForm component can access the state of seats now using the props object. It can access the property state via props.seats. Now, the value of seats is accessible as a prop to the EnrolmentForm component. So it cannot modify the state of seats. To update seats, the EnrolmentForm component needs to tell the parent, App component, to change its state. So we invoke the function setUpdatedSeats using the following:

```
props. setUpdatedSeats(props.currentSeats-1);
```

Now, the App component changes the state:

```
const setUpdatedSeats = (updatedSeats) => {
    setSeats(updatedSeats);
};
```

Using state, you can store data within a component, and you can make the component interactive by updating the state. When you want to communicate with another component, props come into play. If you want to access the state of a component outside of that component, you need to use props to pass that state. Then, other components can access it. But if the component wants to change that state, then it needs to contact the component where the state is defined. Again, it can use a prop to do that communication.

The props are read-only, while the state can be updated. The props are used to pass data through the component tree from top to bottom. We can pass state as props, just like setUpdatedSeats in our example.

Note   The more we move through the chapters, the more you will be familiar with the concepts of props and state and what the best practices are for using them.

React on a Condition

In Chapter 2, we discussed conditional rendering in JavaScript. Conditional rendering means to render components based on conditions. Conditional rendering in React works the same way. You can use operators like if or the ternary operator to update the UI with the required elements based on the state.

Our example showed a logic for displaying seat numbers when enrolling a student. However, we did not differentiate between undergraduates and postgraduates. Imagine we would like to offer 60 undergraduate seats and 40 postgraduate seats. We need to display seats according to the selected program. Let's see how we can achieve this using conditional rendering.

Let us update App.js with the updated code in Listing 3-16. Let me explain the changes in the following. EnrolmentForm.js does not require any further changes.

Listing 3-16. App.js with Conditional Rendering

```
import "./App.css";
import EnrolmentForm from "./EnrolmentForm";
import { useState } from "react";

function App() {
  const [program, setProgram] = useState("UG");
  const [ugSeats, setUgSeats] = useState(60);
  const [pgSeats, setPgSeats] = useState(40);

  const handleChange = (event) => {
    setProgram(event.target.value);
  };
  const setUpdatedSeats = (updatedSeats) => {
    if (program === "UG") {
      setUgSeats(updatedSeats);
    } else {
```

```
        setPgSeats(updatedSeats);
    }
  };
  return (
    <div className="App">
      <div className="programs">
        <label>Remaining UG Seats - {ugSeats}</label>
        <br />
        <br />
        <label>Remaining PG Seats - {pgSeats}</label>
        <br />
        <br />
        <label>Choose Program:</label>
        <select
          className="appDropDowns"
          onChange={handleChange}
          value={program}
        >
          <option value="UG">Undergraduate</option>
          <option value="PG">Postgraduate</option>
        </select>
      </div>
      <EnrolmentForm
        chosenProgram={program}
        setUpdatedSeats={ setUpdatedSeats}
        currentSeats={program === "UG" ? ugSeats : pgSeats}
      />
    </div>
  );
}
export default App;
```

As you can see from the preceding code, we made the following changes:

1. We removed the state variable seats and its associated function
    setSeats. Instead, we introduced two new variables, ugSeats

and pgSeats, each initialized with their initial values, 60 and 40, respectively:

```
const [ugSeats, setUgSeats] = useState(60);
const [pgSeats, setPgSeats] = useState(40);
```

2. We updated the function setUpdatedSeats. If the program selected is UG, we call setUgSeats. Otherwise, we call setPgSeats. This ensures that we update the seats according to the selected program:

```
const setUpdatedSeats = (updatedSeats) => {
    if (program === "UG") {
      setUgSeats(updatedSeats);
    } else {
      setPgSeats(updatedSeats);
    }
  };
```

3. We added one more label element. We updated the text of each label variable to reflect the values of ugSeats and pgSeats, respectively:

```
<label>Remaining UG Seats - {ugSeats}</label>
<label>Remaining PG Seats - {pgSeats}</label>
```

4. In the EnrolmentForm tag, we introduced a ternary operator for the currentSeats prop. If the program selected is UG, we pass ugSeats as the prop value. Otherwise, pgSeats is passed. This enables the EnrolmentForm component to receive the state of corresponding program seats and pass the corresponding argument to the function setUpdatedSeats from the handleSubmit function:

```
currentSeats={program === "UG" ? ugSeats : pgSeats}
```

Go back to the browser and submit a student's information by choosing either the Undergraduate or Postgraduate program. If you select Undergraduate, it will reduce the seats only from the undergraduate quota. If you select Postgraduate, it will reduce the seats from the postgraduate quota. Try submitting multiple enrolments. Refer to Figure 3-17.

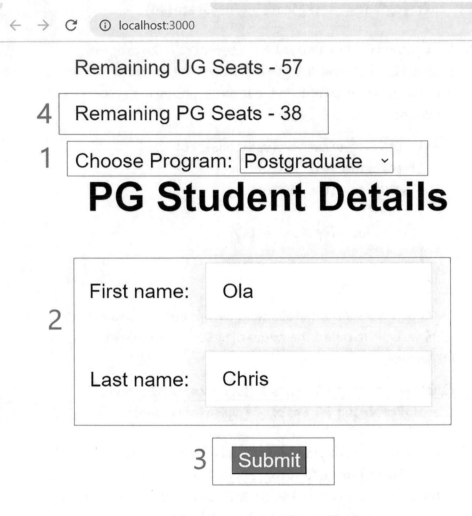

Figure 3-17. *Conditional rendering in a component(Steps: 1, select a program; 2, enter details; 3, click the button; 4, the specified program seats are updated)*

Thanks to conditional rendering, we achieved this functionality with minimal changes. Since the state is now passed conditionally, the corresponding state gets updated.

Note   You can download or clone the entire project at the end of each chapter from the GitHub repository. The final code at the end of each chapter is available in the respective chapter section in the repository. You can access the repository via the book's product page, `https://github.com/Apress/Just_React`. The `just-react` project is located under Chapter 3 ➤ Projects. After cloning, run `npm install`' from the project folder to install all the required node modules before running the code. You can access all listings under Chapter 3 ➤ Listings folder. This book contains listings and code sections that have been tested and verified in VS Code, so there is almost no chance of an error occurring. However, if some code won't work, or functionality is unexpected, due to any unseen formatting issues, ensure that you take the corresponding component code or clone the entire project from GitHub.

Summary

This chapter got you started with React. We created a React application from scratch. We took the hard road and learned how React actually works. You learned about Babel and Webpack. And, finally, you created your first React app.

You created the second app much easier with the help of the outstanding tool create-react-app. Then, we discussed fundamental concepts of React using a simple student enrolment form. We discussed React components, JSX, props, state, and the Virtual DOM. Components are building blocks of a React application. Each component represents a task. A parent component can pass data to a child component through props. JSX describes how a component should look in the browser. The Virtual DOM is the in-memory representation of a component that is described by JSX. State is a JS object that represents the current state of the component. React updates any changes to the state of a React component to the Virtual DOM. React batches the state changes together and compares the Virtual DOM and pre-updated Virtual DOM. Then, it updates the browser DOM, and finally the browser displays the component to the user.

You learned about passing a function as a prop from a parent component to its child component. We discussed how this can update the state of the parent component by calling the function from the child component. Finally, we discussed conditional rendering in React. We illustrated it with a simple example.

We will unpack more into each of the concepts you learned in this chapter. In the next chapter, we will do more component interactions and will build more into our enrolment application by exploring events, props, state, and Hooks. In the process, you will start thinking in React!

CHAPTER 4

Think React

In the previous chapter, you learned some basic concepts of React. We demonstrated these concepts with the help of a student enrolment form project. In this chapter, we will create a fully functional frontend application using the basic concepts of React.

This chapter will expand on the enrolment form project. We will discuss more about React concepts such as props and state, and I will introduce you to lifecycle events in React. Our project will comprise multiple components, and we will learn more about how to deal with the state between them. We will also look at React Hooks in more depth.

The focus of the first section would be to construct the enrolment form by applying some styling and refactoring. You will also gain an understanding of Fluent UI in this chapter. We will add more components to our application and make the components more cohesive. During the next few sections, we aim to design a list that stores and displays student details. We will incorporate the ability to add, delete, and edit items, allowing for more interaction between the form and list components.

This chapter builds a fully functional application by using the most recommended concepts of React. You will become adept at managing state between components by the end of this chapter.

VS Code Extensions

Before we start with the chapter, you may want to install some extensions in Visual Studio Code (VS Code) for better development experience. You can install several extensions in VS Code. Go to the Extensions tab and type in the extension name and install it. I recommend at least installing Prettier, ESLint, ES7 React/Redux/GraphQL/React-Native snippets, VS Code React Refactor, and JS JSX Snippets. Another useful extension is JavaScript Booster. You can always type in React in the Extensions search tab, review details of the extensions, and, if they seem useful, install them. You can see the details of each extension at the bottom, when you select an extension.

© Hari Narayn 2022
H. Narayn, *Just React!*, https://doi.org/10.1007/978-1-4842-8294-6_4

Note   If you want to copy one or more lines of code in VS Code, select the code you want to copy and then press Shift+Alt+down arrow. This will copy the line or set of lines to the bottom.

Restructuring the React Form

In the previous chapter, we built a form where staff can enroll undergraduate and postgraduate students. Let us add some basic styling to it before we continue building. We will also do some code refactoring. Open the project just-react in VS Code. This is the enrolment project we created in Chapter 3. Open App.js, EnrolmentForm.js, and App.css and update as per the following listings. I will explain the changes made to each file after the listings. First, open App.js and replace code as per Listing 4-1.

Note   You can find the final project code of the chapter under the path Chapter 4 ➤ Projects ➤ just-react in the GitHub repository. You can access the repository via the book's product page, https://github.com/Apress/Just_React.

Listing 4-1. App.js

```
import "./App.css";
import EnrolmentForm from "./EnrolmentForm";
import { useState } from "react";

const App = () => {
  const [program, setProgram] = useState("UG");
  const [ugSeats, setUgSeats] = useState(60);
  const [pgSeats, setPgSeats] = useState(40);

  const handleChange = (event) => {
    setProgram(event.target.value);
    setPgSeats(pgSeats);
    setUgSeats(ugSeats);
  };
```

```
const setUpdatedSeats = (updatedSeats) => {
    if (program === "UG") {
      setUgSeats(updatedSeats);
    } else {
      setPgSeats(updatedSeats);
    }
};

  return (
    <div className="App">
      <div className="programs">
      <h3 className="title">Student Enrolment Form</h3>
        <ul className="ulEnrol">

<li className="parentLabels" onChange={handleChange}>
            <input
              type="radio"
              value="UG"
              name="programGroup"
              defaultChecked
            />
            Undergraduate
            <input
              type="radio"
              className="radioSel"
              value="PG"
              name="programGroup"
            />
            Postgraduate
          </li>
          <li>
            <label className="parentLabels">
              Remaining {program} Seats - {program === "UG" ? ugSeats :
              pgSeats}
            </label>
          </li>
```

```
      </ul>
    </div>
    <EnrolmentForm
      chosenProgram={program}
      setUpdatedSeats={setUpdatedSeats}

      currentSeats={program === "UG" ? ugSeats : pgSeats}
    />
  </div>
  );
}

export default App;
```

The following are the changes made to `App.js` since its last listing, which is Listing 3-16 of Chapter 3:

1. Made a syntax change – updated the component function to an arrow function.

2. Added a header with the title as Student Enrolment Form:

   ```
   <h3 className="title">Student Enrolment Form</h3>
   ```

3. Added radio buttons instead of the drop-down menu we had earlier. This is just to improve the styling. We wrapped the radio buttons inside an `</li>` tag. The onChange event of the `<li>` tag calls the handleChange method. For UG, we have the radio button selected by default using the defaultChecked property. Besides this, I added a class name for the PG radio button. This is to have a margin left on it:

   ```
   <li className="parentLabels" onChange={handleChange}>
     <input
       type="radio"
       value="UG"
       name="programGroup"
       checked={true}
     />
   ```

```
Undergraduate
<input
  type="radio"
  className="radioSel"
  value="PG"
  name="programGroup"
/>
Postgraduate
</li>
```

4. Instead of two labels, we now have only one label to display the remaining seats. This will show the remaining undergraduate seats if we select Undergraduate and remaining postgraduate seats if we select Postgraduate. We do not need two labels:

```
<label className="parentLabels">
    Remaining {program} Seats - {program === "UG" ? ugSeats :
    pgSeats}
</label>
```

5. Wrapped all input controls in a <ul> tag to improve the styling:

```
<ul className="ulEnrol">
```

6. Updated the onChange method with two more state updates for setting ugSeats and pgSeats. This will ensure that it updates the respective state variables with the correct number of seats when the user selects a radio button. This will enable the remaining seats label to display the seats corresponding to the selected program:

```
const handleChange = (event) => {
    setProgram(event.target.value);
    setPgSeats(pgSeats);
    setUgSeats(ugSeats);
};
```

7. Added or updated classes in most of the elements. I defined the
    class names in the App.css file, which will follow soon.

Once you updated App.js and digested all the changes we made, update
EnrolmentForm.js as in Listing 4-2.

Listing 4-2. EnrolmentForm.js

```
import { useState } from "react";
import "./App.css";

const EnrolmentForm =(props) => {
  const [firstName, setFirstName] = useState("");
  const [lastName, setLastName] = useState("");
  const [email, setEmail] = useState("");
  const [welcomeMessage, setWelcomeMessage] = useState("");
  const handleClick = (event) => {
    handleInputReset("","","");
    setWelcomeMessage(`${firstName} ${lastName} enrolled. Email sent to -
    ${email}`);
    props.setUpdatedSeats(props.currentSeats - 1);
    event.preventDefault();
  };
//change of input value set method
  const handleInputChange = (setInput, event) => {
    setInput(event.target.value);
  };
//set input fields
const handleInputReset = (fname, lname, email) => {
    setFirstName(fname);
    setLastName(lname);
    setEmail(email);
  };
  return (
    <div>
      <div className="enrolContainer">
        <form className="enrolForm" name="enrolForm" >
            <ul className="ulEnrol">
```

```
<li>
  <label for="firstname"></label>
  <input
    type="text"
    className="inputFields"
    id="firstname"
    name="firstname"
    placeholder="First Name"
    value={firstName}
    onChange={(event) => handleInputChange
    (setFirstName, event)}
  />
</li>
<li>
  <label for="lastname"></label>
  <input
    type="test"
    className="inputFields"
    id="lastname"
    name="lastname"
    placeholder="Last Name"
    value={lastName}
    onChange={(event) => handleInputChange(setLastName, event)}
  />
</li>
<li>
  <label for="email"></label>
  <input
    type="email"
    className="inputFields"
    id="email"
    name="email"
    placeholder="Email"
    value={email}
    onChange={(event) => handleInputChange(setEmail, event)}
  />
```

```
        </li>
        <li id="center-btn">
          <input
            type="submit"
            id="btnEnrol"
            name="Enrol"
            alt="Enrol"
            value="Enrol"
            onClick={handleClick}
          />
        </li>
      <li> <label id="studentMsg" className="message">
      {welcomeMessage}
    </label></li>
      </ul>
    </form>
  </div>
  </div>
  );
}
export default EnrolmentForm;
```

The following are the changes to `EnrolmentForm.js` compared with the last listing we had, which is Listing 3-14 of Chapter 3:

1. Made a syntax change – updated the component function to an arrow function.

2. Removed the header from this file because we placed the header now in the App component.

3. To improve the styling, I wrapped the input controls within a `<ul>` tag. This is like what we did with `App.js`:

   ```
   <ul className="ulEnrol">
   ```

4. Introduced a property, value, to the first name and last name fields. This lets us reset the value to blank once we filled in and submitted the form:

```
value={firstName}
```

5. Changed the onBlur event for both first and last names to the onChange event. Since we now assign the value property to the fields, we must have the onChange event; otherwise, it will not allow typing in the data in the input fields:

```
const handleInputChange = (setInput, event) => {
    setInput(event.target.value);
  };
```

6. The OnChange event of the first name and last name elements now calls the same function handleInputChange with the corresponding set state parameter passed to it. This function sets the input value into the state variable depending on the parameter:

```
onChange={(event) => handleInputChange
(setFirstName, event)}
```

7. Added a new field and state variable for email. The field works just like the first name and last name, except that we specify type as email instead of text. This allows us to validate the email format.

8. As opposed to having a form submit event, we have a button click listener. The code behaves exactly like before. Now, there is no onSubmit event in the form. Instead, there is an onClick event on the button, which calls the same handleSubmit function:

```
<input
                type="submit"
                id="btnEnrol"
                name="Enrol"
                alt="Enrol"
                value="Enrol"
                onClick={handleClick}
            />
```

9. Renamed the `handleSubmit` function to `handleClick` to align with the event from where it is called. Also, I added some additional lines, which I will explain in the following steps:

```
const handleClick = (event) => {
    handleInputReset("", "", "");
    setWelcomeMessage(
      `${firstName} ${lastName} enrolled. Email sent to -
      ${email}`
    );
    props.setUpdatedSeats(props.currentSeats - 1);
    event.preventDefault();
  };
```

10. Added a new function `handleInputReset` that will reset form input values when the user clicks the `Enrol` button. As you can see in Change 9, this is called from the `handleClick` method with empty arguments:

```
const handleInputReset = (fname, lname, email) => {
    setFirstName(fname);
    setLastName(lname);
    setEmail(email);
  };
```

11. As you can see in Change 9, I updated the welcome message slightly and included the email content.

12. Added or updated classes in most of the elements. You can see these classes defined in the following `App.css` file.

That's it for the changes to the JS files. Go through `EnrolmentForm.js` and make sure you got everything right. Then, update `App.css` with the following changes, which define styles for all the classes I added to `App.js` and `EnrolmentForm.js`. Replace the entire `App.css` with the code in Listing 4-3.

Listing 4-3. App.css

```
.App {
  font-family: sans-serif;
  font-size: 26px;
  text-align: left;
  width: 100%;
  padding-top: 30px;
}

.programs {
  position: absolute;
  background: rgba(22, 61, 97, 0.794);
  left: 50%;
  height: 500px;
  width: 40%;
  transform: translate(-50%, 0%);
  text-align: center;
  color: rgba(31, 226, 80, 0.671);
}

.radioSel{
  margin-left: 30px;
}
.parentInputs {
  margin: 15px 0;
  font-size: 16px;
  padding: 10px;
  margin-left: 10px;
  width: 250px;
  border-top: none;
  border-left: none;
  border-right: none;
  background: rgba(245, 240, 240, 0.925);
  color: rgb(5, 19, 66);
  outline: none;
}
```

```css
.title
{
  color:rgba(255, 166, 0, 0.897)
}
.parentLabels {

  padding-bottom: 20px;
}
.enrolContainer {
  position: absolute;
  top: 420px;
  left: 50%;
  transform: translate(-50%, -50%);
  width: 40%;
  height: 450px;
  text-align: center;
  display: flex;
}
.enrolForm {
  width: 100%;
  transition: 0.2s;
}

.inputFields {
  margin: 10px 0;
  font-size: 16px;
  padding: 10px;
  width: 250px;
  border: 1px solid rgb(13, 138, 65);
  border-top: none;
  border-left: none;
  border-right: none;
  background: rgb(245, 240, 240);
  color: rgb(5, 19, 66);
  outline: none;
}
```

```
.ulEnrol {
  list-style-type: none;
  padding: 0;
}
#btnEnrol {
  border: 1px solid ;
  background: rgb(50, 58, 59);
  font-size: 18px;
  color: white;
  margin-top: 20px;
  padding: 10px 50px;
  cursor: pointer;
  transition: 0.4s;
  margin-bottom: 30px;
}
::placeholder {
  color: rgba(83, 70, 70, 0.596);
  opacity: 1;
}
.message {
  color:rgba(31, 226, 80, 0.671);
}
```

Once you update all three files, run the project from your project directory. Open the terminal, navigate to the just-react folder, and run npm start. The form should appear in the browser. You can fill in the details and click the button. The welcome message will appear. At the same time, it will clear the form fields. Refer to Figure 4-1.

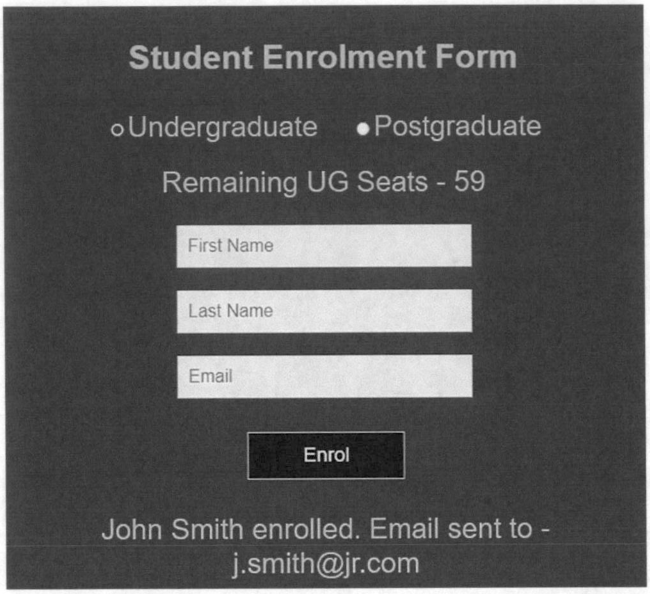

Figure 4-1. *Building a basic form in React*

We have Undergraduate selected by default, and the label displays `Remaining UG Seats - 60`. When you enter the details and click the `button`, the seats will reduce to `59`, and the label will display the welcome message. Refer to Figure 4-1. If you select Postgraduate, the label will display `Remaining PG Seats - 40`. When you submit a student, it will reduce the seats accordingly.

Up to this point, we've added some basic styling to the form and refactored the code. We added one more email field and optimized a few functions. Now let's build a list view to display all the enrolled students and their details.

Combining Reactions

Currently, we have a student enrolment form that allows staff to enter undergraduate and postgraduate student information. But there is no way for us to view the students already enrolled. Let's address that in this section. We can create a view where staff can view enrolled student details. We can put the list view at the bottom of the form. As soon as staff enter student information, it gets added to the view. We will remove the current welcome message since it will not be required when we can display the added student on the list at the bottom.

Note   I am not listing the entire component code in this section and forthcoming sections. I will provide a code section and explanation for each change, so that you can easily digest it. But, sometimes, you may want to copy or refer to the entire component code at each stage. You can find it under the path Chapter 4 ➤ Final chapter code in the GitHub repository(`https://github.com/Apress/Just_React`). You can also download or clone the project `just-react` from the path Chapter 4 ➤ Projects. After cloning, run `npm install` from the project folder to install all the required node modules before running the code.

To add a Details list view, let's create a new component first. Right-click the src folder and create a new file, and name it as `EnrolList.js`. Create another file `EnrolList.css`, just to keep the styles separate.

For the list view, let us use a Fluent UI element instead of a plain HTML element. This will familiarize you with using elements from UI libraries like Fluent UI. It comes with additional features.

Note   Fluent UI is a collection of user experience (UX) frameworks designed by Microsoft using React. You can access the full list here: `https://developer.microsoft.com/en-us/fluentui#/`. There is a section for React elements and styles. You can get into this by selecting Controls/Styles under "React" from the Fluent UI home page.

To begin, install the NPM package for Fluent UI and then run the command `npm i @fluentui/react` from the `just-react` folder. Installing the `@fluentui/react` package enables us to use Fluent UI elements in our component. Copy the following code into `EnrolList.js`. Let's go over the code after the listing.

Listing 4-4. EnrolList.js with a Static List

```
import "./EnrolList.css";
import { DetailsList } from "@fluentui/react/lib/DetailsList";

// Columns for the detail list.
const columns = [
  {
```

```
    key: "fname",
    name: "First Name",
    fieldName: "fname",
    minWidth: 90,
    maxWidth: 200,
    isResizable: true,
  },
  {
    key: "lname",
    name: "Last Name",
    fieldName: "lname",
    minWidth: 90,
    maxWidth: 200,
    isResizable: true,
  },
  {
    key: "program",
    name: "Program",
    fieldName: "program",
    minWidth: 60,
    maxWidth: 200,
    isResizable: true,
  },
  {
    key: "email",
    name: "Email",
    fieldName: "email",
    minWidth: 130,
    maxWidth: 200,
    isResizable: true,
  },
];

// Test items
let items = [];
for (let i = 1; i < 5; i++) {
```

```
  items.push({
    key: i,
    fname: "FirstName " + i,
    lname: "LastName " + i,
    program: "UG",
    email: "Email " + i,
  });
}

const EnrolList = () => {
  return (
    <div className="enrolList">
      <DetailsList items={items} columns={columns} />
    </div>
  );
};
export default EnrolList;
```

In the first few lines, we imported the CSS and classes for using the Fluent UI
DetailsList into the component:

```
import "./EnrolList.css";
import { DetailsList } from "@fluentui/react/lib/DetailsList";
```

Then, we defined an array variable columns for the list columns. The columns are for first
name, last name, program, and email. You can adjust the width of each column individually.
Following that, we created an array of items and added a few static items using a for loop:

```
let items = [];
for (let i = 1; i < 5; i++) {
  items.push({
    key: i,
    fname: "FirstName " + i,
    lname: "LastName " + i,
    program: "UG",
    email: "Email " + i,
  });
}
```

So this loop creates four items in the array, with first name, last name, and email ending with numbers 1–4. Afterward, inside the return function, we added the DetailsList element by specifying the items and columns as the properties. Let us keep it simple for now, providing no additional properties or layouts to the DetailsList:

```
<DetailsList items={items} columns={columns} />
```

This explains the code in the EnrolList.js. For now, we created a static list of four items.

In order to view this list in the browser, we need to call the Enrol list component from the App component. Go to App.js and import the EnrolList component. Add the following statement next to the existing import statements in App.js:

```
import EnrolList from "./EnrolList";
```

Then, scroll down to the bottom and add the <EnrolList /> tag next to the EnrolmentForm tag. Before we go to the browser, let's add some styles to the elements in the EnrolList component. Add the following classes to EnrolList.css. Refer to Listing 4-5.

Listing 4-5. EnrolList.css

```
.enrolList
{
    position: absolute;
    top: 800px;
    left: 50%;
    transform: translate(-50%, -50%);
    width: 40%;
    height: 450px;
    text-align: center;
    display: flex;
}
div[role="checkbox"]
{
    display: none;
}
```

A default checkbox space will appear with the DetailsList. The second class I added is to hide this space, so that it looks better. Otherwise, it will take up space on the left side of the list.

If the code is already running, go to the browser. Else, run npm start, and in the browser, you can see a static list below the enrolment form. Refer to Figure 4-2.

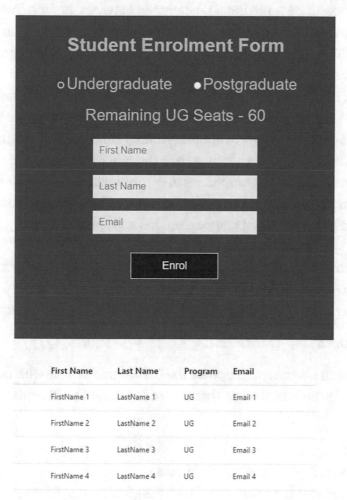

Figure 4-2. *Static list in React*

Now we can see a list below the form. However, it shows some static data, which we provided in the code in EnrolList.js. In the next section, let us make this list dynamic. The list must be empty to begin with. Each time when you add a student, it should get added to this list.

Sibling Reactions

We are calling both EnrolmentForm and EnrolList components in the App component, which enables us to view both the form and the list together in the browser. However, we don't have any EnrolList component tag inside the EnrolmentForm component or vice versa. Hence, there is no direct relationship between the EnrolmentForm and EnrolList components. However, there is a relationship, which is the common parent, App component. The App component connects both these components. So the EnrolmentForm and EnrolList have a sibling relation here.

As part of our requirement, we need to send data from the EnrolmentForm component to the EnrolList component and may also require the opposite. But we cannot send a prop from a sibling to another sibling. However, a sibling can send a prop to its parent, and then the parent can send it to the other sibling.

So, for the EnrolmentForm component to communicate with the EnrolList component, it must send data to the App component. Then, the App component can pass this data to the EnrolList component. Let's see how this sibling interaction plays out.

First, let's make changes to `App.js.` Add a state variable, `studentDetails,` to store student details in `App.js`. It should be an object variable since it needs to hold values like first name, last name, etc. We initialize the variable with an empty object:

```
const [studentDetails, setStudentDetails] = useState({});
```

Then, scroll to the bottom and update the `EnrolmentForm` tag with one new prop, `setStudentDetails`. So now the `EnrolmentForm` tag should be like this:

```
<EnrolmentForm
    chosenProgram={program}
    setUpdatedSeats={setUpdatedSeats}
    currentSeats={program === "UG" ? ugSeats : pgSeats}
    setStudentDetails={setStudentDetails}
/>
```

Now the EnrolmentForm component can access the `setStudentDetails` function using `props.setStudentDetails.` Invoking this function with an object argument will set the passed object value to the state variable, `studentDetails`.

That's all the changes we need to make in `App.js`. Let's move on to `EnrolmentForm.js`. Update the `handleClick` function as shown in the following:

```
const handleClick = (event) => {
    handleInputReset("","","");
    props.setUpdatedSeats(props.currentSeats - 1);
    // Student ID generation
    const randomKey = Math.floor(1000 + Math.random() * 9000);
    let id = randomKey;
    props.setStudentDetails({
      key: id,
      fname: firstName,
      lname: lastName,
      program: props.chosenProgram,
      email: email,
    });
    event.preventDefault();
  };
```

Let me explain the changes we made to this function compared with the last code we had. (Refer to Listing 4-2 for the previous code.)

Within the `handleClick` function, I added a function call to set student details. We set the property fname value to `firstName`. Similarly, a property key and value were added each for last name, email, and program. Apart from this, we generated a four-digit random number for id. Then, we used this id to set the key property of the student details object. The `id` will always be unique.

The student details object is set to the `studentDetails` state variable in the App component as a result of invoking `props.setStudentdetails`. So, now during the button click, the function `handleClick` sets the value to the student details along with the seats.

Earlier, we had a function call to set the welcome message inside the function `handleClick`. I removed this, as we are no longer displaying the message. Also, remove the variable declaration for the welcome message and the `<li>` tag block for the message. We don't need to set the message anymore, since we are going to add student details to the list instead.

The student details information is now passed on from the EnrolmentForm component to the App component when the user submits the enrolment form. The App component then sets the state of the student details accordingly. Next, let's update App.js to pass this updated state to the EnrolList component. Scroll to the bottom and update the EnrolList tag like this:

```
<EnrolList studentDetails={studentDetails} setStudentDetails=
{setStudentDetails} />
```

Here, we passed the studentDetails object and the setStudentDetails function to the EnrolList component. The setStudentDetails function is required for the EnrolList component to empty the student details once it is added to the list.

The last step is to change EnrolList.js to receive these props. Open EnrolList.js and add an import statement for the useEffect Hook:

```
import { useEffect } from "react";
```

Delete the for loop and its contents, which we created earlier for displaying static items. We no longer need these static items as we are now setting up code to receive student details from the App component.

Refer to Listing 4-4 for a comparison with the previous code of EnrolList.js.

The next step is to add a useEffect function above the return function. Look at the following:

```
useEffect(() => {
  const curItemKey = props.studentDetails.key;
  if (curItemKey){
    items = [...items, props.studentDetails];
    props.setStudentDetails({});
  }
} , [props]);
```

During rendering, this useEffect Hook will add the student details received from the App component to the array, items. We access the key using props.studentDetails. key. Then, the function checks if the key is empty or not. If not empty, it adds the student details to the items array. It accesses the student details using props.studentDetails. We use a spread operator to combine the items and props.studentDetails. Finally, after updating the items array, it calls props.setStudentDetails with an empty argument. This will clear the student details object.

The useEffect is not called on every re-render; it executes only if there is a change in the props. We passed props as a dependency. For now, just understand that when we pass a dependency array to useEffect, it gets triggered only if there is a change to that array. Otherwise, it will get triggered on each re-render. I will explain useEffect, the dependency array, and how exactly this works in Chapter 8.

So, when you enter the details of a student and click the button, the EnrolmentForm component sends the student details to the App component. The App component then updates the state of student details. The App component re-renders because of this state update, and it will cause the EnrolList component to receive the new state as a prop. So, when EnrolList renders, because the prop, student details, is changed, useEffect fires and adds the student item to the list. As a result, the DetailsList displays the updated list of students. The process repeats, and the list gets updated whenever a new student is added. Too easy!

View the app in the browser. Select a program, and enter some student details. The student details will get added to the list. The seats also will get updated according to the selected program. Refer to Figure 4-3 where I added three students, and I can see the list at the bottom.

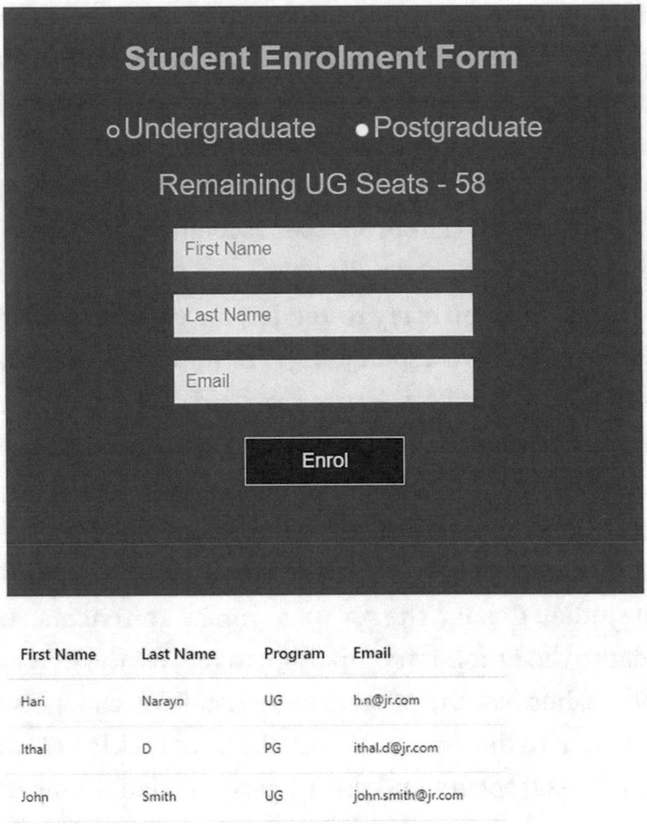

Figure 4-3. *Dynamic list in React*

Here, I added three students, and I can see all their details in the following list. I see that the number of UG seats got updated to 58 on the remaining seats label. The one student I added is of the PG program. Clicking the Postgraduate radio button, I can see that there are 39 seats. The numbers reduced as per the corresponding program.

We have seen how two components interact by passing through their parent. In addition, now you know how to add data from a form to a list. However, what if the component tree is too large and the child components at the bottom of the tree want to interact? It may become too complicated to use this method in that case. The code will become messy. Finding out their common parent up the tree will be an exhausting task for the child components 😊. You don't have to worry about it right now. There are ways to handle these situations. We can make use of Context API, Redux, etc. We will cover those in Chapters 5 and 8.

Next, we will look at a few more component interactions by improving our application. Let us provide edit and delete options for the enrolled student information.

Component Chat Continues...

In order to add editing and deleting options to each row on the list, we need two icons. Let us use the react-icons library for the icons. Open the terminal, and press Ctrl+C followed by Y to stop the server. Install required modules by running npm i react-icons.

Note   React Icons is a consolidated library that has a lot of icons to choose from. You can use any available icons. You can see a full list here: https://react-icons.github.io/react-icons. You can search for the icon name and can see a list of icons. All these libraries get installed as a part of installing the react-icon package. I am using the material design icons in this example.

Add the following import to EnrolmentForm.js after the command completed the installation:

```
import { MdEdit, MdDelete } from "react-icons/md";
```

Add the edit and delete icons to the handleClick function with the following code:

```
const handleClick = (event) => {
    props.setUpdatedSeats(props.currentSeats - 1);
    // Student ID generation
    const randomKey = Math.floor(1000 + Math.random() * 9000);
    let id = randomKey;
    props.setStudentDetails({
      key: id,
      fname: firstName,
      lname: lastName,
      program: props.chosenProgram,
      email: email,
      edit: <MdEdit />,
      delete: <MdDelete />,
    });
    event.preventDefault();
  };
```

With this change, we are sending a delete icon and an edit icon, along with each student row, to the EnrolList component.

Update the columns declaration in EnrolList.js to include two more columns. I added edit as the first column and delete as the last. Refer to the following:

```
const columns = [
  {
    key: "edit",
    name: "Edit",
    fieldName: "edit",
    minWidth: 30,
    maxWidth: 200,
    isResizable: true,
  },
  {
    key: "fname",
    name: "First Name",
    fieldName: "fname",
    minWidth: 90,
    maxWidth: 200,
    isResizable: true,
  },
  {
    key: "lname",
    name: "Last Name",
    fieldName: "lname",
    minWidth: 90,
    maxWidth: 200,
    isResizable: true,
  },
```

```
  {
    key: "program",
    name: "Program",
    fieldName: "program",
    minWidth: 60,
    maxWidth: 200,
    isResizable: true,
  },
  {
    key: "email",
    name: "Email",
    fieldName: "email",
    minWidth: 130,
    maxWidth: 200,
    isResizable: true,
  },
  {
    key: "delete",
    name: "Delete",
    fieldName: "delete",
    minWidth: 50,
    maxWidth: 200,
    isResizable: true,
  },
];
```

Those were the changes to the UI. If you add students from the form, the rows will appear as in Figure 4-4. Note that there may be a horizontal scroll bar at the bottom of the list, if you are using a smaller screens, as there are now several columns.

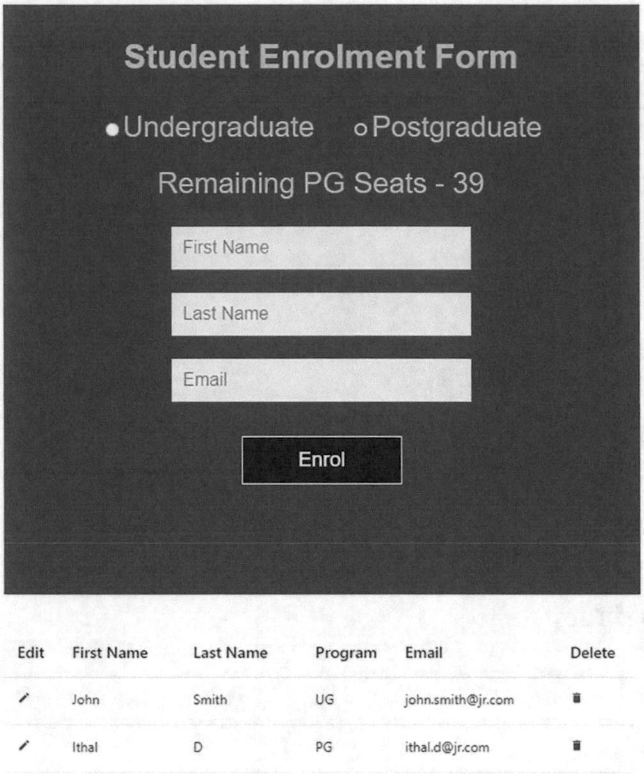

Figure 4-4. *Actions on a list*

Let us now implement the functionalities for editing and deleting student information. Let us start with the delete option first. To delete a student row, we need to attach an `onClick` event to the delete icon. We need to define this `onClick` event in the EnrolmentForm component. This is because we are passing edit and delete as the properties of the student details object from the EnrolmentForm component.

In the event listener function, there needs to be logic to remove the specific row from the `items` array. Importantly, this should update the details list. Of course, we can use the student id as a key to identify the row.

First, let's add an event listener to the `<MdDelete />` tag in the `handleClick` function inside `EnrolmentForm.js`. Open `EnrolmentForm.js` and edit the `handleClick` function to add a click event to the delete icon. Refer to the following:

```
const handleClick = (event) => {
    handleInputReset("","","");
    props.setSeats(props.currentSeats - 1);
```

```
// Student ID generation Student ID generation
const randomKey = Math.floor(1000 + Math.random() * 9000);
let id = randomKey;
props.setStudentDetails({
  key: id,
  fname: firstName,
  lname: lastName,
  program: props.chosenProgram,
  email: email,
    edit: <MdEdit className="actionIcon" />,
  delete: <MdDelete className="actionIcon" onClick={() => props.handle
  ItemSelection("delete",id)}/>
});
event.preventDefault();
};
```

We are now passing the handleItemSelection function on the onClick event of the delete icon with the action name and id as arguments. Also, we added a class to the two icons to provide some styling. The following is the change we made in the function handleClick with respect to the deletion:

```
<MdDelete className="actionIcon" onClick={() => props.handleItemSelection
("delete",id)}/>
```

So this expects a new prop, handleItemSelection, to be passed from the App component. Before modifying App.js, let us update App.css by adding the following class to give some styles for these edit and delete icons.

Add the following to App.css:

```
.actionIcon {
  font-size: 16px;
  color: rgb(77, 133, 141);
  cursor: pointer;
}
```

Now, let us update App.js. First, add two state variables. The first one is for the action and the second one for the id. Add the following declarations below the previous useState declarations:

```
const [action, setAction] = useState();
const [selItemId, setSelItemId] = useState();
```

Next, let's define a function handleItemSelection. Add the following function below or above the existing handleChange function in App.js:

```
const handleItemSelection = (action, id) => {
   setAction(action);
   setSelItemId(id);
 }
```

Here you can see that the function updates both the action and the id state variables using the received parameters.

Next, define another function restoreSeats:

```
const restoreSeats = (pgm) =>
 {
   pgm === "UG" ?setUgSeats(ugSeats+1) : setPgSeats(pgSeats+1);
   setAction("");
 }
```

This function is to restore the number of available seats when a deletion occurs. When restoreSeats is called, it restores the seats to its original state. If we delete a UG seat, it will restore the UG seats by adding 1; and if we delete a PG seat, it will restore the PG seats. We can pass this function as a prop to the EnrolList component, so that it can restore the number of available seats once the user deletes a row from the list.

Scroll down to the bottom and update the EnrolmentForm tag inside the return function to include the handleItemSelection function as a prop. This will allow the EnrolmentForm component to access the above-defined handleItemSelection function:

```
<EnrolmentForm
        chosenProgram={program}
        setSeats={setUpdatedSeats}
        currentSeats={program === "UG" ? ugSeats : pgSeats}
```

```
setStudentDetails={setStudentDetails}
handleItemSelection={handleItemSelection}
/>
```

From the EnrolmentForm component, the handleItemSelection function is invoked when we click the delete icon using props.handleItemSelection.

So, if the user clicks Delete, it invokes handleItemSelection inside the App component. When the function executes, we will have the word delete stored into the variable action and the selected item id in the selItemId variable.

Thereafter, let us pass those values to the EnrolList component, so that the EnrolList component can identify the action and the id of the row to be actioned. Open App.js and update the EnrolList tag with the following code:

```
<EnrolList
        studentDetails={studentDetails}
        setStudentDetails={setStudentDetails}
        selectedItemId={selItemId}
        action={action}
        restoreSeats ={restoreSeats}
    />
```

Now we added three more properties to the EnrolList tag. We are passing the action and the id. Besides that, we are passing the function restoreSeats as a prop. The EnrolList can call it after the deletion, so that it will restore the number of available seats.

Go to EnrolList.js and replace the useEffect code block with the following. Let us look at the changes after the code section:

```
useEffect(() => {
    const curItemKey = props.studentDetails.key;
    if (curItemKey) {
      items = [...items, props.studentDetails];
      props.setStudentDetails({});
    }
    // Execute deletion on the selected item.
```

133

```
  if (props.action === "delete") {
    // filter the selected item
    const deleteItem = items.filter(
      (item) => item.key === props.selectedItemId
    )[0];

    // Remove from the list
    items = items.filter((item) => item !== deleteItem);
    // update seats
    props.restoreSeats(deleteItem.program);
  }
}, [props]);
```

The added code checks if the action is delete. If yes, the filter function filters out the item object using the key. We had the key set as the item id before. Therefore, we can identify the selected item by comparing item.key with props.selectedItemId. The props.selecteditemId has the value of item id. We had set this in App.js:

```
const deleteItem = items.filter(
    (item) => item.key === props.selectedItemId
  )[0];
```

After finding out the item to be deleted, the code removes the corresponding item from the items array using the filter method. This updates the students' list:

```
items = items.filter((item) => item !== deleteItem);
```

Finally, it calls props.restoreSeats to restore the number of available seats based on the program of the deleted student. This sets the state of the respective program seats in the App component:

```
props.restoreSeats(deleteItem.program);
```

Run npm start if you haven't already. Try adding multiple items and deleting items. It should remove the corresponding student details from the list and update the seats accordingly.

To sum up, in order to achieve the delete functionality, we built a multicomponent interaction in the application. The EnrolmentForm component builds the student details rows, along with edit and delete buttons. We pass these to the EnrolList component when the user clicks the Enrol button. If a student row is to be deleted, the

EnrolmentForm component starts the action and passes the details to the EnrolList component via the App component. The EnrolList component then deletes the item and updates the student list. It restores the state of the seats using a communication between the EnrolList and App components. React does all these things quite fast by changing state within components and by making communication possible between the components. You can feel how quickly these actions happen in a browser screen. I know you are excited! Let us move on to implement the edit functionality next and keep on learning React.

Reacting to Edits

As we have all the required information within the EnrolmentForm component and are updating the information using the form, implementing edit details does not require a back-and-forth component interaction like deleting.

As soon as the user clicks the edit icon, we need to bring the details into the text fields, so they can edit them and click the button to update. This should update the details on the students' list. We need to change the button's text from Enrol to Update if the action is edit. Last, we need a cancel button so the user can cancel the changes if they want.

Go to EnrolmentForm.js and make the following changes.

First, add a state variable for handling the button text. Initialize it with Enrol as the value:

```
const [btnValue, setBtnValue] = useState("Enrol");
```

Create a new state variable to store the selected student id. Initialize it with zero. Add this just below the preceding line. We will store the generated random ID into this variable before sending it to the EnrolList component:

```
const [studentID, setStudentID] = useState(0);
```

Now create a new function handleEdit and place it above the handleClick function:

```
const handleEdit = (stId) => {
    handleInputReset(firstName, lastName, email);
    setStudentID(stId);
    setBtnValue("Update");

};
```

We will set this function to be invoked when the user clicks the edit icon. First, it calls handleInputReset, which sets the field values of the selected row to the first name, last name, and email text fields. In the next line, the function sets the selected student id to the state variable. Because of this, we ensure that the right row gets updated when the user clicks the Update button. Also, this function changes the button text from Enrol to Update. This differentiates it from submitting a new student.

Next, update the handleClick function as follows. I will explain each line of code after:

```
const handleClick = (event) => {
    handleInputReset("", "", "");
    props.setSeats(props.currentSeats - 1);
    // Student ID generation
    const randomKey = Math.floor(1000 + Math.random() * 9000);
    let id = randomKey;
    setStudentID(randomKey);
    // For Enrol, use the randomKey variable and for Update use the state
variable
    id = btnValue === "Enrol" ? randomKey : studentID;
    props.setStudentDetails({
      key: id,
      fname: firstName,
      lname: lastName,
      program: props.chosenProgram,
      email: email,
      edit: <MdEdit className="actionIcon" onClick={() =>
      handleEdit(id)} />,
      delete: (
        <MdDelete
          className="actionIcon"
          onClick={() => props.handleItemSelection("delete", id)}
        />
      ),
    });
    setBtnValue("Enrol");
    event.preventDefault();
  };
```

We added the following two lines just above `props.setStudentDetails`:

```
setStudentID(randomKey);
id = btnValue === "Enrol" ? randomKey : studentID;
```

In the first line, we are updating the state variable `studentID` using `setStudentID(randomKey)`. We are setting the random number value to the `studentID` variable here. This is the same number that we are storing in the variable id and passing as the key during click on the edit.

The second line specifies a condition. It says to use the random generated number as the student id if the button is `Enrol` and use the state variable `studentID` value if it is `Update`. This is because, if the button is `Update`, we cannot use the random number since it would create a new item instead of updating. So we specified to use the state variable `studentID` there. This variable will have the selected student ID.

We update the state for `studentID`, but it will not get reflected to the variable immediately. Therefore, we are using the random number itself as the key if the button text is `Enrol`. That means during a new student enrolment.

The next update we made to the `handleClick` function is to include the function call in the edit icon. If you look at the `props.setStudentDetails` section, we updated the edit property like this:

```
edit: <MdEdit className="actionIcon" onClick={() => handleEdit(id)}/>,
```

Here, we added an `onClick` event and pointed it to the `handleEdit` function and passed the selected student ID as a parameter. If you look at the `handleEdit` function we defined earlier, you see that it sets the `studentID` variable to the selected student id. Also, it sets the button text to `Update`. So this ensures that when the edit icon is clicked, the button text is changed to `Update`.

Last, we set the button value to `Enrol` inside the `handleClick` function, so that after the update, the button value resets to `Enrol`:

```
setBtnValue("Enrol");
```

Next, create a new function handleClickCancel and place it above the handleClick function. We will set this function to the onClick event of the Cancel button so that when we click the Cancel button, this function gets invoked. This function will reset the input fields to empty and set the button value back to Enrol.:

```
const handleClickCancel = (event) =>
  {
    handleInputReset("","","");
    setBtnValue("Enrol");
    event.preventDefault();
  }
```

So until now we created two new functions handleEdit and handleClickCancel. Also, we changed the handleClick function. Next, let us change the JSX to include the changes to the Enrol button properties and to add a new button. Replace the <li> tag for the Enrol button to the following one. Keep other <li> tags as they are. Only replace the <li> with id center-btn:

```
<li id="center-btn">
                <input
                  type="submit"
                  id="btnEnrol"
                  name="Enrol"
                  className="btn"
                  alt="Enrol"
                  value={btnValue}
                  onClick={handleClick}
                />
                <input
                  type="submit"
                  id="btnCancel"
                  name="Cancel"
                  className="btn"
                  alt="Cancel"
                  value="Cancel"
                   onClick={handleClickCancel}
                />
</li>
```

Compared with the previous code, there are two buttons now. The Enrol button now has an assigned class, btn. The button text is now dynamic, and we initialized it with the value Enrol. The Cancel button has the same class but a different id.

Let us define these classes in App.css. Replace the #btnEnrol section with the following:

```css
.btn
{
  border: 1px solid;
  background: rgb(50, 58, 59);
  font-size: 18px;
  color: white;
  margin-top: 20px;
  padding: 10px 50px;
  cursor: pointer;
  transition: 0.4s;
  margin-bottom: 30px;
}
#btnCancel {
 margin-left:20px;
}
```

Now we have a defined class to define styles for both the Enrol button and the Cancel button. If you view this form in a browser, the form will still look like before. However, there will also be a Cancel button.

Next, let us move on to update the EnrolList component to implement the update logic there. Go to EnrolList.js and replace the useEffect block with the following code:

```javascript
useEffect(() => {
    // Execute deletion on the selected item.
    if (props.action === "delete") {
      // filter the selected item
      const deleteItem = items.filter(
        (item) => item.key === props.selectedItemId
      )[0];
      // update seats
```

```
    props.restoreSeats(deleteItem.program);
    // Remove from the list
    items = items.filter((item) => item !== deleteItem);
  }
// Update the list items with the student details after rendering
  const curItemKey = props.studentDetails.key;
  if (curItemKey) {
    const i = items.findIndex((item) => item.key === curItemKey);
    if (i > -1) {
      items = items.map((item) =>
        item.key === curItemKey ? props.studentDetails : item
      );
    } else {
      items = [...items, props.studentDetails];
    }
    props.setStudentDetails({});
  }
});
```

Let us look at the changes. First, we added a condition to check between update and create. If the items exist in the list, it is considered as an update; else, create. The findIndex function is used to look up the index of the selected item in the items array. If it finds the item, it replaces the item with the updated item object:

```
const i = items.findIndex((item) => item.key === curItemKey);
    if (i > -1) {
      items = items.map((item) =>
        item.key === curItemKey ? props.studentDetails : item
      );
```

Otherwise, the function just adds the item to the items array as before:

```
items = [...items, props.studentDetails];
```

When you click Edit on any row in the list, the selected student details will now appear on the screen along with the Update and Cancel buttons. You can change any field value, first name, last name, or email. When you click the Update button, the corresponding list row gets updated. Clicking Cancel will clear the field values and display the Enrol button again. Let's look at the app in the browser. Refer to Figure 4-5.

Note   Run npm start if it's not already running. You can keep it running and view the changes in the browser as and when you type.

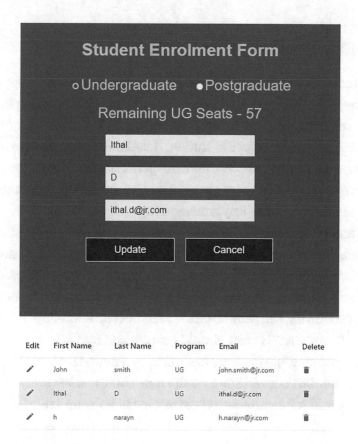

Figure 4-5. *Editing a list*

For example, when I clicked the edit icon against the second row, the details got displayed in the form to edit. At the same time, the button text got changed to Update. If I make any changes and click Update, the corresponding row gets updated. Otherwise, if I click Cancel, the form gets cleared. After Update or Cancel, the button text will get reset to Enrol. Try to create multiple items and try to edit and delete them.

However, we did not yet complete the edit implementation. Only, the student details we can edit at this stage. We are yet to work on implementing a solution for updating the program and seats details. The program and seat details will not get updated as expected now. Let us implement that next.

More Reactions to the Parent

The students belong to two kinds of program in this app, Undergraduate and Postgraduate. Imagine adding a postgraduate student and later editing it. At this time, the radio button selection may not be on postgraduate. We are only sending data to the enrolment form to display the selected student details. However, we are not sending data to the App component to choose the corresponding program of the student. Also, we need to update seats when a student switches a program from undergraduate to postgraduate or vice versa. Let us implement that.

Selecting a student and editing it should auto-select the corresponding program radio button. Also, the user should be able to change the program and save it back on the list. Importantly, all this should display the remaining seats accordingly. For example, let's say you added a UG student, and the seats got changed to 59. The next time, when you are editing and moving the same student to the PG program, the UG seats should get updated back to 60, and the PG seats should get reduced by 1.

We will start by editing App.js by introducing two new state variables. The first one isUGChecked is to handle checked state for the radio buttons. We initialize it with the value true. The second state variable isRestoreSeats is for updating seat numbers correctly:

```
const [isUGChecked, setIsUGChecked] = useState(true);
const [isRestoreSeats, setIsRestoreSeats] = useState(false);
```

Afterward, update the `<li>` tag for the radio buttons as follows. Be careful not to remove the `<li>` tag of the remaining seats. Replace only that of the radio buttons:

```
<li className="parentLabels" onChange={handleChange}>
        <input
          type="radio"
          value="UG"
          name="programGroup"
          checked={isUGChecked}
        />
        Undergraduate
        <input
          type="radio"
          className="radioSel"
          value="PG"
          name="programGroup"
          checked={!isUGChecked}
        />
        Postgraduate
      </li>
```

We set the `checked` property for both radio buttons. For UG, we set it to the value of the `isUGChecked` variable; and for PG, we set it to the opposite value of the `isUGChecked` variable. We initialized the `isUGChecked` variable with the value true. Because of this, we will have Undergraduate selected by default.

Now, in `App.js`, define a new function `setSelectedProgram`:

```
const setSelectedProgram = (selProgram) => {
   selProgram === "UG" ? setIsUGChecked(true) : setIsUGChecked(false);
   setProgram(selProgram);
   setIsRestoreSeats(true);
 };
```

The function receives a parameter `selProgram`. If `selProgram` is UG, it will set the state variable `isUGChecked` to `true`, which means the Undergraduate radio button gets selected. If the `selProgram` is PG, it will set `isUGChecked` to false, which means the Postgraduate radio button gets selected. Next, we set the `program` variable to the selected program to display the correct label. This ensures the label will display the remaining UG seats or PG seats as per the program. Last, we set the isRestoreSeats variable to true. This implies that we need to set the number of available seats accordingly. We will handle this later in the handleChange function, that is, when a program is switched.

The preceding function setSelectedProgram must be called from the EnrolmentForm component when you select an item for editing. To achieve this, add a new property setSelectedProgram to the EnrolmentForm tag, as shown in the following. Calling this from the EnrolmentForm component will invoke the preceding function:

```
<EnrolmentForm
        chosenProgram={program}
        setSeats={setUpdatedSeats}
        currentSeats={program === "UG" ? ugSeats : pgSeats}
        setStudentDetails={setStudentDetails}
        handleItemSelection={handleItemSelection}
        setSelectedProgram={setSelectedProgram}
    />
```

Open EnrolmentForm.js and update the edit property inside props. setStudentDetails of the handleClick function. This is to pass program as a parameter along with the id. The updated line follows:

```
edit: <MdEdit className="actionIcon" onClick={() => handleEdit(id, props.
chosenProgram)} />
```

As a result, clicking the edit icon will pass an additional argument to the handleEdit function, which is the program of the selected item. Now, update the handleEdit function as follows:

```
const handleEdit = (stId, program) => {
    handleInputReset(firstName, lastName, email);
    setStudentID(stId);
    setBtnValue("Update");
    props.setSelectedProgram(program);
  };
```

The props.setSelectedProgram(program) line will invoke the setSelectedProgram of the App component by passing the value of the program into it. This will pass the program of the selected item to the App component. Subsequently, the function setSelectedProgram in the App component will select the radio button accordingly.

Finally, we need to switch back to App.js to make one more change in order to handle the number of available seats. Update the handleChange function as in the following in App.js:

```
const handleChange = (event) => {
    setProgram(event.target.value);
    setIsUGChecked(!isUGChecked);
    if(isRestoreSeats)
    {
      event.target.value === "UG" ? setPgSeats(pgSeats + 1) :
          setUgSeats(ugSeats + 1);
      setIsRestoreSeats(false);
    }
};
```

When we select a student to edit and if we change their program from UG to PG or vice versa, this part of the handleChange function is called. This increases the number of seats in the previous program by 1.

Let me explain the concept with an example. Let's say you added two new UG students, John and Ithal. The number of UG seats now gets reduced to 58. When you click edit on any of those students, say John, handleEdit will be called. Inside handleEdit, we are calling props.setSelectedProgram. This invokes the setSelectedProgram function in the App component. We have a line in this function to set isRestoreSeats to true. Suppose you changed John's program from UG to PG. Now, the handleChange function is called. It checks if isRestoreSeats is true, and it finds it is. Then, it checks John's current program, which is PG. Therefore, it increases the previous program, UG, seats by 1. This way, it restores the previous program seats when you switch programs.

As soon as a seat gets increased, the function sets IsRestoreSeats to false. This ensures that if a user clicks a radio button multiple times, it won't increase the seats again. Afterward, if the user clicks edit on any student, the function will set IsRestoreSeats back to true.

Go to the app and try to create a program change scenario, as shown. For example, I added two UG students and one PG student. The seats will read 58 and 39, respectively. Click edit against a UG student and switch the program to Postgraduate using the radio button. If you click back the Undergraduate radio button, the UG seats will be 59 now. Even if you switch back and forth several times, the seats will remain at the same number. If you keep it in Postgraduate and save the form, the PG seats will become 38. You will see one UG student and two PG students on the list now. At the same time, it will display the corresponding remaining seats.

We completed a working React frontend application at this stage. You can experiment with different scenarios.

Note   As mentioned in Chapter 3, this book contains listings and code sections that have been tested and verified in VS Code, so there is almost no chance of an error occurring. However, due to unseen formatting issues, if some code won't work or functionality is unexpected, ensure that you take the corresponding component file code or clone the entire project, from GitHub. As mentioned before, you can access the repository via the book's product page, `https://github.com/Apress/Just-React`. There you can find the final project code and each listing of the chapter under the folder Chapter 4.

Summary

In conclusion, we focused primarily on coding in this chapter. My goal was to familiarize you with the component interactions and make you think the React way.

We began by building on top of the student enrolment form, which we started in the last chapter. We talked about Fluent UI controls. Afterward, we discussed how a component can interact with another through their common parent component. We built a complete frontend form for student enrolment. You learned about adding items to a list, working on selected list items, etc. You learned how to achieve all these without having to touch the DOM. We implemented all these features purely using state management. You learned the better usage of concepts like props, state, Hooks, etc.

This chapter was primarily based on the enrolment form application. We constructed the application by relying on the basic React concept of components and state management. Each component represents a single task, and the components communicate to keep the app together. The enrollment form has the functionality of adding/updating details, and the enrollment list component displays them as a list. The App component holds these two components together and also handles updates to seats and programs.

In the next chapter, we will discuss a few more advanced concepts in React. You will learn about React Lazy, Suspense, props drilling, Context API, etc. In addition to improving this enrolment app, we will create a new React project to illustrate the concepts. Think React and prepare to rethink in the next chapter!

CHAPTER 5

Rethink React

In the previous chapter, we built a complete frontend project for a student enrolment form. This chapter is about "re-": rethink, redesign, rebuild, and restructure React apps in React way. We will discuss mostly about rebuilding things in a better way. You will learn more advanced concepts of React in this chapter. We will check how these features can improve our existing solution.

The first thing we will do is learn about code splitting. You will learn about the Lazy function and the Suspense component. We will apply code splitting into our enrolment application. Next, we will discuss potential issues in our application. You will learn about props drilling and how to solve a potential issue with that by redesigning components.

In the next section, we will create a new single-page application (SPA). The application will support multiple user views. The application will teach us more about component interaction. We will talk about React fragments.

Then, we will explore a relatively new feature of React, which was introduced with React 16.3. The React Context provides an easy way to manage the state between components without drilling through them. We will learn to use the useContext hook.

At the end of this chapter, you will be proficient in designing and creating React apps following the most recommended and most current approaches.

Note To find out which version of react and react-dom you are using, type `npm view react version` and `npm view react-dom version` from the Visual Studio Code (VS Code) terminal of the project. We are using React 18 for all projects in this book.

© Hari Narayn 2022
H. Narayn, *Just React!*, https://doi.org/10.1007/978-1-4842-8294-6_5

React Lazy and Suspense

Think about our enrolment form project. We have the form and list components. When you first load the page, do you need the list to load? Not really. Even though the list is empty, we do not require it to load.

Both the components are child components of their parent component, App. The browser can load only the form component and can load the list component later. We can achieve this goal by splitting our App component here to allow it to load at different times in the browser. We refer to this as code splitting. This is an important functionality of React, especially for large single-page applications (SPAs).

This will not make a significant performance improvement in our simple project. However, this can be quite useful for larger applications. Imagine our application is large. Webpack bundles all the files and includes them on the web page when it loads. For larger applications, this bundle can get very large and slow down the application. We can break this bundle into smaller chunks. When loading a page, it will load only the required chunk first. Other parts will load later. That's the concept of lazy loading. With the Lazy function and the Suspense component, we can achieve this code splitting.

Let me illustrate this with our enrolment form project. Open the `just-react` project (enrolment application project) in VS Code from where you left in the last chapter.

Note   Refer to the GitHub repository Chapter 4 section for the latest code of the `just-react` project. You can access the repository via the book's product page, `https://github.com/Apress/Just_React`. All code listings and final component codes of all projects are available there.

Before making any changes, let's inspect how the component currently loads using the Chrome developer tools. Using `npm start`, the localhost will appear in the browser. I'm using Chrome here as the browser. Press F12 to open the developer tools, and then press Ctrl+Shift+P to open the Run command window. Type in `coverage`, and then select `Show Coverage`. Figure 5-1 illustrates this.

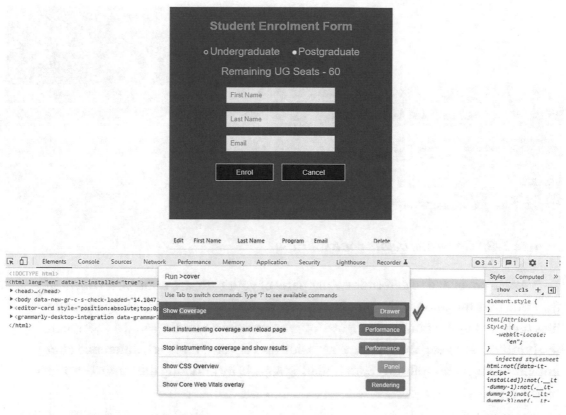

Figure 5-1. *Show Coverage*

After you click Show Coverage, a new window opens in the developer tools below the existing one. You can either click the reload button inside the coverage window, or you can reload it from the browser's top. Once you reload it, the coverage will look like Figure 5-2.

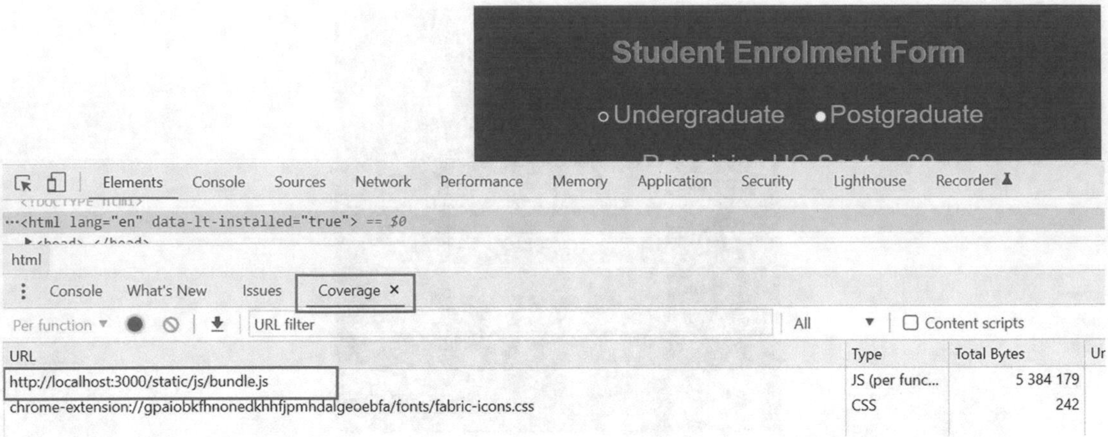

Figure 5-2. *Coverage before code splitting*

We use coverage to determine what parts of your code are unused. It shows all the code files included in the bundle. Therefore, we use it here to identify the code files included in the bundle. In Figure 5-2, you can see a bundle.js and a CSS file in the bundle. Let's keep this information aside and check if there is a difference after implementing code splitting. Start updating App.js by updating the import section as follows:

```
import "./App.css";
import React, { useState, Suspense } from "react";
import EnrolmentForm from "./EnrolmentForm";
const EnrolList = React.lazy(() => import("./EnrolList.js"));
```

Compared with the previous code we had, I added a React.lazy() function to import the list component. This lets you load the list component lazily. In addition, I added React and Suspense to import from the React library. This is required to use the Lazy function and the Suspense component. Scroll down and replace the EnrolList tag with the following:

```
<Suspense fallback={<div> Enrolled student details loading......
</div>}><EnrolList
        studentDetails={studentDetails}
        setStudentDetails={setStudentDetails}
        selectedItemId={selItemId}
```

```
action={action}
restoreSeats={restoreSeats}
/></Suspense>
```

I wrapped the EnrolList inside a Suspense component. This is required by the Lazy function to wrap the lazy component. I also added a fallback property. With this, I ensure that if the lazy-loaded component cannot load, it will display the fallback div. In our case, the fallback div contains only a message.

Using Lazy and Suspense, we implemented code splitting in our project. If you run the code with npm start, you can see the application performs exactly as before. If you run it on a slow network, you observe that the fallback message appears before the list component headers. To simulate a slow network, open the developer tools in Chrome and go to the Network tab. Select the drop-down against "No throttling" and change it to "Fast 3G." I highlight this in Figure 5-3.

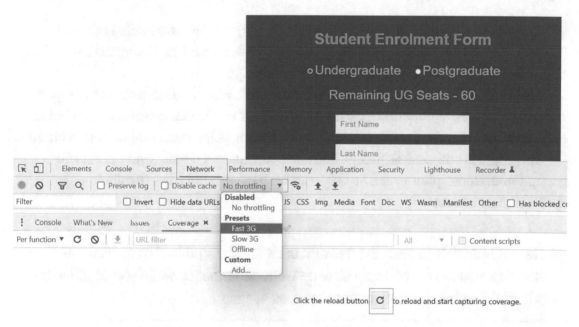

Figure 5-3. *Simulating a slow network*

After setting the network, click the reload button inside the coverage.

You will see the message "Enrolled student details loading..." for a second before the coverage loads. This shows it loaded the EnrolList component after the initial load.

If you look at the coverage, now there are two more files under the Coverage tab. Refer to Figure 5-4.

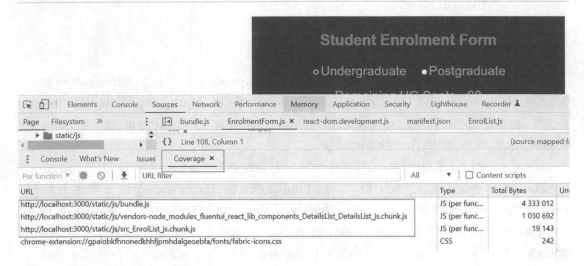

Figure 5-4. *Coverage after code splitting*

Compared with the previous version (Figure 5-2), the browser loaded two more files, `src_EnrolList_js.chunk.js` and `vendors-noder_modules_fluentui-react_lib_components_DetailsList_DetailsList_js.chunk.js`.

So, here, initially the web page loaded the bundle without the `EnrolList` component. Then the EnrolList component and the `DetailsList` inside that component loaded in two additional chunks. This shows how code splitting helps load components in chunks.

The app will still work as before. You can enter student details, and the list will get updated. Code splitting can be very useful when we build complex single-page applications in React.

Note   Remember to reset the network back to "No throttling" from "Fast 3G." Otherwise, you may experience slow network performance while you continue to work on the enrolment project from the next section.

Props Drilling Issue

By props drilling, we mean sending props from a higher-level component to a lower-level component. In Chapter 4, in the enrolment project, we passed props down the component tree. For example, the user can select a program, undergraduate or postgraduate, and we pass this value down to the EnrolmentForm component. This is because we need to know what program we selected when saving the student details on to the list. Here's the catch: do we really need the value of the program in the EnrolmentForm component? No. In the EnrolmentForm component, we are entering student information. We designed the component for this data entry. It does not need to know about the selected program. We are capturing it in the EnrolmentForm component only to pass it on to the EnrolList component where this program value is required. That is passing props through a component that doesn't need them at all. This is a major disadvantage of props drilling. The same is true for seats. We can handle seat management between the App and EnrolList components without passing it through the EnrolmentForm component.

If your application is complex, imagine what it would be like. Managing the application through props drilling will be extremely difficult due to the large component tree. By using a concept called React Context, we can avoid this issue with props drilling. Context is an API built into React, and it provides an alternate and more easy way to pass data between components without having to use the props. We will learn more about Context in the later sections of the chapter.

In this section, we will look at how to fix flaws in component interactions. We can fix the preceding issue without using Context. We can improve the way of passing the prop program, for example. To avoid this props drilling problem, I recommend analyzing the component tree and looking for ways to improve it. With respect to the enrolment app, let's look at how we can do this.

Continuing from where you left off in the previous section, open the just-react project. Our plan is to modify this project to avoid the existing props drilling issue. By making the App component pass the program directly to the EnrolList component, we won't have to go through EnrolmentForm.

To ensure that you can easily capture the changes, we will modify the component code of these three components in three steps.

Step 1: We modify App.js. The goal is to avoid passing program and seat information to the EnrolmentForm component, but instead, pass them to the EnrolList component.

At the bottom, locate the EnrolmentForm tag and replace it with the following:

```
<EnrolmentForm
        setStudentDetails={setStudentDetails}
        handleItemSelection={handleItemSelection}
/>
```

We previously passed six parameters to the `EnrolmentForm` tag. Now, we are passing only the two functions `setStudentDetails` and `handleItemSelection` as the props. Let's recap what these two functions do. The `setStudentDetails` sets the entered student details to the state variable `studentDetails`. The `handleItemSelection` sets the selected student id and the selected action to the respective state variables.

Earlier, we were passing four more props to EnrolmentForm: `chosenProgram`, `setSelectedProgram`, `currentSeats`, and `setSeats`. The `chosenProgram` and `currentSeats` are the values of the selected program and the seats available for that program. The functions `setSelectedProgram` and `setSeats` are the function props the child component can use to set the selected program and the number of seats available. Our goal is to pass the program, seats, and these functions to EnrolList instead of EnrolmentForm. For this reason, we removed all these four properties. We now need to add these four props to the `EnrolList` tag.

Update the `EnrolList` tag like this:

```
<EnrolList
          studentDetails={studentDetails}
          setStudentDetails={setStudentDetails}
          selectedItemId={selItemId}
          action={action}
          restoreSeats={restoreSeats}
          setUpdatedSeats={setUpdatedSeats}
          currentSeats={program === "UG" ? ugSeats : pgSeats}
          chosenProgram ={program}
setSelectedProgram={setSelectedProgram}
          />
```

So now we have a total of nine props passed to the EnrolList component. We are passing seats, program, and the two function props directly to the EnrolList component.

Step 2: Next, let us update `EnrolmentForm.js`. The goal is to remove all references to the program and seats from the EnrolmentForm component. Furthermore, when the user clicks Edit, the selected student's id needs to be passed to the App component. First, locate and update the function `handleEdit`. Replace the function with the following:

```
const handleEdit = (stId) => {
    handleInputReset(firstName, lastName, email);
    setStudentID(stId);
```

```
    setBtnValue("Update");
    props.handleItemSelection("edit", stId);
};
```

Let us look at the changes done in the function. From the existing code, we removed the `program` parameter and the call to the `setSelectedProgram`.

Note   At this point, you can find the latest code for each component of the just-react project in the Chapter 4 section of the GitHub repository. You can access the repository via the product page of the book at `https://github.com/Apress/ Just_React`.

Additionally, I added `props.handleItemSelection("edit", stId)`. It's the same thing we did earlier for delete. Now the `handleItemSelection` function in the App component will be triggered every time the user selects a student for editing. This will update the values of the state variables `action` and `id` in the App component. We already passed these variables as props to the EnrolList component. So the EnrolList component will receive the updated state.

Next, locate the `handleClick` function and replace it with the following. We will discuss the changes after this:

```
const handleClick = (event) => {
    handleInputReset("", "", "");
    // Student ID generation
    const randomKey = Math.floor(1000 + Math.random() * 9000);
    let id = randomKey;
    setStudentID(randomKey);
    // For Enrol, use the randomKey variable and for Update use the state
        variable
    id = btnValue === "Enrol" ? randomKey : studentID;
    props.setStudentDetails({
        key: id,
        fname: firstName,
        lname: lastName,
        email: email,
        edit: <MdEdit className="actionIcon" onClick={() => handleEdit(id)} />,
```

```
      delete: (
        <MdDelete
          className="actionIcon"
          onClick={() => props.handleItemSelection("delete", id)}
        />
      ),
    });
    setBtnValue("Enrol");
    event.preventDefault();
  };
```

Previously, in this function, we were setting available seats using `props.setUpdatedSeats(props.currentSeats - 1)`. We removed this as our objective is not to have references to seats in this component. We will set this up in the EnrolList component.

In the previous version of this function, available seats were set by `props.setUpdatedSeats(props.currentSeats - 1)`. As we want to do this from within the EnrolList component, I deleted this line.

Next, let us remove all the references to `program` from this function. The next change is that we removed the `program` property from the `props.setStudentDetails` method. Additionally, we updated the `handleEdit` call of the edit key to remove `program` from the arguments. The edit property looks like the following, with only the student id as an argument:

```
edit: (
        <MdEdit
          className="actionIcon"
          onClick={() => handleEdit(id)}
        />
      )
```

That's all the changes to the EnrolmentForm component now. Now, we removed all program and seats references inside the component. Also, we updated the `handleEdit` function to pass the action and student id during an edit.

Step 3: Next, we need to update `EnrolList.js` to read the program and set the seats as per the edits. First, we need to add the following two lines at the bottom of the `useEffect` method:

```
props.studentDetails.program = props.chosenProgram;
props.setUpdatedSeats(props.currentSeats - 1);
```

The first line sets the selected program to the `studentDetails` object. The EnrolmentForm component no longer passes the program. So we set the student's program in this component based on the program selected. In the second line, the function prop `setUpdatedSeats` is invoked to reduce the seats by one according to the selected program. The number of seats is reduced by one when we add a new student. This was previously done in the EnrolmentForm component during the button click.

With the preceding changes, the delete function will now work. For the edit to work, we need to add a `useEffect` method to the EnrolList component.

The existing `useEffect` will get triggered whenever there is a change in the `props`, since we passed the entire `props` object as the dependency. However, we want the edit to be triggered only when the `handleEdit` is called from the EnrolmentForm component. The `handleEdit` updates the state of the action and student id in the App component. So we need to create another block with `props.studentId` or `props.action` as the dependency. Let us use student id.

So add the following code block above the existing `useEffect` method:

```
useEffect(() => {
  if (props.action === "edit") {
    const currentItem = items.filter(
      (item) => item.key === props.selectedItemId
    )[0];
    props.setSelectedProgram(currentItem.program);
  }
}, [props.selectedItemId]);
```

Here, we are getting the selected item similar to what we did for the delete. After that we are invoking the function prop `setSelectedProgram` with the current item program as the argument. This will update the radio button selection to the corresponding program and will restore the seats. This function we have already defined in `App.js`.

Note   If you would like to view the complete component code at any time, refer to the GitHub repository (`https://github.com/Apress/Just_React`). You can find each component code under the path Chapter 5 ➤ Final chapter code ➤ just-react.

That's all the changes we needed make in all three component codes. In conclusion, we pass the id and action from the EnrolmentForm component to the EnrolList component through the App component. The EnrolList component then communicates with the App component to update the program and seats. The EnrolmentForm component is no longer connected to the program and seats.

Run npm start and view the app in the browser. Add, edit, and delete students and change program. All should work as expected. Refer to Figure 5-5, where I added one UG and one PG student and later changed the program of the PG student to UG.

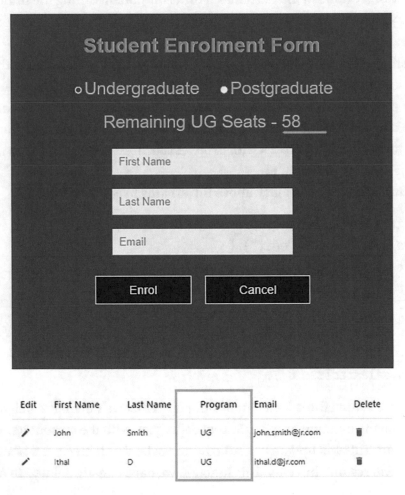

Figure 5-5. *Right way to pass the props*

We redesigned the app to work better. We avoided the props drilling issue with the program and seats props and still achieved all the functionalities. You can keep the enrolment project aside for now. Next, let us create a single-page application with multiple user views.

Multi-view React App

In this section, we'll create a single-page app with multiple views. The end user will experience it as a multi-page website, but we will implement it on a single page without having any navigation to any other pages. We take care of loading and unloading components through state management. As I mentioned before, Netflix, Airbnb, PayPal, etc. are examples of single-page applications (SPAs).

Imagine you are running a small food shop. You have preprepared chicken burgers, veg burgers, chips, and ice creams available for sale. The customers can only order food online with the option for pickup. Customers can only pay cash during pickup. You want to develop a React application to handle sales.

In the root component, say App, we store a list of food items and their respective remaining quantities. In another component, say Foods, we display the list of food items. Customers can view this page and click each item. Whenever a user clicks any food item, the user will get into an item page that displays only the selected item. Customers can select the quantity and click Submit Order. We will have another component called FoodOrder for this item page. Upon ordering, it should decrease the respective food item's quantity, depending on how many of the item the customer ordered.

Let us create a React project using these three components. Your VS Code terminal might be at the `just-react` folder at this stage. Go a step back to the root folder by running `cd...` Then run `npx create-react-app just-food`. The name of our project here is `just-food`. Once the command finishes executing, open the project folder in VS Code using File ➤ Open Folder from the top. We have the `App.js` created by default under the `src` folder. Let's define the food items and their quantities in this App component. Replace the code in App.js with that in Listing 5-1.

Listing 5-1. Just Food – App.js

```
import "./App.css";
import React, { useState } from "react";
const App = () => {
    const [menuItems, setMenuItems] = useState([
    {
      id: 1,
      name: "Chicken Burger",
      quantity: 40,
      desc: "Fried chicken burger - lettuce, tomato, cheese and
      mayonnaise",
      price: "24",
      image: "cb.jpg",
    },
    {
      id: 2,
      name: "Veg Burger",
      quantity: 30,
      desc: "Plant-based burger - lettuce, tomato, vegan cheese and
      mayonnaise",
      price: "22",
      image: "vb.jpg",
    },
    {
      id: 3,
      name: "Chips",
      quantity: 50,
      desc: "Potato chips fried to perfection",
      price: "7",
      image: "chips.jpg",
    },
    {
      id: 4,
      name: "Ice Cream",
      quantity: 30,
```

```
        desc: "Ice cream - Vanilla ice cream double scoop",
        price: "4",
        image: "ic.jpg",
      },
    ]);
  return (
      <div className="App">
        <h3 className="title">Just Food Online Shop</h3>
        <h4 className="subTitle">Menu Availability</h4>
        <ul className="ulApp">
          {menuItems.map((item) => {
            return (
              <li key={item.id} className="liApp">
                {item.name} - {item.quantity}
              </li>
            );
          })}
        </ul>
      </div>
    );
};
export default App;
```

The menuItems object array variable contains the initial quantity of each of the four food items in our menu. The setMenuItems function can update the menu items or existing item's properties. For example, we can use this to set the item quantity after the user placed orders. In the JSX code, we have a menu element (<ul>) besides the title sections. I added a map function to loop over the array menuItems and create <li> tags for each menu item with its name and quantity.

The id property serves as a key to the <li> element. In addition, we have defined a description, price, and image for each of the menu items. This will be handy when we develop further components. Now, replace the default code in App.css with the following. Refer to Listing 5-2.

Listing 5-2. Just Food – App.css

```
.App {
  font-family: "Segoe UI", Tahoma, Geneva, Verdana, sans-serif;
  text-align: left;
  width: 100%;
  margin-top: 30px;
  position: absolute;
  background: rgb(22, 61, 97);
  left: 50%;
  height: 630px;
  width: 40%;
  transform: translate(-50%, 0%);
  text-align: center;
  color: white;
}

.title {
  color: rgba(235, 232, 51, 0.993);
  font-weight: 400;
  font-size: 44px;
}
.subTitle {
  color: rgba(85, 191, 233, 0.993);
  font-weight: 400;
  font-size: 34px;
  margin-bottom: 0px;
}
.ulApp {
  list-style-type: none;
  padding: 0;
  font-size: 28px;
}
.liApp {
  padding-bottom: 10px;
}
```

```
.toggleButton
{
  float:left;
  margin: 5px 0px 0px 5px;
  align-items: center;
  padding: 6px 14px;
  border-radius: 8px;
  border: none;
  color: #fff;
  background-color:#367AF6;
  cursor: pointer;
}
```

You now have a static app displayed on the browser. Refer to Figure 5-6.

Figure 5-6. *App component with static object values*

If you want to add another menu item, you can just add it to the menuItems array in the code, and the app will have it immediately reflected.

So we created a component that allows you, the food shop owner, and staff to view the current menu availability. Customers cannot see this. Let us create another component, say Foods. The component will display all the four items along with a small description, price, and image. This will be the customer's home page. We will have a button to switch between the foods display and the availability display.

Let us prepare the images before we create the Foods component. Right-click the src folder and select New Folder. Name the folder images. Within the images folder, add four images named cb.jpg, vb.jpg, chips.jpg and ic.jpg. Make sure the names match those of the image property of the menuItems object in the App component.

Note   You can access the images that I used from the GitHub repo (`https://github.com/Apress/Just_React`). The images are located under Chapter 5 ➤ Food images. All the four images are from unsplash.com, and those images are free to use.

Next, right-click the src folder and create a new file named Foods.js. Add the following code into it. Refer to Listing 5-3.

Listing 5-3. Foods.js

```
import React, {Fragment, useState } from "react";
import "./Foods.css";
const Foods = (props) => {
  return (
  <Fragment>
      <h4 className="foodTitle">Choose from our Menu</h4>
      <ul className="ulFoods">
        {props.foodItems.map((item) => {
          return (
            <li key={item.id} className="liFoods">
              <img
                className="foodImg"
                src={require(`./images/${item.image}`)}
                alt={item.name}
              />
```

```
        <div className="foodItem">
          <p className="foodDesc">{item.desc}</p>
          <p className="foodPrice">{item.price}$</p>
        </div>
      </li>
    );
  })}
    </ul>
  </Fragment>
 );
};
export default Foods;
```

The Foods component expects a prop from the parent component, from which it is called. Here, we need to pass menuItems from the App component to the Foods component. The prop is foodItems. By looping through the foodItems, it creates a view of the food image, description, and price. Like in App.js, we use object properties here for the image and other content.

We wrapped all the elements in the return statements in a React fragment (<Fragment></Fragment>). It is not possible to keep multiple child elements without a container element inside a JSX expression. Hence, we wrapped all child elements inside the return function using a fragment. Also, instead of using the syntax <Fragment> </Fragment>, you can also use <></>.

Fragments in React allow us to group items without having to wrap them inside another element, such as a div. Here, in our case, there is no need to add a new div. Instead, we can use a fragment. It is important to note that fragments do not add extra DOM nodes, whereas a plain <div> naturally does. If we want to add styles to the container or if it serves some other purpose, we can use a div element as a container. It is unnecessary to add an extra node otherwise. We can instead use a fragment. You can see there isn't an extra node for the fragment if you run the application in the browser. Press F12 and see the HTML under the dev tools.

To view the Foods component in the browser, we need to add it to App.js. To do this, let's first create a button that will switch the view between food availability and food selection. In a real-world scenario, the availability of food is only visible to admin users, such as the shop owner or staff. We will deal with this in Chapter 9 when we learn about authentication.

To import the Foods component, go back to App.js and add a new import statement. Also, import Fragment as we need it for wrapping JSX child elements:

```
import React, {Fragment, useState } from "react";
import Foods from "./Foods";
```

Now, add a new state variable below the menuItems variable declaration. Set its initial value to false:

```
const [isChooseFoodPage, setIsChooseFoodPage] = useState(false);
```

Now, update the return statement to reflect the following. Refer to Listing 5-4.

Listing 5-4. App.js Return Function with Toggle

```
return (
  <div className="App">
    <button className="toggleButton" onClick={() => setIsChooseFoodPage
    (!isChooseFoodPage)}>
      {isChooseFoodPage ? "Availability Check" : "Order Food"}
    </button>
    <h3 className="title">Just Food Online Shop</h3>
    {!isChooseFoodPage && (
      <Fragment>
        <h4 className="subTitle">Menu Availability</h4>
        <ul className="ulApp">
          {menuItems.map((item) => {
            return (
              <li key={item.id} className="liApp">
                {item.name} - {item.quantity}
              </li>
            );
          })}
        </ul>
      </Fragment>
    )}
    {isChooseFoodPage && <Foods foodItems={menuItems}></Foods>}
  </div>
);
```

Let us look at the changes we made in the return function. We added a button there. The button text is based on the state variable isChooseFoodPage. If isChooseFoodPage is true, it will say Availability Check; otherwise, it will display Order Food:

```
<button className="toggleButton" onClick={() => setIsChooseFoodPage
(!isChooseFoodPage)}>
        {isChooseFoodPage ? "Availability Check" : "Order Food"}
</button>
```

By default, isChooseFoodPage is false. Because of that, the button text will show Order Food by default. When you click the button, the text will switch. I already defined the styles of the button in App.css in Listing 5-2.

Next, we added a condition around the Menu Availability header text and menu items. Here we have a condition that says if isChooseFoodPage is false, then display the component. We wrapped the header text and the <ul> tag for menu items inside a fragment. Here we have a JSX expression, !isChooseFoodPage. We define the menu items list and the header text elements inside that expression. We cannot keep the multiple child elements without a container inside a JSX expression. So we added an argument. As the title Just Food Online Shop is the same in both scenarios, we kept it outside of the !isChooseFoodPage expression.

The last change is that we added the Foods component and passed menuItems as a prop to it. We added a condition to display the Foods component, which is the opposite condition of the preceding scenario, where we displayed menu items and the availability header .

If isChooseFoodPage is true, the Foods component gets displayed by default. If the user clicks the Order Food button, it changes the text to Availability Check, and it will display the Foods component.

Before viewing the app in the browser, let us add some styles to the Foods component. You might have noticed that we imported Foods.css in the preceding Foods.js. Create a new file Foods.css under the same src folder and copy Listing 5-5.

Listing 5-5. Foods.css

```
.foodTitle {
  color: rgba(85, 191, 233, 0.993);
  font-weight: 400;
  font-size: 34px;
  padding-bottom: 10px;
}
```

```css
.ulFoods {
  list-style-type: none;
  padding: 0;
  font-size: 28px;
  height: 75%;
}
.liFoods {
  width: 100%;
  height: 18%;
  float: left;
  margin-left: 20%;
  text-align: center;
  margin-top: -3%;
  word-wrap: normal;
  margin-bottom: 5%;
  cursor: pointer;
}
.foodImg {
  width: 12%;
  height: 85%;
  float: left;
  margin-right: 10px;
}
.foodItem {
  width: 70%;
  text-align: left;
  font-size: 18px;
  height: 25%;
}
.foodDesc {
  margin: 0;
}
```

```
.foodPrice {
  margin: 0;
  color: rgba(85, 191, 233, 0.993);
  font-weight: 600;
}
```

Run npm start and view the app in your browser. We will have the Menu Availability page displayed by default. Click the top-left button with the text Order Food. When you click it, it displays the Foods component, and the button text changes to Availability Check. Now you can view the four food items with their images, descriptions, and prices. Refer to Figure 5-7 for details.

Figure 5-7. *Foods component*

Whenever you move your mouse over any of the food items, a cursor appears. We added a cursor style to the food items. You can click Availability Check and switch back to the Menu Availability view.

Our next task is to create a component that can display individual food items so that the customer can order food. Keeping it simple, we're going to allow customers to order only one item at a time. Customers will need to select one or more quantity, provide their name and mobile number, and then click Submit Order. Once ordered, a message will appear on the customer's screen. In the back end, we should reduce the availability accordingly. If they want another item, they need to go back to the Order Food page (Choose from our Menu) from our menu availability page to select the item again, select quantity, provide details, and place a separate order.

Note   Assume the customer gets a message or a call once the order is ready. The customer can pick up multiple orders together. Obviously, we are not handling this part of the process in our app 😊.

Now, let us create the component for ordering the individual food, the FoodOrder component. Right-click the src folder, create a new file, and name it FoodOrder.js. Copy the following code into it. Refer to Listing 5-6. We will go into the code details in the following.

Listing 5-6. FoodOrder.js

```
import React, {Fragment, useState } from "react";
import "./FoodOrder.css";

const FoodOrder = (props) => {
  const selectedFood = props.food;
  const [quantity, setQuantity] = useState(1);
  const [totalAmount, setTotalAmount] = useState(selectedFood.price);
  const [isOrdered, setIsOrdered] = useState(false);

  const handleQuantityChange = (event) => {
    setTotalAmount(selectedFood.price * event.target.value);
    setQuantity(event.target.value);
  };
```

```
const handleClick = () => {
  setIsOrdered(true);
  props.updateQuantity(selectedFood.id, quantity);
};

return (
  <Fragment>
    <h4 className="selFoodTitle">{selectedFood.name}</h4>
    <img
      className="selFoodImg"          src={require(`./images/$
                                      {selectedFood.image}`)}
      alt={selectedFood.name}
    />
    <ul className="ulFoodDetails">
      <li>
        <p className="selFoodDesc">{selectedFood.desc}</p>
      </li>
      <li>
        <p className="selFoodPrice">{totalAmount}$</p>
      </li>
      <li className="selQuantity">
        <label>Quantity</label>
        <input
          type="number"
          defaultValue={1}
          className="quantity"
          min="1"
          max="10"
          onChange={handleQuantityChange}
        />
      </li>

      <li className="liDetails">
        <label for="name"></label>
        <input
          type="text"
          className="inputFields"
```

```
              id="name"
              name="name"
              placeholder="Your Name"
          />
        </li>
        <li>
          <label for="mobile"></label>
          <input
            type="text"
            className="inputFields"
            id="mobile"
            name="mobile"
            placeholder="Your mobile number"
          />
        </li>

        <li>
          <button className="btn btnOrder" onClick={handleClick}>
            Submit Order
          </button>
          <button className="btn btnReturnMenu" onClick={props.returnToMenu}>
            Return to Menu
          </button>
        </li>
        {isOrdered && (
          <li className="liMessage">
            <label>
              Order Submitted! You will receive an SMS to once ready
              for pickup.
            </label>
          </li>
        )}
      </ul>
    </Fragment>
  );
};
export default FoodOrder;
```

Let us look at the JSX we defined first. We have the image, the description, and the price of the selected food displayed in this component. It is expecting a prop, selectedFood, from its parent component. So here we expect the Foods component to pass the selected food item object. The FoodOrder component retrieves properties from the object, like the name, image, etc.

Below that, there is an option to select quantity. By default, the quantity will be 1. As soon as the user changes the quantity, the price will increase accordingly. For this purpose, we have defined two state variables:

```
const [quantity, setQuantity] = useState(1);
const [totalAmount, setTotalAmount] = useState(selectedFood.price);
```

We initialized the quantity to 1 and the price to that of the selected food. For example, if you select Ice Cream, both the quantity and price will be 1 and $4, respectively.

In the next step, we have a handleQuantityChange function. This gets called when the user changes the input field for Quantity:

```
const handleQuantityChange = (event) => {
    setTotalAmount(selectedFood.price * event.target.value);
    setQuantity(event.target.value);
  };
```

As soon as the customer selects a quantity, the state variable totalAmount gets updated with the selected quantity multiplied by the amount. Besides that, it sets the selected quantity to the variable quantity.

Look at the JSX again. Below the quantity input element, we have text inputs for name and mobile number. There are no operations set for these fields; it is just for entering the data. Finally, we have two buttons at the bottom. First, let's inspect the right-hand-side button, which is the Return to Menu button.

Upon clicking this button, we need to hide the FoodOrder component and display the Foods component to order food items. This button calls a callback function props.returnToMenu. We will need to define this function in the Foods component and pass it as a prop.

The other button on the left-hand side is for submitting orders. When a customer clicks it, the handleClick function gets called:

```
const handleClick = () => {
    setIsOrdered(true);
    props.updateQuantity(selectedFood.id, quantity);
 };
```

In the first line, the function sets the IsOrdered variable to true. We defined this variable and initialized it with false. If IsOrdered is true, we will display a label underneath the buttons that says you submitted the order. We defined a label with a condition below the buttons for this purpose.

In the second line, the handleClick invokes props.updateQuantity with two parameters, the id of the selected food item and the selected quantity. By calling this function, it invokes a function in the parent component, Foods, to set the quantity.

So this means, in the Foods component, we need to pass three props to the FoodOrder component: the selected item and two function props for returning to the menu and updating the quantity.

Next, let's update the Foods component again to include the FoodOrder component and pass the required props.

Replace the Foods component code with that in Listing 5-7.

Listing 5-7. Foods.js with the Option to Select an Item

```
import React, { Fragment, useState } from "react";
import "./Foods.css";
import FoodOrder from "./FoodOrder";
const Foods = (props) => {
  const [selectedFood, setSelectedFood] = useState("");

  const handleSelect = (event) => {
    setSelectedFood(
      props.foodItems.find((item) => {
        return item.id === parseInt(event.currentTarget.dataset.id);
      })
    );
  };
```

```
return (
  <Fragment>
    {!selectedFood && (
      <Fragment>
        <h4 className="foodTitle">Choose from our Menu</h4>
        <ul className="ulFoods">
          {props.foodItems.map((item) => {
            return (
              <li
                key={item.id}
                className="liFoods"
                data-id={item.id}
                onClick={handleSelect}
              >
                <img
                  className="foodImg"
                  src={require(`./images/${item.image}`)}
                  alt={item.name}
                />
                <div className="foodItem">
                  <p className="foodDesc">{item.desc}</p>
                  <p className="foodPrice">{item.price}$</p>
                </div>
              </li>
            );
          })}
        </ul>
      </Fragment>
    )}
    {selectedFood && (
      <FoodOrder
        food={selectedFood}
        returnToMenu={() => setSelectedFood("")}
        updateQuantity={(id, quantity) => props.updateQuantity
        (id, quantity)}
```

```
        />
      )}
    </Fragment>
  );
};

export default Foods;
```

In the Foods component, we introduced a new state variable `selectedFood`, which can store the selected food item details:

```
const [selectedFood, setSelectedFood] = useState("");
```

In the return statement, we enclosed the food details and title in a fragment. This section will only display if `selectedFood` is empty. This means that when the customer selects a food, we hide the Choose from our Menu section from the user.

Below that, we added the FoodOrder tag with three props. We imported the component on top. The FoodOrder component will only appear if `selectedFood` has a value:

```
<FoodOrder
        food={selectedFood}
        returnToMenu={() => setSelectedFood("")}
        updateQuantity={(id, quantity) => props.updateQuantity
        (id, quantity)}
        />
```

We have the food details such as name, price, and image stored in the `selectedFood` property. The callback function `returnToMenu` calls `setSelectedFood` with an empty parameter. Therefore, when the child component invokes the `returnToMenu` function, the `selectedFood` variable becomes empty. Because of this, the app displays the Choose from our Menu section and not the FoodOrder component.

The third property, `updateQuantity`, is a callback function. This function invokes `updateQuantity` of the App component using `props.updateQuantity`. This means we will have to pass a new function prop from the App component. We will do it shortly.

We are passing the selected item id and ordered quantity from the Foods component. The Foods component receives the same from the FoodOrder component as parameters to this function prop.

Besides all this, we have a new function handleSelect, which sets the selected food upon clicking any food item. This function is called from the onClick event of each <li> tag:

```
const handleSelect = (event) => {
    setSelectedFood(
      props.foodItems.find((item) => {
        return item.id === parseInt(event.currentTarget.dataset.id);
      })
    );
};
```

We defined data-id of each <li> tag as item id. This function loops through the food items and compares the id with the data-id of the <li> tag. Finally, it sets the matched food item to the selectedFood variable. As soon as this happens, the FoodOrder component gets loaded, and Choose from our Menu disappears. This is because we set a condition around these sections to make the FoodOrder component visible if selectedFood has value.

In the App component, we need to include the quantity update. As we defined the quantity there, we need to update it there. We just need to make two changes. First, we need to create a new function updateMenuItemQuantity and place it above the return function:

```
const updateMenuItemQuantity = (id, orderQuantity) => {
    const updatedMenuItems = menuItems.map((item) => {
      if (item.id === id)
        return {
          ...item,
          quantity: item.quantity - orderQuantity,
        };
      return item;
    });
    setMenuItems(updatedMenuItems);
};
```

This function receives the id and orderQuantity parameters. It copies the array of menu items to the updatedMenuItems variable. Then, it finds the ordered menu item using the id and updates the quantity by subtracting the orderQuantity. It then sets the updatedMenuItems to the menuItems variable using the setMenuItems method. This updates the menu items by reducing the quantity of the ordered food item.

We now need to pass a function prop to the Foods component to invoke the preceding updateMenuItemQuantity function. Scroll down to the bottom and update the Foods component to include the new callback property:

```
<Foods
    foodItems={menuItems}
    updateQuantity={updateMenuItemQuantity}>
</Foods>
```

We already updated the Foods component to call props.updateQuantity when its child, FoodOrder, invokes its function prop updateQuantity.

That's all. Now the user will be able to select food, see the details in a new view, increase quantity, and submit the order. The price will increase according to the quantity. Upon submitting order, a message will be printed. The user can go back to the menu using the Return to Menu button. Before we see this browser, let us put some styling. Create a new file FoodOrder.css and copy the following CSS code from Listing 5-8. We already imported this into the FoodOrder component.

Listing 5-8. FoodOrder.css

```
.selFoodTitle {
  color: rgba(85, 191, 233, 0.993);
  font-weight: 400;
  font-size: 34px;
  margin-top: -5%;
  text-align: center;
  margin-left: 10%;
  width: 80%;
}
.selFoodImg {
  width: 40%;
  height: 30%;
```

```
    float: left;
    margin-left: 10%;
    margin-top: -5%;
}
.ulFoodDetails {
    list-style-type: none;
    padding: 0;
    width: 70%;
    margin-left: 20%;
    text-align: center;
    font-size: 18px;
    height: 25%;
}
.selFoodDesc {
    margin-top: -5%;
    margin-left: 45%;
    text-align: center;
}
.selFoodPrice {
    color: rgba(235, 232, 51, 0.993);
    font-weight: 600;
    font-size: 22px;
}
.liDetails {
    margin-top: 10px;
}
.inputFields {
    margin: 10px 0;
    font-size: 16px;
    padding: 10px;
    width: 250px;
    border: 1px solid rgb(13, 138, 65);
    border-top: none;
    border-left: none;
    border-right: none;
```

```
  background: rgb(245, 240, 240);
  color: rgb(5, 19, 66);
  outline: none;
}

.quantity {
  margin: 10px 10px;
  font-size: 16px;
  padding: 10px;
  width: 50px;
  border: 1px solid rgb(13, 138, 65);
  border-top: none;
  border-left: none;
  border-right: none;
  background: rgb(245, 240, 240);
  color: rgb(5, 19, 66);
  outline: none;
}
.btn {
  background-color: #0095ff;
  border-radius: 3px;
  box-shadow: rgba(255, 255, 255, 0.4) 0 1px 0 0 inset;
  box-sizing: border-box;
  color: #fff;
  cursor: pointer;
  display: inline-block;
  font-size: 16px;
  font-weight: 400;
  line-height: 1.15385;
  margin: 0;
  outline: none;
  padding: 8px 0.8em;
  position: relative;
```

```css
  text-align: center;
  white-space: nowrap;
  margin-top: 5%;
  border: 1px solid rgba(235, 232, 51, 0.993);
}
.btnOrder {
  margin-right: 20px;
}
.btn:hover,
.btn:focus {
  background-color: #07c;
}
.btn:active {
  background-color: #0064bd;
  box-shadow: none;
}
.liMessage {
  margin-top: 10px;
  color: rgba(235, 232, 51, 0.993);
}
```

Run npm start to view the app in the browser. Click Order Food and select one of the food items. When you select it, individual food details appear with the option to submit order. If you increase the quantity, the price will increase accordingly. When you submit, you will get a confirmation message. If you click Return to Menu, all the food items will be available to select again.

Refer to Figure 5-8, where I ordered three ice creams.

Figure 5-8. *FoodOrder component(Steps: 1, enter quantity; 2, enter details; 3, submit order; 4, receive message; 5, check availability)*

Imagine that I received a confirmation message on the app 😊. When I click Availability Check, I can see there are now only 27 ice creams. Refer to Figure 5-9.

Figure 5-9. App component updated from the FoodOrder component

The quantity updated based on the ordered quantity of the respective item. You can experiment with other food items and order different quantities. The availability should update based on that.

The app works as expected. But as you may have already noticed, we have a props drilling issue in this quantity update. We are sending the ordered food item id and quantity through the Foods component, which does not require these values at all.

As compared to the enrolment project, there is no redesign we can do here to avoid the drilling issue. The only way to transfer these data from the App component to the FoodOrder component is through the Foods component. So how can we avoid the issue with props drilling? Let's see.

React Context

As part of the student enrolment project, we fixed the props drilling issue by designing the components in a better way. We had an App component and its two child components. This allowed us to redesign, passing the props directly to the right component. However, for the just-food project, the third component, FoodOrder, is nested within the second component, Foods. So, here, we cannot pass the properties from the root component, App, to the third component without passing the properties through the second component, Foods.

Because the second component does not require the props, we have a props drilling issue. We can solve this by using Context. As we mentioned before, Context is an API built into React that provides an alternate and more convenient method of passing data between components.

Using Context, we can create a kind of global state that can be used by all components. To implement Context, we need three steps. Create a context, provide it from a component, and then consume it from any other component that requires it.

To help you better understand this, let us fix the props drilling in our just-food project with the help of Context.

Before we proceed, let us remove the update quantity function we implemented through props drilling. Remove the respective sections from all components. Go to App. js and delete the updateMenuItemQuantity function. Then scroll down and remove the property from the <Foods> tag. The tag should look like the following now:

```
<Foods foodItems={menuItems}></Foods>
```

Move on to Foods.js and remove the updateQuantity property from the <FoodOrder> tag. We should now have only two properties:

```
  <FoodOrder food={selectedFood} returnToMenu={() =>
setSelectedFood("")} />
```

To update the handleClick function, open FoodOrder.js, and delete the props. updateQuantity function. The handleClick should look like the one shown in the following:

```
const handleClick = () => {
    setIsOrdered(true);
 };
```

We have now removed all the code for updating quantity. If you run the app now, you observe that it will not update the quantity on the Menu Availability page after you ordered an item. Let's reintroduce this feature in a better way using Context.

First, let's create a context. Go to App.js and add the following line just below the imports:

```
export const foodItemsContext = React.createContext();
```

This step creates a context using the method `createContext`. We created the context and stored it in the variable `foodItemsContext`. We are exporting this in a variable, so that we can use it in our FoodOrder component.

Next, we will wrap the JSX component tree inside the context provider. Scroll down to the return function and wrap the entire JSX within the following tag:

```
<foodItemsContext.Provider value={menuItems}>
 </foodItemsContext.Provider>
```

This means that our parent div element, including its children, is now included inside of the preceding tag. In this context provider, we put the value as `menuItems`. Therefore, the `menuItems` object is now provided in this context.

The last step is to change the FoodOrder component to consume the context from there. We can use a a React Hook, `useContext` for that. Add the following two lines to `FoodOrder.js`:

```
import { useContext } from "react";
import { foodItemsContext } from "./App";
```

Now we've imported the `useContext` hook. Besides that, we imported the `foodItemsContext` from the App component. We created the `foodItemsContext` earlier in the App component and imported the reference here. The `useContext` Hook enables us to access this context. So declare a variable to read the food context. Put this next to the `useState` declarations inside the component:

```
const menuItems = useContext(foodItemsContext);
```

Now the variable contains the menu items provided by the `foodItemsContext`. Next, update the `handleClick` function as follows:

```
const handleClick = () => {
    setIsOrdered(true);
    menuItems.map((item) => {
      if (item.id === selectedFood.id) {
        item.quantity = item.quantity - quantity;
      }
    });
  };
```

Now, the function checks menuItems and updates the quantity if the id matches that of the ordered item.

You can view the app in the browser now. Try ordering items, and you can observe that quantity gets updated exactly as before, this time without drilling props through the Foods component! We haven't done any coding in the Foods component for this purpose. The Foods component does not have to worry about the quantity here, as we pass the context from the App component directly to the FoodOrder component. When you update the menuItems from the FoodOrder component, the Availability Check page gets updated with the quantity of the ordered item. Context changes, like state changes, cause a re-render of the components. The context solution has fixed the props drilling problem, and the app now looks much cleaner.

Figures 5-10 and 5-11 illustrate how we avoided the props drilling issue by using Context in the just-food app.

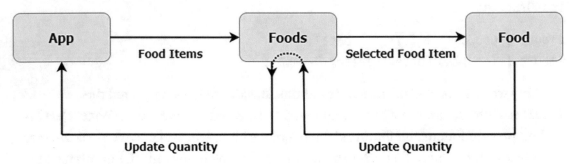

Figure 5-10. *App design without Context*

Figure 5-11. *App design with Context*

> **Note**   You can visit the GitHub repository (`https://github.com/Apress/ Just_React`) to view the project code at the end of each chapter. The just-food project with Context implementation is located under Chapter 5 ➤ Projects. You can download or clone the entire project at the end of each chapter from the GitHub repository. After cloning, run `npm install` from the project folder to install all the required node modules before running the code.

Summary

Our focus in this chapter was rethinking in React way. We did a lot of practicing in this chapter. We began in a lazy mode by learning about code splitting using Lazy and Suspense. React's code splitting feature can be extremely useful when coding complex applications.

Our next discussion focused on a common issue with React, which is with props drilling. After that, we went back and reanalyzed our student enrolment code. Props drilling and a few other issues we found there led us to redesign the components. Finally, we built it by eliminating the props drilling issue.

In the subsequent section, we built a different application called just-food. There are multiple views in the application. We built everything on a single page. You learned more about component interactions and conditional display. You learned about React fragments.

After another rcthink, we found the props drilling problem that we could not fix with any kind of redesign because of the nested component structure. This is where another React feature, React Context, came into play. We redesigned the app using Context. This allowed us to bypass the middle component and share the state between the first and third components. You met with the Hook "useContext".

I guess we can relax a bit in the next two chapters. We will focus on debugging and styling React applications there. I will introduce you to a few helpful tools and libraries in the next two chapters. More advanced features of React await you in Chapters 8 and 9. See you then debugging React in the next chapter!

CHAPTER 6

React to Bugs

This chapter discusses different ways to debug React applications. It is mostly about how you, as a developer, react to bugs and issues in React applications.

In this chapter, we will start with the Chrome developer tools, which most of you should already be familiar with. If you are already proficient in the Chrome developer tools, you may skip that section. From there, we will move to our just-food application, which we developed in our last chapter. We'll break the just-food app by creating some errors and then look at how the Chrome tools can help us fix them.

We will discuss error boundaries and realize that they are not applicable to our functional components. But don't fret. We will create a friendly error page for our users.

We will then explore and learn how to use the React DevTools. You will learn about using the Components tab and how to change props and state on the go. We will then discuss finding performance glitches with the help of Profiler. We will conclude this chapter by discussing debugging within Visual Studio Code (VS Code). You will learn how to set breakpoints, do debugging, and log in VS Code.

By the end of this chapter, you will be more excited about debugging React applications than developing them. This chapter will be a smooth and relaxing ride compared with our code-rich chapters.

Chrome Reacts

During our initial chapters, we covered the Chrome dev tools, a set of web developer tools that comes with the Chrome browser. This tool has a lot of powerful features for debugging web applications. It's your go-to tool for finding issues such as bugs, style issues, performance issues, etc.

Let's look at our existing just-food project to check if there are any potential bugs or issues. You can run npm start to open the app in the Chrome browser. Press F12 to open the dev tools once the browser loaded the app. The dev tools will open on the right

© Hari Narayn 2022
H. Narayn, *Just React!*, https://doi.org/10.1007/978-1-4842-8294-6_6

side by default if you are launching it for the first time. Close the second console at the bottom, as highlighted in Figure 6-1. Then, you can position the tools to the bottom by clicking Settings ➤ Dock to bottom. I like it at the bottom, but you can place it wherever you like. Even you can keep it as a separate window if you prefer that way. Refer to Figure 6-1.

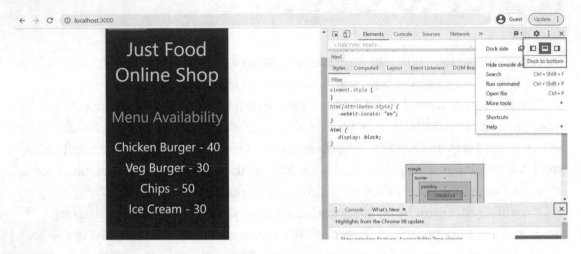

Figure 6-1. *Open the Chrome DevTools*

From the Elements tab, we can make out that the browser rendered JSX elements as HTML elements. On the right, we will have the styles defined for each class. You can resize the tabs to keep more space for the Elements tab, so that you can see all elements. You can do it by dragging the splitter to the right using the mouse. Refer to Figure 6-2.

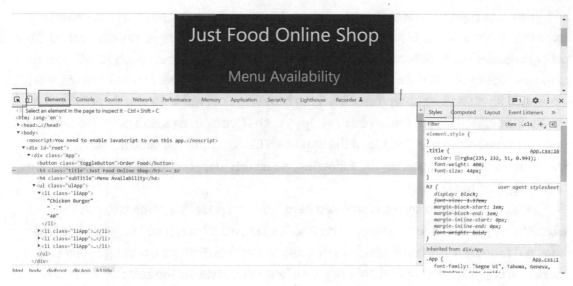

Figure 6-2. *Elements tab*

You can look at each HTML element using the inspect icon at the top left. Using the inspect icon, you can select a specific HTML element from the screen. The element markup and styles will be highlighted in the dev tools when you inspect an element. Click the inspect icon, then click the app, and then click the HTML element you want to select. This will highlight the element under the Elements tab. We can spot the styles in the pop-up window and in the right-side window. Refer to Figure 6-3.

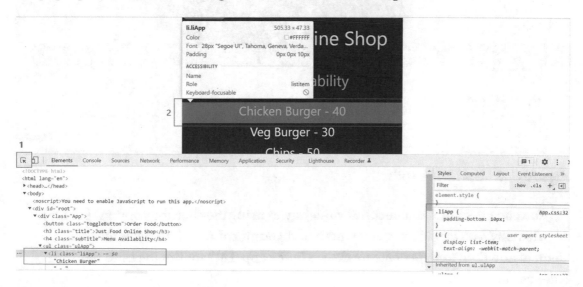

Figure 6-3. *Inspecting an element*

From the right window, you can change the styles. For example, you can change padding-bottom of the liApp class to 25px. You can add a new style, say color:Red. This will get immediately reflected in the app. This way, you can inspect each HTML element and view the updated style in the browser. The style will be active for the browser session only, and it will be lost once you refresh the browser. This will help you determine the desired look for the app. Once you are happy with it, you go back and copy the updated style into the respective CSS file of the app in VS Code. I updated padding-bottom and the color of the liApp class in the following. Since this class is common to all food items, it gets applied to all items.

If you only want to style the selected item, you can do it by adding styles to the element.style block. If you add a style inside element.style, it will only apply to the selected food item element, which in this case is Chicken Burger. Creating a new CSS class and copying this style will allow you to keep that style for the selected element. Then, apply the CSS class to that element only in the JS file. I have highlighted in Figure 6-4 how styles apply to elements.

Figure 6-4. *Updating styles*

You can check and uncheck individual styles using the checkbox option (in blue).

This way, you can inspect elements and determine the desired styles for each element and then update or create classes in the app. Let's look at the third tab, Sources, next.

Don't React, Debug First

This section shows how to debug React code by using the DevTools. To do so, we will use the Foods component, which we built for customers to order food. Click the Order Food button at the top and select any of the food items from the resulting page. When you select the item, it opens the food order page with the details of the selected item.

Now, click the Sources tab from the DevTools. From the left-hand-side window, expand the js folder under localhost. Then go down the tree as highlighted in Figure 6-5 and then locate FoodOrder.js. When you click FoodOrder.js, you can view the complete code of the file in the middle window. Just click the line number on the first line inside the handleChange and handleClick functions to put debug points. We have the line numbers highlighted now. Also, you can view breakpoint details on the right window.

I highlighted all the preceding steps in Figure 6-5.

Figure 6-5. *Sources*

When you change the quantity, the debugger will pause on line 14, where you set the breakpoint earlier. When you hover over selectedFood.price, you would notice the value 24 there, if you had selected Chicken Burger. Similarly, you can check the value of event.target.value. On the top, you can see the message paused in debugger. Next to that you can see two buttons.

The first one is to resume script execution. Clicking it will continue the execution, and it will move to the next breakpoint if you have one. Otherwise, it will get completed. You can use the F8 key as an alternative to do this. For example, when you click the script execution button, when you are at line 14 in the preceding example, it will move to line 19, where you set the next breakpoint.

The second one is to step over to the next line. We can use the F10 key instead of this. Pressing F10, you can observe the blue line move over to the next line. Here in this example, if you click the step over button (or press F10), the `setTotalAmount` gets executed, and the debugger will step into line 15. This way, you can check the point-in-time values at each line of the code. This helps you find out which line needs to be changed in case of an error or unexpected results. Refer to Figure 6-6.

Figure 6-6. *Debugging the source*

While debugging a line, if you switch over to the tab Console, you can print out the value at that moment in time. For example, if you type `selectedFood.price` or `event.target.value` at the console and then press Enter, it will print the value. The console will display the `selectedFood` object value if you type in `selectedFood` and hit Enter. Refer to Figure 6-7.

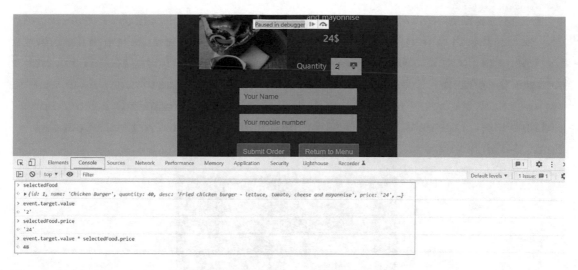

Figure 6-7. *Viewing point-in-time values at Console*

We can continue execution by pressing the F8 key. When you click the Submit Order button, it will hit the breakpoint at line 19. You can navigate through menu items to check how the map function works over there. You can remove a breakpoint by clicking the line again. By using breakpoints and the console effectively, you can uncover bugs and performance glitches and update your code accordingly.

Console Reactions

You can view any errors and warnings in the Console tab. It also provides the detailed error messages in red with the line number and other details. In addition, you can log any results into the console by adding the logging into the code. Let's look at how these things work with an example.

In FoodOrder.js, add the following lines to the handleQuantityChange function:

```
console.log(`The price of the selected food is ${selectedFood.price}`);
console.table(selectedFood);
```

```
console.log(`The total price  is ${selectedFood.price* event.target.
value}`);
```

In the first line, we are logging selectedFood.price into the console. In the second line, we are logging the selectedFood object in table format. View the app in the browser and open the Console tab in the DevTools. Select Order Food, choose a food item, and increase the quantity. Now, the console will display the price, the food details, as well as the total price. It displays the food details in a table format. We can find the line number and filename on the right. If you click the line number, it will take you to the code file. Figure 6-8 highlights these details.

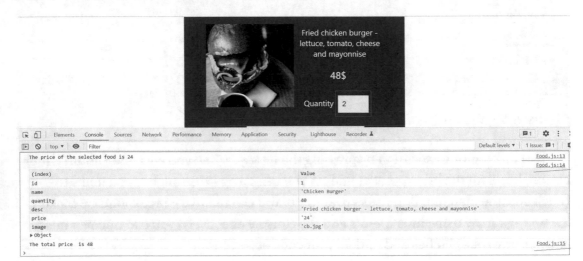

Figure 6-8. *Logging into the console*

You can remove these console logs from the code now. Next, let's create an error and check how the console displays it.

Go to FoodOrder.js and add parentheses around the handleQuantityChange call in FoodOrder.js. To do this, update the <li> tag for the quantity like this:

```
<li className="selQuantity">
        <label>Quantity</label>
        <input
          type="number"
          defaultValue={1}
          className="quantity"
          min="1"
```

```
        max="10"
        onChange={handleQuantityChange()}
      />
</li>
```

I have only added parentheses to the handleQuantityChange method. Open the app in the browser, keep the DevTools open, select the Order Food button from the top, and select an item. You will spot a few errors immediately in the console. The selected item will not load. Refer to Figure 6-9.

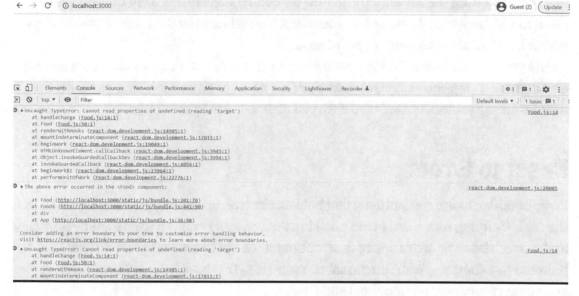

Figure 6-9. *Console errors*

Besides the details, the error provides an idea of how to track it down. Also, you can spot the filename and code line on the right. If you examine the error, you can see that the handleQuantityChange function was called before you updated the quantity. And it didn't find any value for the event, so it threw the error "Cannot read properties of undefined (reading 'target')."

When you add parentheses to a function call, it actually evaluates the function and tries to assign its result to the onChange call. This is not what we're after. We want to add a reference to the function to the onChange property, so that the function will be invoked when we change the quantity. We can achieve this by either of the following two methods:

1. onChange={handleQuantityChange} – Here the event is passed by default.

2. onChange={(event)=> handleQuantityChange(event)} – If we use an arrow function like this, we need to pass an event specifically.

So these are the two ways to include a reference to the function call. When we do onChange={handleQuantityChange()}, that calls the function itself instead of referring. That throws the error immediately.

The preceding was an example of how we could detect errors from the console and use it to resolve issues. Now, before you revert the code and fix the error, let us display a fallback interface to the user in case of an error.

As you can observe from Figure 6-9, the browser gives us a suggestion in the second error, where it suggests that we consider adding an error boundary. That's actually a wonderful suggestion, but let's see if we can do it in the next section.

React to Errors

Error boundaries are components that help us catch errors and display a different UI to the user. By doing so, we can avoid breaking the app and display a user-friendly interface to the user. However, we cannot use error boundaries in functional components. We built the just-food app with functional components. This book's focus is on building apps using functional components and Hooks.

Let's use the JavaScript method of try-catch blocks and insert some state behavior into it. We can also use it to handle error handling.

Create a new component in the just-food project. Right-click src ➤ New File and name it ErrorFunctionalBoundary.js. Copy Listing 6-1 into the file.

Listing 6-1. ErrorFunctionalBoundary.js

```
const ErrorFunctionalBoundary = () => {
  return <h1  align="center" >We'll be back shortly! Please check
  back</h1>;
};
export default ErrorFunctionalBoundary;
```

This component returns a heading with a user-friendly message. Of course, we can add images and style this better. We will keep it simple for now. Next, add the following statement to FoodOrder.js to import ErrorFunctionalBoundary:

```
import ErrorFunctionalBoundary from "./ErrorFunctionalBoundary";
```

Create a new state variable and initialize it with a false value:

```
const [isErrorCatched, setIsErrorCatched] = useState(false);
```

Incorporate a try-catch block in the handleQuantityChange function as shown in the following:

```
const handleQuantityChange = (event) => {
  try
  {
   setTotalAmount(selectedFood.price * event.target.value);
   setQuantity(event.target.value);
  }
  catch{
   setIsErrorCatched(true);
  }
};
```

Whenever an error occurs, it will set the state variable isErrorCatched to true.

The next step is to add the ErrorFunctionalBoundary component inside the return function. Also, wrap it inside a condition so that it will display only if isErrorCatched is true:

```
 {isErrorCatched && <ErrorFunctionalBoundary />}
```

Similarly, add a Fragment for existing JSX elements, and wrap it around a condition so we will display it only if isErrorCatched is false. Refer to Listing 6-2 for the updated return function of FoodOrder.js.

Listing 6-2. Return Function – FoodOrder.js

```
return (
    <Fragment>
      {!isErrorCatched && (
```

```
<Fragment>
<h4 className="selFoodTitle">{selectedFood.name}</h4>
<img
  className="selFoodImg"
  src={require(`./images/${selectedFood.image}`)}
  alt={selectedFood.name}
/>
<ul className="ulFoodDetails">
  <li>
    <p className="selFoodDesc">{selectedFood.desc}</p>
  </li>
  <li>
    <p className="selFoodPrice">{totalAmount}$</p>
  </li>
  <li className="selQuantity">
    <label>Quantity</label>
    <input
      type="number"
      defaultValue={1}
      className="quantity"
      min="1"
      max="10"
      onChange={handleQuantityChange()}
    />
  </li>

  <li className="liDetails">
    <input
      type="text"
      className="inputFields"
      id="name"
      name="name"
      placeholder="Your Name"
    />
  </li>
  <li>
```

```
          <input
            type="text"
            className="inputFields"
            id="mobile"
            name="mobile"
            placeholder="Your mobile number"
          />
        </li>

        <li>
          <button className="btn btnOrder" onClick={handleClick}>
            Submit Order
          </button>
          <button
            className="btn btnReturnMenu"
            onClick={props.returnToMenu}
          >
            Return to Menu
          </button>
        </li>
        {isOrdered && (
          <li className="liMessage">
            <label>
              Order Submitted! You will receive an SMS to once ready
              for pickup.
            </label>
          </li>
        )}
      </ul>
    </Fragment>
  )}
  {isErrorCatched && <ErrorFunctionalBoundary />}
</Fragment>
);
```

> **Note**   The just-food project with the ErrorFunctionalBoundary
> component implementation is located under Chapter 6 ➤ Projects in the GitHub
> repo (https://github.com/Apress/Just_React).

Now, open the app in the browser. Click through and select a food item. You will spot the message that we set in the error boundary. Refer to Figure 6-10.

Figure 6-10. *Handling errors*

You will no longer view this specific error in the console since we handled it in the application. You can always comment on the try-catch sections during development if you want to view console errors. Once the build is complete, you can enable it again.

As a best practice, include the ErrorFunctionalBoundary component in all other components. Then, use try-catch blocks to capture errors and set state. Hopefully in the future, there will be some better ways to handle errors with new React versions.

Don't forget to revert your onChange function to the working one. And make sure that the application works correctly now as before:

```
onChange={handleQuantityChange()}
```

React Developer Tools

The React developer tools are an extension to the Chrome DevTools. This provides a better view of component trees for debugging, as well as the ability to inspect and edit props and states. Using our just-food app, we'll make out how it works.

We need to install the extension first. Search for React Developer Tools in your Chrome browser and click the first link. This will open up the React Developer Tools page. Click Add to Chrome. A pop-up will appear. Click Add extension. Refer to Figure 6-11.

Figure 6-11. *Adding the React Dev Tools extension*

Now that you have opened the app and pressed F12, you can see two more tabs: Components and Profiler. Restart your browser in case you don't see them.

Click through to select a food item in the app. We can view the component tree, props, Hooks, etc. from the Components tab of the DevTools. Refer to Figure 6-12.

Figure 6-12. *React DevTools – Components*

You can view all the props of the selected component. Expand it to view the details. If you edit the values, the changes will get updated in the browser.

The Hooks section shows the context and all the state variables of the selected component. You can change the state and look at what happens. If you click the checkbox against the third state (in Figure 6-12), the message `Order Submitted` appears, which is because it sets the `isOrdered` variable to `true`. Upon ticking the checkbox against the fourth state variable, the application displays the `ErrorFunctionalBoundary` component as `isErrorCatched` is now `true`. You will notice the message `We'll be back shortly`. This way, you can test the component behavior in the browser. This makes the development quite easy.

It is also possible to select other components from the component tree in the left pane. You can read and update props and states from the browser.

We can measure the performance of our applications with Profiler. Let me illustrate with an example. To use Profiler, refresh the app, click the Profiler, tab and click the record button. Refer to Figure 6-13.

Figure 6-13. *React DevTools – Start profiling*

After you start profiling, click through the app to order a food item. For instance, I selected Chips of quantity 4 and ordered. Once you place the order, stop profiling. Refer to Figure 6-14.

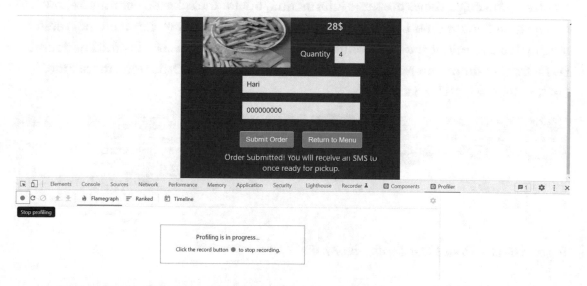

Figure 6-14. *React DevTools – Stop profiling*

Immediately after stopping the profiling process, we can view some data in the Flamegraph tab. Click the Flamegraph tab after stopping the profiling process. Refer to Figure 6-15. Let's digest this information and learn more about profiling.

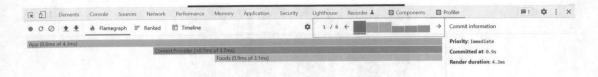

Figure 6-15. *React DevTools – profiling data*

React has two aspects: renders and commits. A render determines what changes need to be made to the DOM. React calls the render and compares the results with the previous render. After comparing, React decides what changes should apply to the DOM and then applies those changes. This is called a commit.

Figure 6-15 shows six commits. These are displayed as a bar chart on the right side. By default, it will have the first commit selected. We can click each bar to view all the commits one by one.

There is a Flamegraph. A Flamegraph shows you the current state of the app at a given commit. The width of a bar shows how long it took to render a component and its children. The color shows the same information, but for the selected commit. Yellow means it took more time, blue means it took less time, and gray means it did not render during this commit. If you click commit 2, for example, you can see only the Foods and FoodOrder components rendered. Foods was faster, and FoodOrder took more time. Refer to Figure 6-16 for details.

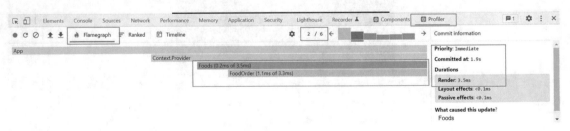

Figure 6-16. *React DevTools – commits*

The right-hand-side window shows the total render and commit time of a specific commit. Also, if you click the Ranked tab, you can view the components ordered with FoodOrder at the top as it took the longest time to render in commit 2. The Ranked tab displays data specific to a commit. Refer to Figure 6-17.

Figure 6-17. *React DevTools – Ranked*

When your application is large and you want to view only the commits that took longer to commit, you can use the filter commit option from the settings. Refer to Figure 6-18.

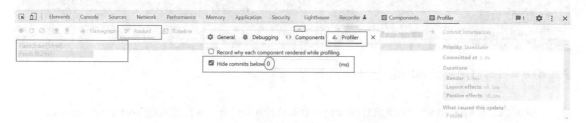

Figure 6-18. *React DevTools – commit filter*

Despite what we have discussed, React Profiler capabilities do not end here. There is a lot to explore when you become more and more experienced in React. But for now, we have covered a good amount of information on Profiler regarding advanced React development.

That was all about the powerful and the impressive React developer tools. In the next section, let's jump on to VS Code for some in-house debugging there to make a developer's life easier and more exciting!

React to Bugs Within VS Code

I showed how to debug React apps using the Chrome developer tools in the first section. Would it be easier sometimes to debug using VS Code? Yes, there are built-in debugging features in VS Code, and we will use them to debug our just-food app.

The first step is to click the Run and Debug section in VS Code. Next, click "create a launch.json file." Refer to Figure 6-19. The launch.json is where you configure the debugger.

Figure 6-19. *Create launch.json*

Select Chrome from the list that appears. Refer to Figure 6-20 for more information.

Figure 6-20. *Select an environment for the debugger*

It will create the file with some default content. The type is "pwa-chrome". This identifies the debugger for the Chrome browser. The only change we need to make is to change the port to 3000, which is the localhost port we are using. Listing 6-3 shows what your final launch.json should look like in Listing 6-3.

Listing 6-3. launch.json

```
{
    "version": "0.2.0",
    "configurations": [
        {
            "type": "pwa-chrome",
            "request": "launch",
            "name": "Launch Chrome against localhost",
            "url": "http://localhost:3000",
            "webRoot": "${workspaceFolder}"
        }
    ]
}
```

We can now debug just like we did in Chrome. Go to FoodOrder.js and click the line number that corresponds to the first line in the handleQuantityChange function. This will set a breakpoint there. Make sure npm start is running. Now, press F5 to debug. The browser will open the app. Click through and select a food item. When you increase the item quantity, it will hit the debug point in FoodOrder.js in VS Code. You can view the point-in-time values as in Chrome debugging. Refer to Figure 6-21.

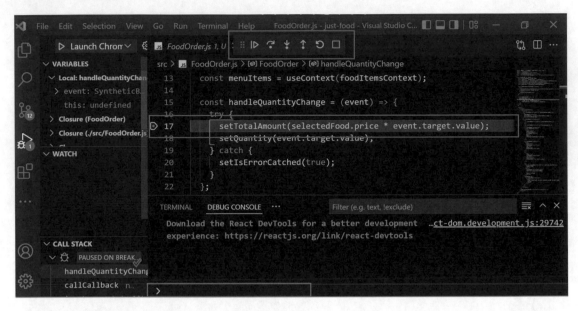

Figure 6-21. *Debugging in VS Code*

In the top bar, you'll find buttons for stepping through the code, restarting, stopping, etc. At the bottom, we have a Debug Console. You can do console logs at the arrow point, and it will appear in the console.

The Watch option is on the left side of the screen. With Watch, you can observe the real-time value of variables and expressions. We can see the value of the object selectedFood when you select an item and see how it changes when the browser loads the selected item.

To illustrate this, put a breakpoint inside Foods.js in the handleSelect function. Then click F5 to debug. Then, go to the Watch section. Click + to add a variable there. Type in selectedFood and hit Enter. Then, switch to the browser, click the Order Food button on the home page, and select a food item. Then, it reaches the breakpoint, and you observe selectedFood is undefined at this point. Refer to Figure 6-22.

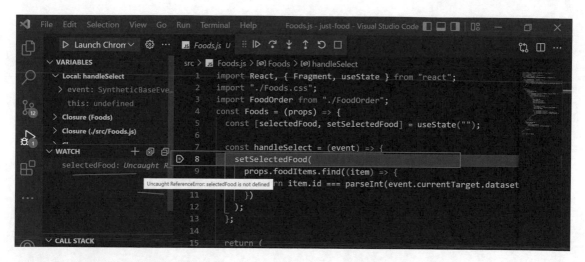

Figure 6-22. *Using Watch*

Press F8 to continue debugging, and now it will open the food item page in the browser. Now, try to increase the quantity, and it will hit the breakpoint at FoodOrder.js. Now, you can view the current value of the selectedFood in the Watch section. Refer to Figure 6-23 for the example.

Figure 6-23. *Watch evaluation*

This way, you can watch the point-in-time variable value without having to enter it in the console and check every time.

> **Note**   You can visit the GitHub repository to view final chapter project code (`https://github.com/Apress/Just_React`). Also, all the listings of this chapter are located under the path Chapter 6 ➤ Listings. You can also download or clone the entire project at the end of each chapter from the GitHub repository. After cloning, run `npm install` from the project folder to install all the required node modules before running the code.

Summary

During this chapter, we discussed error catching and different ways to debug your application. We began with learning about the Chrome developer tools. We discussed different tabs of the tool and how to easily debug your application using this incredible tool. In the next section, we designed a way to catch errors and display a friendly error interface to the user. We created a custom error boundary component for our functional component in the app.

Following that, we talked about the React developer tools. We discussed the Components tab and how you can use it to change props and states in a browser in real time. Then, we discussed profiling. Profiling is an excellent way of measuring how well a React application is performing.

Last but not least, we discussed VS Code's debugging capabilities. You learned how to debug without leaving our lightweight but heavily packed VS Code.

I will introduce you to different ways you can style React components in the next chapter. We will practice some basic Cascading Style Sheets (CSS) as well. In Chapters 8 and 9, we will continue to explore more advanced React concepts, such as Hooks, authentication in React, Redux, etc.

CHAPTER 7

Reacting in Style

Until now, we have learned about JavaScript, React, debugging, and more. You learned how to create an app with multiple components and how to manage state and props. While building apps, we added some styles. However, we never discussed styling in depth. We will discuss different ways of styling components and their pros and cons in this chapter. I will also introduce you to some tools that can help you choose styling for your React apps.

Cascading Style Sheets (CSS) is an essential part of any application. We cannot create a good-looking React application without CSS. It is crucial that your app looks good, not just okay, but great. There is no point in having a superfunctional app if it is unsightly.

Let's inspect some basic styling concepts in this chapter. There are many ways you can style a React app. This chapter will not guide you through styling your React app using CSS. Instead, it gives you an overview of different methods and best practices to present your app.

We will discuss the CSS-in-JS pattern, which puts the styling in JavaScript (JS) itself. During our discussion, we will examine one of the component elements of the just-food project. We will learn how to use Styled Components in our React components and then explore further into CSS and how we use them in our applications.

Next, we will discuss the shortcomings of CSS and how we can overcome those. Finally, we will go over Sassy CSS (SCSS). We will cover the advanced features that SCSS brings with it.

You will learn about CSS modules and how they can address the global scoping issue that plain CSS faces. Then, this will be illustrated with an example from the project just-food. We will then update our app's styling using CSS modules. We will discuss some useful tools that can help improve the way you develop and design React apps. Last but not least, we'll explore how to make your application mobile-friendly, and I'll introduce you to a new React Hook.

By the end of this chapter, you will understand the different ways to style React apps and the choices to make.

© Hari Narayn 2022
H. Narayn, *Just React!*, https://doi.org/10.1007/978-1-4842-8294-6_7

CSS-in-JS

CSS-in-JS is an approach where we create CSS using JS and define it in the JS file itself instead of having an external CSS file. This method may have larger performance effects and look untidy. You will get to know why this is the case as we go through this section. However, this approach provides an advantage of allowing you to use expressions while defining styles within JS. Additionally, it can be a convenient way to create something for quick testing or similar purposes.

Note   Keep a backup of App.js before you change it in the sections "CSS-in-JS" and "Styled Components." When we start the "CSS" section, you can restore this file back. CSS-in-JS and Styled Components files are available in separate folders under the Chapter 7 section of the GitHub repo (https://github.com/Apress/ Just_React).

Let's use the top button from the just-food project as an example. We used that button to toggle between the Order Food and Menu Availability sections. The button uses a class called toggle button. When we use inline styling, we do not need that class. Rather, we can refer to the style within the JS file.

There are two ways of doing CSS-in-JS mode styling in React. The first would be to apply inline styling. See the following. I removed the className toggleButton and applied the styles directly inline:

```
    <button
style={{  float: 'left',  marginTop: '5px', marginLeft: '3px',  alignItems:
'center', paddingTop:'6px', paddingRight: '14px',    borderRadius: 8,
border: 'none',  color: '#fff',  backgroundColor: 'red',    cursor:
'pointer' }}
        onClick={() => setIsChooseFoodPage(!isChooseFoodPage)}
      >{isChooseFoodPage ? "Availability Check" : "Order Food"}</button>
```

The attribute names must be in camel case when you apply styles inline. For example, we use the attribute background-color in a CSS class, but here, we used backgroundColor instead.

A second way for CSS-in-JS is to extract these styles into a const variable and then apply them to a particular element. Declare the following variable right above the return function in `App.js`. The styles are the same, except that we changed the background color from red to green just to differentiate the changes:

```
const toggleButtonStyles = {
    float: "left",
    marginTop: "5px",
    marginLeft: "3px",
    alignItems: "center",
    paddingTop: "7px",
    paddingRight: "14px",
    borderRadius: 8,
    border: "none",
    color: "#fff",
    backgroundColor: "green",
    cursor: "pointer",
  };
```

After that, assign the variable name to the element as follows:

```
<button
        style={toggleButtonStyles}
        onClick={() => setIsChooseFoodPage(!isChooseFoodPage)}>
        {isChooseFoodPage ? "Availability Check" : "Order Food"}
      </button>
```

You should see the same appearance if you view the app in a browser now. The only difference would be the button background color, which we made intentionally. We just changed the styling to CSS-in-JS rather than using a CSS class.

Styled Components

Styled Components is a library built in for styling React apps. They built it based on CSS-in-JS. So it is basically a tool to use the CSS-in-JS type of styling. Its syntax is somewhat tricky. Let us replace our previous CSS-in-JS code by using a styled component.

Install Styled Components by running `npm install styled-components`. Once successfully installed, add the following import statement into `App.js`:

```
import styled from "styled-components";
```

Instead of the `toggleButtonStyles` variable, add the following variable:

```
const StyledtoggleButton = styled.button`
  float: left;
  margin: 5px 0px 0px 3px;
  align-items: center;
  padding: 6px 14px;
  border-radius: 8px;
  border: none;
  color: #fff;
  background-color: #367af6;
  cursor: pointer;
`;
```

It uses the same structure as a class in a CSS file. The only difference is that it requires a prefix `styled`. Additionally, we need to specify what type of element is to follow. For example, for a `button`, we add the prefix `styled.button`, and for a `div`, we would add `styled.div`.

Next, change the `button` element to the styled component `StyledtoggleButton`:

```
<StyledtoggleButton
        onClick={() => setIsChooseFoodPage(!isChooseFoodPage)}>
        {isChooseFoodPage ? "Availability Check" : "Order Food"}
    </StyledtoggleButton>
```

After you run `npm start`, check if the app looks as it did previously. If you inspect using the F12 key, you will notice that it generated the button's class name randomly. This is because the styled component generates a unique class name.

In comparison with plain CSS-in-JS, the advantage of Styled Components is that we can reuse them easily, because they create a component-based style. In addition, the classes will be unique, which will avoid the global scoping issue. We will discuss the global scoping issue in the next section.

Additionally, you can provide the styles in CSS format instead of adding a camel case style for each. As an example, you can use the CSS attribute `background-color` itself rather than using `backgroundColor`.

Now, revert back App.js as it was before the start of this section. Let us move on to the next section.

CSS

CSS describes how elements should be displayed on a browser. Let us take the example of our just-food app. How did we style this app? We used CSS. Let me demonstrate by taking the App component as an example.

If you open the just-food project and open App.js, you will observe the class ulApp assigned to the <ul> tag. We defined this class ulApp in App.css, which we already imported into App.js. We assigned it the <ul> tag using the className attribute.

So adding style using a CSS file takes three steps.

Step 1: Create a CSS file and define the class there. In our App component, we already created App.css and defined the ulApp class as in the following:

```
.ulApp {
  list-style-type: none;
  padding: 0;
  font-size: 28px;
}
```

Step 2: Add the CSS file to the component file (.js). We did this by using the import statement:

```
import "./App.css";
```

Step 3: Assign the class to the element using the className attribute:

```
<ul className="ulApp">
```

This way, we can define all the classes for the App component in App.css and assign to any element as needed. If we want to, we can create different CSS classes for different components.

We use this model throughout our book because it is simple to use and easy to understand, especially for small applications. There are some disadvantages for larger applications, including the fact that the CSS files may become large and it will be difficult to maintain or clean them up later. In addition, naming the class for each element will be challenging.

We must be extremely cautious when writing in CSS classes, as it may otherwise cause issues due to CSS's global nature. CSS gets applied globally to common markup elements. For example, imagine you added a new color to an h1 element in a CSS class like this:

```
. h1
{
color:Blue
}
```

This would set all h1 headings in the application to blue. This shows how CSS's global nature can be dangerous if we don't pay attention to it. However, the global nature of CSS is one of its greatest strengths too. The global scope of CSS provides consistency to the websites and apps.

Imagine that you have around 10–20 CSS files. When you are naming a class, you must think if you gave the same name in another CSS file. If you do, that might override the style of another element. It can be extremely difficult to track down these definitions in larger applications.

I will explain this with an example from our just-food app. We will put the same class names in App.css and FoodOrder.css.

Before we apply the changes, run npm start and view the app in the browser. Click through the app and select a food item. It should look like Figure 7-1.

Figure 7-1. *Different class names*

The heading Chicken Burger appears as intended on top. We defined a class selFoodTitle for it in FoodOrder.css. Also, press F12 to check the class and its styles in the DevTools.

Now, if you look at App.js, you can see we applied a class subTitle to the h4 element there:

```
<h4 className="subTitle"> Menu Availability</h4>
```

Consider a scenario where you forgot you had a class name subTitle in App.css and put the same class in FoodOrder.css.

In FoodOrder.css, rename the class selFoodTitle to subTitle:

```
.subTitle {
  color: rgba(85, 191, 233, 0.993);
  font-weight: 400;
  font-size: 34px;
  margin-top: -5%;
  text-align: center;
  margin-left:10%;
  width: 80%;
}
```

Update the h4 heading in FoodOrder.js to the following to reflect the new class name:

```
<h4 className="subTitle">{selectedFood.name}</h4>
```

Now, view the app in the browser and select a food item. I selected Chicken Burger again. You will notice the heading Chicken Burger came down and sit on top of the image. Refer to Figure 7-2.

221

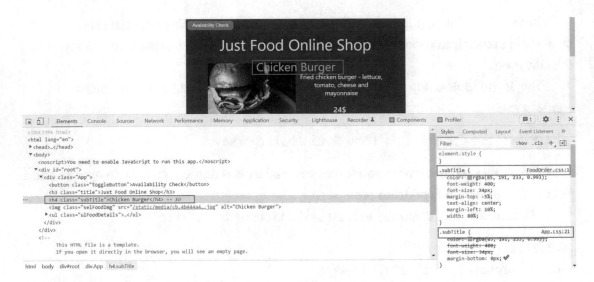

Figure 7-2. *Global scope issue with same class names*

Here, both `subTitle` classes apply to the heading Chicken Burger. As the App component is a parent component, its CSS files will obviously get loaded into the child components. Technically, the Foods component is embedded in the App component. Therefore, the Foods component loads both classes and applies a mixed style. This is not what we wanted. This is the global scope issue with CSS. We need to be careful while naming the classes; they cannot be the same as what we defined before. This can be one of the major drawbacks of styling with CSS.

Another factor to be aware of is that child elements will always inherit the styles from the classes of their parents unless we specify otherwise. For example, in the App component, the `li` elements inherit padding and font size from the class of `ul` (`ulApp`). It was necessary to define the `liApp` class for `li` elements and provide `padding-bottom` to override the parent's style there.

This section's goal was to introduce you to CSS. We also outlined some of the troubles you may run into while styling with CSS. Next, let's discuss SCSS before we get to CSS modules.

Sassy CSS (SCSS)

Sassy CSS (SCSS) is another way to style React components. SCSS refers to a modern syntax of a language called Syntactically Awesome Style Sheets (SASS). SASS is a language that is compiled into CSS. It is a language built on top of CSS. Besides having all the features of CSS, SCSS has some additional features.

Let's check how these features work by creating and using an SCSS file in our just-food app. To begin, you will need to install the node-sass library. Run the following command in the terminal:

```
npm install node-sass
```

Having done that, right-click the src folder, then create a new file, and name it as App.scss. As soon as you rename it, the filename will get updated in Explorer with a pink icon. Copy the following code in Listing 7-1 into that file. We will dig deeper in the following.

Listing 7-1. App.scss

```
$fullwidth:100;
$colorAqua: rgba(85, 191, 233, 0.993);
$colorYellow: rgba(235, 232, 51, 0.993);
$colorBlue: rgb(22, 61, 97);
$colorChooseButton: purple;

.App {
  font-family: "Segoe UI", Tahoma, Geneva, Verdana, sans-serif;
  text-align: left;
  width: ($fullwidth*2/5)*1%;
  margin-top: 30px;
  position: absolute;
  background: $colorBlue;
  left:($fullwidth/2)*1%;
  height: 630px;
  transform: translate(-50%, 0%);
  text-align: center;
  color: white;
}
.title {
  color: $colorYellow;
  font-weight: 400;
  font-size: 44px;
```

```scss
}
h4 {
  color: $colorAqua;
  font-weight: 400;
  font-size: 34px;
  margin-bottom: 0px;
}
.ulApp {
  list-style-type: none;
  padding: 0;
  font-size: 28px;
}
.liApp {
  padding-bottom: 10px;
}
div {
  button {
    float: left;
    margin: 5px 0px 0px 3px;
    align-items: center;
    padding: 6px 14px;
    border-radius: 8px;
    border: none;
    color: #fff;
    background-color: $colorChooseButton;
    cursor: pointer;
  }
}
```

Change the import statement in App.js from import "./App.css" to import "./
App.scss";. So we are no longer importing the CSS file but using the SCSS file. Run
npm start and view the app in the browser. You will not find any difference in the app
interface, except that the Order Food button background color is now purple instead
of the light blue we had earlier. We intentionally changed this color to highlight that
we have made a change. Unlike the CSS file, we used variable definitions here. We
could define some variables at the top and then use these variables in class definitions.

This might not seem necessary for our application, but it can be useful in many large applications:

```
$fullwidth:100;
$colorAqua: rgba(85, 191, 233, 0.993);
$colorYellow: rgba(235, 232, 51, 0.993);
$colorBlue: rgb(22, 61, 97);
$colorChooseButton: purple;
```

You may also notice that we have defined the top button style with a nested class. The class says, "Apply style to all buttons within a div":

```
div {
  button {
    float: left;
    margin: 5px 0px 0px 3px;
    align-items: center;
    padding: 6px 14px;
    border-radius: 8px;
    border: none;
    color: #fff;
    background-color: $colorChooseButton;
    cursor: pointer;
  }
}
```

Previously, we had defined this in the CSS file as the `.toggleButton` class. If you want to add another button inside the `div`, you don't have to define a class name for each one. Instead, you can use this nested method. This is also an advantage of SCSS over plain CSS.

Furthermore, SCSS supports mathematical calculations. For example, I set a variable `$fullWidth` to 100 and set the width of the App class as `($fullwidth*2/5)*1%;` and the left margin as `($fullwidth/2)*1%;`. This means the width would be 40% and the left margin 50%. Therefore, it gives the same style as the `App.css` file.

Another useful feature is the import capability. You can import a style sheet into an SCSS file. For example, if you convert `Foods.css` into an SCSS file, you can import `App.scss` into `Foods.scss` using the following statement:

```
import "./App.scss";
```

In this way, you can refer to only `FoodOrder.scss` in the `FoodOrder.js` file and reuse the classes from `App.scss`. Similarly, you can import styles from third-party libraries such as Fluent UI, Bootstrap, etc. into an SCSS file.

We talked about how SCSS has more features such as nesting, variables, importing, math, etc. than plain CSS. However, it has the same disadvantages as using a plain CSS. Files can grow very large, and maintenance will be difficult.

The global scope issue still exists. Whenever you define a class, you need to think if it affects any other place. Let's look at how we can overcome this problem by using CSS modules.

CSS Modules

You can write classes that are scoped locally using CSS modules. CSS modules will autogenerate a unique class name. We can solve the global scope problem using CSS modules. CSS modules are extremely useful in React applications. This is the same as a plain CSS file, but the extension is module.css. Let me explain what CSS modules are again by using our app. We will fix the issue with the Chicken Burger title overlapping with the image that we encountered earlier.

Before you begin, revert the import reference of `App.js` to `App.css` instead of `App.scss` as in the following. We can create SCSS modules as well. However, let us use CSS modules:

```
import "./App.css";
```

Let's check how the class names are appearing in the browser DevTools before we make any changes to implement CSS modules. View the app in the browser, press F12, and look at them. Refer to Figure 7-3.

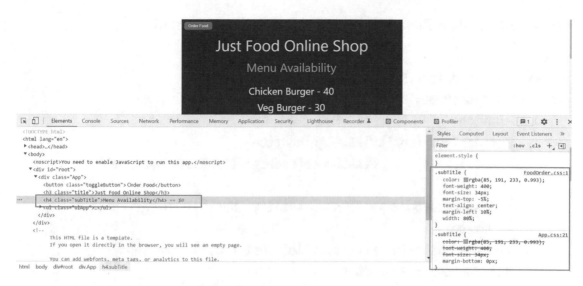

Figure 7-3. *Elements with plain CSS classes*

It displayed each class name with the same name as we defined it.

Let's implement CSS modules now. Select `App.css` from Visual Studio Code (VS Code) Explorer, press F2, and rename it to `App.module.css`. Afterward, change the import statement in `App.js` as in the following:

```
import appStyles from "./App.module.css";
```

This is how we import the CSS module file. The `appStyles` object contains the styles from the `App.module.css` file. You can name it whatever you want. As a convention, put `styles` at the end. I called it `appStyles`. This object contains all the classes that we defined in `App.module.css`.

Now, we need to update the `className` attributes of all elements. For example, previously we defined the class name for the root `div` element like this:

```
<div className="App">
```

When we use CSS modules, the definition will change to this:

```
<div className={appStyles.App} >
```

So here we fetch the class names from the imported `appStyles` object.

Now, let us replace the `className` attributes of all elements like this. The updated return statement of `App.js` now should be as in Listing 7-2.

Listing 7-2. App.js Elements with CSS Module Implementation

```
return (
    <foodItemsContext.Provider value={menuItems}>
      <div className={appStyles.App}>
        <button
          className={appStyles.toggleButton}
          onClick={() => setIsChooseFoodPage(!isChooseFoodPage)}
        >
          {isChooseFoodPage ? "Availability Check" : "Order Food"}
        </button>
        <h3 className={appStyles.title}>Just Food Online Shop</h3>
        {!isChooseFoodPage && (
          <>
            <h4 className={appStyles.subTitle}>Menu Availability</h4>
            <ul className={appStyles.ulApp}>
              {menuItems.map((item) => {
                return (
                  <li key={item.id} className={appStyles.liApp}>
                    {item.name} - {item.quantity}
                  </li>
                );
              })}
            </ul>
          </>
        )}
        {isChooseFoodPage && <Foods foodItems={menuItems}></Foods>}
      </div>
    </foodItemsContext.Provider>
  );
```

Figure 7-4 shows how the class names appear in the DevTools when you open the browser and press F12.

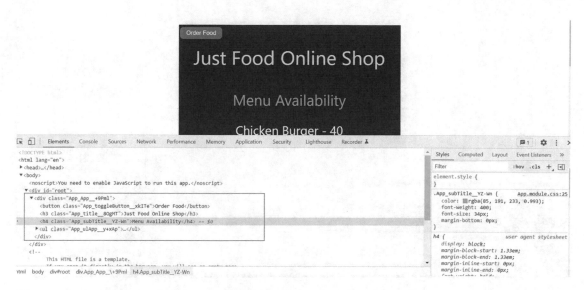

Figure 7-4. *CSS module–generated classes*

You have the same look and feel, while at the same time, you have unique names for each class. You can spot a prefix, which is the component name, and a random generated suffix for each class name.

Now, if you navigate to order a food item, you won't experience any issues with the food item header, as in Figure 7-2. As the class subTitle we defined for the App component now has a unique name, it will not interfere with the one we defined in FoodOrder.css. See Figure 7-5 for details.

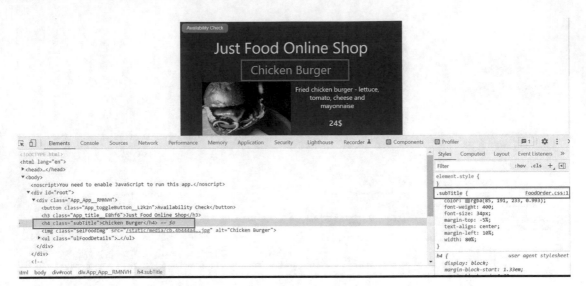

Figure 7-5. CSS module resolving the global scope issue

Because of the App component having unique classes, its classes will not mix up with its child components. With CSS modules, you do not have to worry about other classes while naming your CSS classes.

You can now implement CSS modules for the Foods and FoodOrder components as well, just like we did for the App component. The first step will be to rename both CSS files to Foods.modules.css and FoodOrder.module.css, respectively. Next, replace the respective import statement for the CSS file. For Foods.js, the CSS import now will be

```
import foodStyles from  "./Foods.modules.css;
```

And for FoodOrder.js, the import will be

```
import foodOrderStyles from  "./FoodOrder.module.css";
```

Then replace the class names of each element with the module format like we did for App. In FoodOrder.js, you will see there are multiple classes defined for few elements. To add more than one class to an element, use the following format. The following is an example from the FoodOrder component:

```
className={`${foodOrderStyles.btn} ${foodOrderStyles.btnOrder}`}
```

We can create SCSS modules in the same way as CSS modules. I prefer CSS modules over plain CSS, SCSS, SCSS modules, inline styling, CSS-in-JS, or Styled Components. All methods have their own advantages and disadvantages.

In the next section, we'll examine a few third-party libraries and tools that can help you set up a good-looking UI quickly while creating React apps.

Note   You can visit the GitHub repository to view the project code at any time during the learning. You can access the repository via the book's product page, `https://github.com/Apress/Just_React`. The `just-food` project with CSS module implementation for all components is located under Chapter 7 ➤ Projects. You can refer to individual component code and also download or clone the entire project. After cloning, run `npm install` from the project folder to install all the required node modules before running the code.

CodeSandbox

The online code editor CodeSandbox is a very useful tool for you to quickly set up your React app. You can create your own React coding sandbox using this tool.

You can set up a React project in CodeSandbox by visiting `https://codesandbox.io/`. Scroll down and click the button `</> Start coding for free`. A pop-up will appear, so click the "Create Sandbox" button. Now, there will be many templates to choose from. See Figure 7-6.

Figure 7-6. *Sandbox templates*

You can select React, and it will create a sandbox for you. The project setup will be like what we have when we create a React project using create-react-app. It will create the App component, as shown in Figure 7-7.

Figure 7-7. *React CodeSandbox*

This tool will be very handy for development.

Material UI

Material UI (MUI) is a library of advanced components, which can style React applications quickly. You can visit `https://mui.com` for details on the installation, examples, different components, etc. There are so many options available.

When you click a component, you can see the different options and code for that component. For example, if you want to try out the Grid, you can find it at the bottom of the layout section. There are different options for using the Grid. You can also open and edit the code directly from here in CodeSandbox. See Figure 7-8.

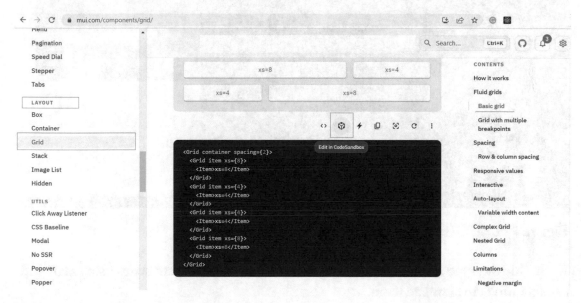

Figure 7-8. *MUI components*

If you click Edit in CodeSandbox, it will open the code in CodeSandbox.io. In this example, you can directly edit the code on the left and see changes on the right. In this way, you can finalize the component styles and layout and then copy to your project. Refer to Figure 7-9 where I slightly changed the Grid code and styles.

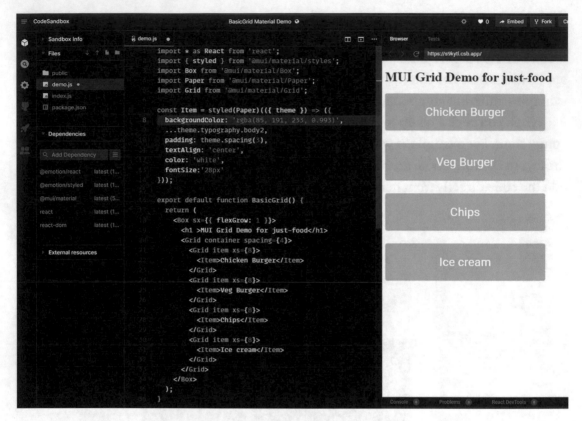

Figure 7-9. *MUI components – CodeSandbox*

In this way, you can try out different components and different styles using MUI and CodeSandbox to simulate them.

Responsive React

Within this chapter, we focused on desktop/laptop styling of React apps. Nowadays, most traffic for a website comes from mobile devices, making it important that your app is mobile-ready. Responsive design is an approach where we design our web pages in such a way that they adapt based on the device. In this section, we will look at the basics of responsive design. As usual, we will illustrate this with our just-food project. In this example, we will only focus on the home page, the App component.

Note   Keep a backup of `App.js` before you change it in this section and then restore it back after the section. We will continue to use this project in Chapter 9 to illustrate authentication. At that time, we will use the code prior to this section as we don't require responsive code there to keep the changes simple. In the GitHub repo (`https://github.com/Apress/Just_React`), you will see two copies of the just-food project: one before the responsive changes (`just-food`) and one with the responsive changes (`just-food-responsive`). We will use the former in Chapter 9.

Using the Chrome developer tools, we can simulate mobile experience. Run npm start and view the app in the browser. Press F12 to open the developer tools. When you click Toggle Device Toolbar at the bottom, the device toolbar will appear at the top. In the Dimensions section, you can select your desired device. Our app will display based on it. When you select the `Responsive` option, you will be able to enter your own width and height. See Figure 7-10 where I chose the iPhone 12 Pro.

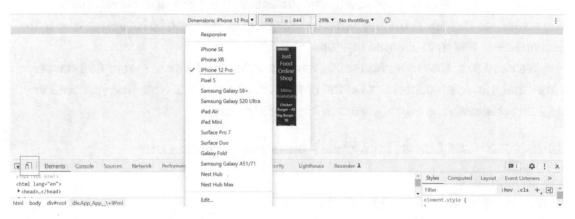

Figure 7-10. *Device toolbar*

It is possible to select or unselect devices from the toolbar using the Edit link at the bottom. You can see our app isn't mobile-friendly at this point. If you select iPad Air, at least the whole content on the page will be visible.

Let's use this example to illustrate responsive design. In this example, we will focus on mobile and make our home page readable on mobile devices and desktops/laptops.

We will use a hook called useMediaQuery from an npm package `react-responsive` to implement responsive design. Media queries are one of the most popular methods for specifying distinct style according to screen size. The `react-responsive` package makes it easy to implement media queries in a React app.

To start with, stop running `npm start` and install the `react-responsive` package using the following command:

```
npm install react-responsive
```

Once the package is installed, add the following import statement to `App.js`:

```
import { useMediaQuery } from "react-responsive";
```

The next step is to define two Boolean variables, one for mobile and one for desktop. Define this inside the App function, where you defined state variables earlier:

```
const isLapOrDeskTop = useMediaQuery({
    query: "(min-width: 1224px)",
  });
  const isMobile = useMediaQuery({ query: "(max-width: 480px)" });
```

When using the hook `useMediaQuery`, the `isLapOrDesktop` variable returns true if the screen size is greater than or equal to 1224px. Likewise, `isMobile` returns true if the screen size is less than or equal to 480px.

We need to define styles for mobile next. I created the following set of CSS classes. Copy that into `App.module.scss` at the bottom. See Listing 7-3. Note that you need to add this classes to the existing styles in `App.module.scss`.

Listing 7-3. CSS Classes for Mobile – update App.module.scss

```
.titleMobile {
  color: rgba(235, 232, 51, 0.993);
  font-weight: 400;
  float: left;
  font-size: 26px;
  padding-bottom: 30px;
}
.ulAppMobile {
  list-style-type: none;
  padding: 0;
  padding-top: 50px;
```

```
  font-size: 16px;
}
.subTitleMobile {
  color: rgba(85, 191, 233, 0.993);
  font-weight: 400;
  font-size: 24px;
  margin-bottom: 0px;

}
.liAppMobile {
  padding-bottom: 30px;
}
```

Now, we have the CSS classes available for desktop and mobile devices.

The last step is to update the return statement in App.js to include mobile experience as well. Ideally, it is a good idea to create a separate component for mobile. We will keep things simple for now. Let's copy the root div with its child elements and assign the classes for mobile. Refer to Listing 7-4 for the updated return statement of App.js.

Listing 7-4. App.js Return Statement

```
return (
    <foodItemsContext.Provider value={menuItems}>
      {isMobile && (
        <div className={appStyles.App}>
          <button
            className={appStyles.toggleButton}
            onClick={() => setIsChooseFoodPage(!isChooseFoodPage)}
          >
            {isChooseFoodPage ? "Availability Check" : "Order Food"}
          </button>
          <h3 className={appStyles.titleMobile}>Just Food Online Shop</h3>
          {!isChooseFoodPage && (
            <>
              <h4 className={appStyles.subTitleMobile}>Menu
              Availability</h4>
              <ul className={appStyles.ulAppMobile}>
```

```
            {menuItems.map((item) => {
              return (
                <li key={item.id} className={appStyles.liAppMobile}>
                  {item.name} - {item.quantity}
                </li>
              );
            })}
          </ul>
        </>
      )}
      {isChooseFoodPage && <Foods foodItems={menuItems}></Foods>}
    </div>
  )}
{isLapOrDeskTop && (
  <div className={appStyles.App}>
    <button
      className={appStyles.toggleButton}
      onClick={() => setIsChooseFoodPage(!isChooseFoodPage)}
    >
      {isChooseFoodPage ? "Availability Check" : "Order Food"}
    </button>

    <h3 className={appStyles.title}>Just Food Online Shop</h3>
    {!isChooseFoodPage && (
      <>
        <h4 className={appStyles.subTitle}>Menu Availability</h4>
        <ul className={appStyles.ulApp}>
          {menuItems.map((item) => {
            return (
              <li key={item.id} className={appStyles.liApp}>
                {item.name} - {item.quantity}
              </li>
            );
          })}
        </ul>
      </>
```

```
      )}
      {isChooseFoodPage && <Foods foodItems={menuItems}></Foods>}
    </div>
  )}
</foodItemsContext.Provider>
);
```

We now have two div's: one will render if isMobile is true, and the other will render if isLapOrDesktop is true. Run npm start and view the app. Press F12 and select any mobile device. (Refer to Figure 7-10.) If you were in desktop mode before, just refresh the screen after making these settings. You will see that it looks readable now in a mobile device. Refer to Figure 7-11.

Note   This is just an example of how you can implement a responsive design. I just created some basic CSS and have added no additional styling to make the app look great. You can always try to improve the styling for practice. You can implement responsive design for other components as well. As I mentioned before, while developing larger applications, it is ideal to have different components and CSS modules for mobile, tablet, and desktop/laptop devices. Then, we can use useMediaQuery to implement responsive design, like we did here.

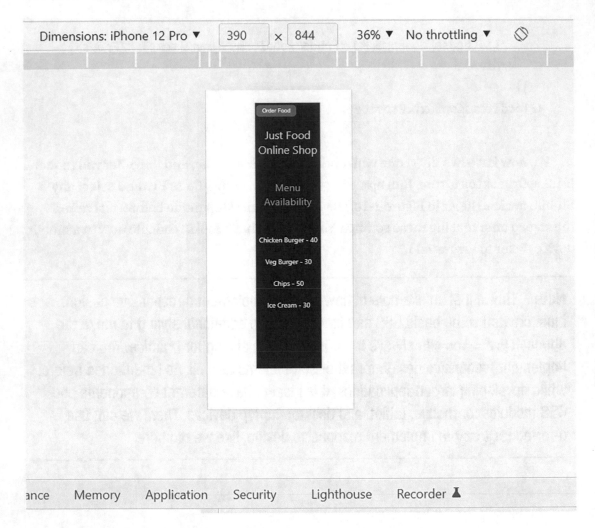

Figure 7-11. *Responsive design*

When you close the device toolbar and refresh the browser, it will still work as before and open in the browser without breaking the view. This means now the app is adapting to the environment in which it is rendered. This is the concept of responsive design.

Note   All the code of this section is available in the GitHub repo (https://github.com/Apress/Just-React). The entire code of App.js and App.css is available under Chapter 7 ➤ Listings, and the project is under Chapter 7 ➤ Projects ➤ just-react-responsive.

Summary

This chapter dealt with styling. Much like the previous chapters, this chapter also based most of its learning on our just-food React app. We began by learning about CSS-in-JS and its uses. Then we discussed Styled Components before moving on to learn how CSS works. There was a section to discuss some potential drawbacks of CSS when it comes to developing React applications.

After discussing the global scoping issue, we moved on to implementing SCSS-based styling. We briefly discussed several features of SCSS. Our next discussion was about CSS modules. We implemented CSS modules into just-food app components. In addition, we have discussed how CSS modules can overcome the global scoping issue. We talked about CodeSandbox and Material UI; we saw how these tools can be very helpful during the development phase of React apps. Lastly, we have discussed responsive design and seen how to implement it with the help of the react-responsive package.

In this chapter, we discussed the pros and cons of the different styling methods. I do not mean the chapter to make recommendations on which method you should use for your React app, but to shed light on how a React app reacts to different styling methods. According to my experience, CSS modules work better with React. However, always choose the best method based on your app. For example, a React app with nested elements may benefit more from SCSS modules, based on how comfortable you are with debugging SCSS styles.

In the next chapter, let us talk about one of React's most exciting features, Hooks! We have already learned about Hooks in our previous chapters. We have used the `useState` hook many times. However, in Chapter 8, let us hook more into Hooks and try to build few custom Hooks!

CHAPTER 8

Hook into React

The last two chapters covered debugging and styling React apps. In this chapter, we will continue learning React concepts from where we left off in Chapter 5. This chapter is about React Hooks. You already learned about Hooks from the previous chapters. We will dive deeper into Hooks in this chapter, and I can assure you it is going to be an interesting read. Hooks are the engine of modern React development.

We will begin by examining a class component's lifecycle. After transforming it into a functional component, we will look at how Hooks can add state to it. We will discuss the state Hook and how it is used to manage the state in functional components. You will learn more about the effect the Hook and how it functions to emulate lifecycle events in functional components.

We will discuss refs in React and how important it is to not manipulate the Document Object Model (DOM). I will introduce you to the useRef hook, and then we will look at the useReducer Hook. We will learn complex state management with this Hook.

Next, we will discuss useContext with an example. Then, we'll move on to memorization techniques. We'll discuss the higher-order component (HOC) React Memo and the two memory Hooks, useMemo and useCallback. A detailed example will show you how to use these three techniques. Before we move on to the last section on custom hooks, we will discuss the remaining hooks. By the end of this chapter, you will be a Hook master.

Life of a Class

In the following sections, let us investigate the back story behind the birth of Hooks. To get there, we need to learn about class components and its lifecycle events.

© Hari Narayn 2022
H. Narayn, *Just React!*, https://doi.org/10.1007/978-1-4842-8294-6_8

By creating a class component, we can investigate how the lifecycle events such as componentDidMount, componentDidUpdate and componentWillUnmount works. We will then see how Hooks can achieve the same goal with function components. We will use CodeSandbox for this demo. To get started, go to `https://codesandbox.io/` and create a new React sandbox. Assuming you are already in CodeSandbox, click the three lines on the top left and then choose File ➤ New Sandbox. Refer to Figure 8-1.

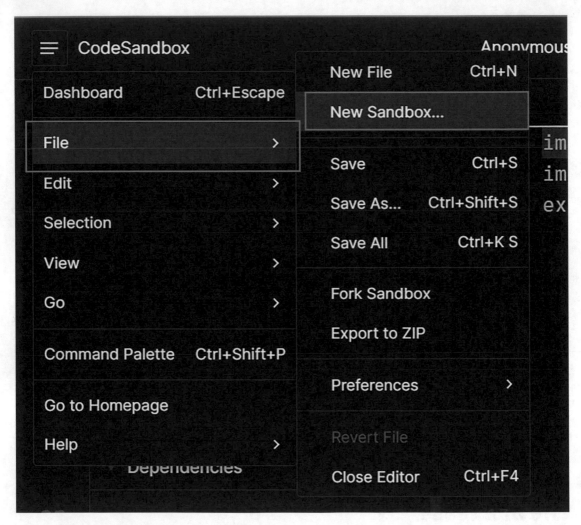

Figure 8-1. *Creating a new sandbox*

Select React from the pop-up, and it will create App.js automatically. Create a new component, called Time. Right-click the src folder and create a file and name it Time.js. Copy Listing 8-1 into Time.js.

Note   Code used in each listing is available in the book's GitHub repository, https://github.com/Apress/Just_React. You can refer to it from the path Chapter 8 ➤ Projects ➤ respective folder name.

Listing 8-1.   Time.js

```
import React from "react";
class Time extends React.Component {
  constructor(props) {
    super(props);
    this.state = {
      currentTime: new Date().toLocaleString(),
      close: false
    };
  }
  componentDidUpdate(prevState) {
    if (prevState.currentTime !== this.state.currentTime) {
      console.log("Time is changing.");
    }
  }
  componentWillUnmount() {
    console.log(`The Time component is going to be unmounted at ${this.
    state.currentTime}`);
  }
  componentDidMount() {
    console.log(`The Time component is mounted at ${this.state.
    currentTime}`);
    setInterval(() => {
      this.setState({
        currentTime: new Date().toLocaleString()
```

```
      });
    }, 1000);
  }
  render() {
    return <h1>{this.state.currentTime}</h1>;
  }
}
export default Time;
```

Here we display the current time in a label. To do that, we used a `setInterval` method that changes the time every 1000 milliseconds. We placed this `setInterval` method inside the event `componentDidMount`.

`componentDidMount()`is a React lifecycle method that runs when a component is rendered for the first time. It calls `setInterval` to set the state for the current time. When the state is set, it re-renders the component, and the screen gets updated with the current time. Because of the state update getting repeated every 1000 milliseconds, it always updates the time on the screen. We've also added a console log inside the `componentDidMount` method that prints the message that the Time component is mounted at the current time.

There is also a `componentDidUpdate` event here. Inside this method, we are logging a message to the console that the time is changing at the current time. The `componentDidUpdate()` fires immediately after every render of a component except the first one.

Last, we defined a `componentWillUnmount()` method, invoking which will log a message to the console that the Time component is going to be unmounted at the current time. The `componentWillUnmount` event gets invoked when the component is about to be removed from the DOM. When you click a button from a child component to go back to the parent component, the child component unmounts. Just before that unmount, `componentWillUnmount` gets fired.

So now we have all three lifecycle methods in this component. Let's update `App.js` so that it will call the Time component. Copy the code from Listing 8-2 into `App.js`.

Listing 8-2. App.js

```
import React from "react";
import Time from "./Time";
export default class App extends React.Component {
```

```
constructor(props) {
  super(props);
  this.state = {
    open: true
  };
}

render() {
  return (
    <div>
      {this.state.open && (
        <>
          <Time />
          <button onClick={() => this.setState({ open: false })}>
            Close Time
          </button>
        </>
      )}
      {!this.state.open && <h1>Time display closed</h1>}
    </div>
  );
}
}
```

Let us inspect the code inside App.js. We defined a state variable open and set its value to true by default. In the return statement, wc display the Time component only if the variable open is true. To close the time display, we have a button Close Time, which sets the variable open to false. The screen displays the button only when the variable open is true, which means when the time is visible. We wrapped both elements in a fragment.

As a result, by default, the browser renders the Time component, and the Time Closed display is not visible. When we click the button, it reverses.

During initial rendering of the App component, it mounts the Time component. This triggers componentDidMount. After mounting it, the time keeps updating, which triggers componentDidUpdate. Upon clicking the Close Time button, the Time component will be unmounted and trigger componentWillUnmount before unmounting. This summarizes the lifecycle events of the Time component.

Visualize this using CodeSandbox. Refresh the browser screen. You will see the message that the Time component is mounted at the current time. Keep the time running for some time. This will keep logging the message `Time is changing` to the console.

After clicking the Close Time button, the screen will display the header `Time display closed,` and it will stop displaying the time. At the same time, the code will log the console to show that the Time component is going to be unmounted at the current time. For an example run, see Figure 8-2 where I kept the time running for about 4 minutes.

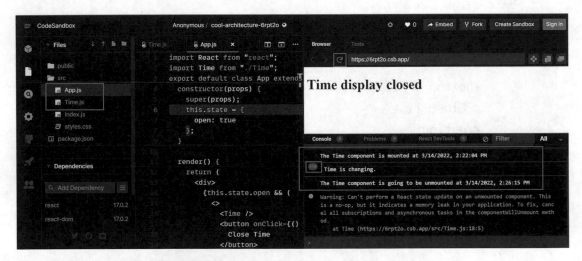

Figure 8-2. *React component lifecycle*

So we have seen how lifecycle methods work within a React class component. You can see that the `Time is changing` message got logged 250 times in around 4 minutes. This is because `componentDidUpdate` gets called every time the component is re-rendered. After the time display has been closed, you must refresh the screen for it to be displayed once again. This will restart the lifecycle.

Note   There is a warning at the bottom regarding state update on an unmounted component. This is because the time interval is still running on the Time component while it is unmounted. This causes continuous state updates. We will fix this issue when we convert this to a functional component and use Hooks in the following section. Ignore it for now.

The following explains how the lifecycle works in the class component Time when it is called by the App component:

1. React creates a new instance of the Time component when it is called by the App component, during initial render:

    const TimeInstance = new Time()

2. This invokes the Time component's constructor and renders the component for the first time:

    TimeInstance.render()

3. This causes componentDidMount to be triggered, and the time updates. Note that componentDidMount only gets triggered on the initial render:

    TimeInstance.ComponentDidMount()

4. The componentDidMount event calls the setInterval method. This method updates state, which causes the component to re-render. Re-rendering causes componentDidUpdate to fire. As we update state of the time every 1000 milliseconds, componentDidUpdate is called every 1000 milliseconds:

    TimeInstance.render() -> TimeInstance. ComponentDidUpdate ()

    TimeInstance.render() -> TimeInstance. ComponentDidUpdate ()
    ....
    ....
    ....

5. When we click the Close Time button, it will set the state variable open to false. This will trigger componentWillUnmount(), and the TimeInstance will be unmounted. As a result, the time is no longer displayed on the screen. This ends the lifecycle of the TimeInstance:

    TimeInstance.ComponentWillUnmount()

Life of a Function and the Birth of Hooks

Imagine a function component. The lifecycle of a function component is much simpler than that of a class component. Let's see how that works. Let's define a function component, as in the following:

```
const App = (props) => {
  return <h1>Function Component</h1>;
};
export default App;
```

In React, it renders this function component by calling App(props). If we don't specify any props, the arguments will be empty. If React needs to re-render this component, it will call App(props) again. This component does not have lifecycle events like a class component does, so it is impossible to manage the state. We cannot have a timer that is continuously changing on this component like we did in the previous section.

Let us redesign the App and Time components as function components, so that we can explore what we can and cannot accomplish in these components. Create a new React sandbox, or you can just update the code in the existing sandbox. Choose React from the pop-up, and it will create App.js by default. Create Time.js as we did before and copy Listing 8-3 into it.

Note   In CodeSandbox, you can sign up for free and save your work, as we will use it for all the examples in this chapter. To create a new sandbox, if you are inside one already, click File and New Sandbox, as shown in Figure 8-1 at the start of the chapter.

Listing 8-3. Function Component – Time.js

```
let currentTime = new Date().toLocaleString();
const Time =(props) => {
  return <h1>{currentTime}</h1>;
};
export default Time;
```

In this component, we get the current time and return it. We don't have the ability to change it continuously. To get the updated time, React needs to call this component again. Copy Listing 8-4 into your App.js file.

Listing 8-4. Function Component – App.js

```
import Time from "./Time";
const App =(props) => {
  let open = true;
  const closeTime = () => {
    console.log("closeTime called");
    open = false;
  };
  return (
    <div>
      {open && (
        <>
          <Time />
          <button onClick={closeTime}>Close Time</button>
        </>
      )}
      {!open && <h1>Time display closed</h1>}
    </div>
  );
};
export default App;
```

This App component imports the Time component. The variable open is true by default, so the Time component and button Close Time will render by default. If we set the variable open to false, the heading Time display closed will appear. Refer to Figure 8-3. We defined a function closeTime to set the variable open to false. When we click the button, this function is called and sets the variable to false.

Look at the result in the CodeSandbox screen and see if it works as per the expectations. You will notice two issues:

1. The time does not change at all. This is because we call the Time component once and we do not have the option to call it repeatedly inside the App component.

2. Close Time does not function. When we click the Close Time button, the time display does not close. It calls the function `closeTime` and sets the variable open to false. You can see this on the console shown in Figure 8-3. Everything is fine so far, but the App component does not re-render because there is no state change. The App component renders based on the previous value of the variable open.

Note   We will refer to these issues in the following section as issue 1 and issue 2.

Figure 8-3. *React functional components*

What we observe here is that function components are simple. They accept props and can return JSX. If you have only render methods on your components, you can create them as function components. But what if you have state management on your components as well, like the preceding example?

The only way to achieve this functionality was using class components. Here comes Hooks, the concept that was born to address this issue. Hooks enable function components to hook into React state and lifecycle.

Before React 16.8, React developers were habituated to coding with class components and lifecycle methods. One fine day, it became clear that building React apps with class components wasn't the way forward. As the developers adapted to the new hero in town, React Hooks, their life became a lot easier. Hooks made the code more readable and reusable. Thanks to Hooks, now we can manage the state without writing a class.

In Chapter 4, we saw an example of Hooks being used by converting a class component to a function component. Let's enable these Time and App components to have state and lifecycle events by utilizing Hooks.

Note   You can use either regular or arrow function syntax while defining function components. In most of the following examples, I used regular function syntax.

---

useState

We will begin learning Hooks with the most popular, useState, the state Hook. As the name suggests, useState allows you to have state variables in function components. You can import useState from the react library with the following statement:

```
import { useState } from 'react';
```

As an argument to useState, we can pass the initial value of the state. It returns an array. If you want to create a state variable for the variable open we used earlier, just declare it as in the following:

```
const open = useState(true);
```

You must include this declaration within the component. You might wonder why you can't put the declaration of the state variable outside of the component declaration. I'll explain. A state variable stores data about the component. The component re-renders when the state changes. Before a re-render can be triggered, React needs to see the state and decide what has changed. Thus, we must declare state within a component for React to be able to control it.

Now, the variable open will have an array value. If you print out open[0], you will get the value true, but if you print open[1], you will get a function. Refer to Figure 8-4, where I logged these values into the console.

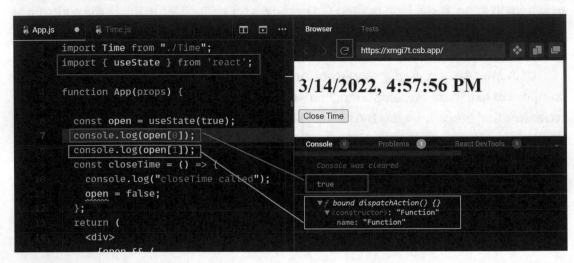

Figure 8-4. *Return values of useState*

A second element is a function that can change the value of the variable. If we apply simple array destructuring to the declaration, it will look like this:

```
const [open, setOpen] = useState(true);
```

Now, the variable open will have the value true, and the setOpen will contain the function. The variable open is now considered a Boolean type and has the value true. If you call setOpen(false), it sets the value of open to false.

In App.js, let's update the state variable declaration and closeTime function as follows:

```
const [open, setOpen] = useState(true);
const closeTime = () => {
  setOpen(false);
};
```

During this step, we added the state Hook to set the value for the variable open. Run the code in CodeSandbox. Click the Close Time button. You should see the message that the time display is closed. See Figure 8-5.

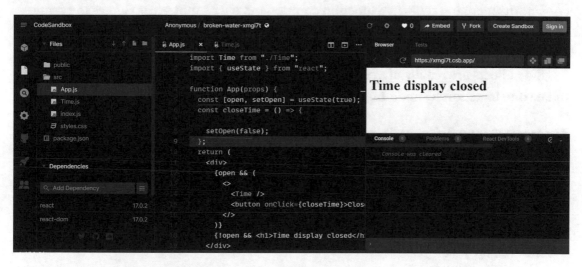

Figure 8-5. *useState and re-render*

Now we have resolved issue 2 mentioned in the preceding section. The useState Hook updated the variable's state, which caused the component to re-render. This thus closed the time display. The state Hook preserves the value of the state variable during re-render. When we called setOpen(false), it set the value of the variable to false, and the component re-rendered. During re-render, it checks the value of open, sees it as false, and then displays the elements accordingly. If you refresh the browser screen, it will display the time again because the value of open again initializes as true.

Now, we can switch between time display and the closed message with the help of the state Hook. This resolves issue 2 that we mentioned in the preceding section. Issue 1 remains unresolved, because the time is not changing. We are only seeing fixed time until refresh. Let us fix that in the next section when we learn the effect Hook.

useEffect

Using the `componentDidMount` lifecycle event of the class component, we could display constantly changing time. In a function component, we cannot access lifecycle events, but we can hook into them. The Hook `useEffect` handles side effects in functional components, as the name implies.

Side effects are results of a change outside the scope of a function or expression. Let us see one in action by updating the Time component as follows. Refer to Listing 8-5.

Listing 8-5. useEffect in Time.js

```
import { useState, useEffect } from "react";
function Time(props) {
  const [currentTime, setCurrentTime] = useState(new Date().
  toLocaleString());
  useEffect(() => {
    console.log(" I am useEffect and I got invoked");
    setInterval(() => {
      setCurrentTime(new Date().toLocaleString());
    }, 1000);
  });

  return <h1>{currentTime}</h1>;
}
export default Time;
```

The Hooks were imported into the Time component here. We defined a state variable to hold current time. We added the Hook `useEffect`, within which we are logging a message to the console. In addition, we defined the `setInterval` method inside `useEffect`, which updates the current time continuously.

Now if you update the code and refresh the browser screen, you see that the time is continuously changing. From the console logs, you can see that the `useEffect` gets fired when the initial render occurs.

However, if you keep the screen for a few minutes, you can see in the console that the `useEffect` call gets triggered again and again. This is because every re-render produces a side effect, which triggers `useEffect`. You can see in Figure 8-6 that the first console log line inside the `useEffect` method got logged 422 times!

Figure 8-6. *useEffect*

The setInterval method sets the current time every 1000 milliseconds, so there is frequent re-rendering and thus frequent useEffect calls. When you add logging in the setInterval method, you see that there is a call loop going on in both useEffect and setInterval. Refer to Figure 8-7.

Figure 8-7. *useEffect calls on every render*

Even though the time gets updated, this is not a clean way to use the effect Hook here. The setInterval periodically updates the time. Thus, we should call setInterval only once during the initial render. Therefore, we want useEffect to get triggered during this initial render only.

We can accomplish this by passing an argument to useEffect. Let's see how it works. Update the useEffect function, as shown in the following:

```
useEffect(() => {
    console.log(" I am useEffect and I got invoked");
    setInterval(() => {
      console.log("Time changing");
      setCurrentTime(new Date().toLocaleString());
    }, 1000);
  },[]);
```

Check in CodeSandbox, and you can see that the useEffect function is called only during initial render. The screen displays current time as before. Refer to Figure 8-8.

Figure 8-8. *useEffect only on initial render*

The only change is that we passed an empty array as a second argument to have the useEffect call only on initial render. This works just like the componentDidMount in a class component. We simulated the behavior of the ComponentDidMount event by using the effect Hook.

Here's how it works. The second argument that we are passing to useEffect is basically a dependency. If you specify a dependency array, the useEffect will run only if there is a change in the dependency array values. During the first render, the array is empty, and useEffect runs. When the component re-renders, the array is again empty, so there is no change, and the effect will not run. During the second re-render, there is still no change in array values. This stops the effect from running during any re-rendering.

This empty array will never update, so the effect will not be called again. This is how passing an empty array as a dependency makes useEffect only run on the initial render. With this, we have achieved the same result in a function component as in the class component.

Now, let's try to implement a function to display the current time in the console when the time display is closed, as we did by using the ComponentWillUnmount event in the class component. In essence, implementing that will give us a cleanup function to use before the Time component unmounts.

Let's update Time.js by updating the useEffect function. Refer to Listing 8-6. Let me explain the code after. I added a return statement, as you can see from the following code. Also, I updated the log message in the initial render to say the component is mounted at the current time.

Listing 8-6. Time.js with useEffect

```
import { useState, useEffect } from "react";
function Time(props) {
  const [currentTime, setCurrentTime] = useState(new Date().
  toLocaleString());
  useEffect(() => {
    console.log(`The Time component is mounted at ${currentTime}`);
    setInterval(() => {
      console.log("Time is changing");
      setCurrentTime(new Date().toLocaleString());
    }, 1000);

    return () => {
      console.log(
        `The Time component is going to be unmounted at ${ new Date().
        toLocaleString()}`
      );
    };
  }, []);

  return <h1>{currentTime}</h1>;
}
export default Time;
```

I updated the log message in the initial render to display the current component time. Also, I added a return statement inside useEffect. In any callback function, the return is being called on the unmount event. When we return a function inside useEffect, it will run just before the component is unmounted.

Run the code and keep it running for a few minutes. If you click the Close Time button, the time display will close, and the console will log the unmount message with the current time. Refer to Figure 8-9 for further information.

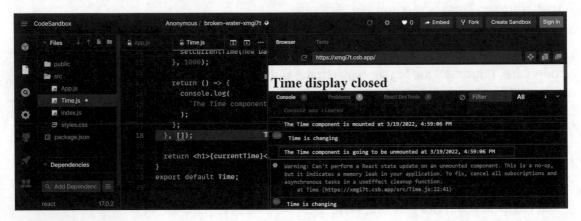

Figure 8-9. *useEffect during unmount*

We unmounted the component, and we got the unmount message logged. However, the state updates are still going on, and we can see the Time is changing message on the console. Also, there is a warning on the console. We saw the same warning when we did the class component. As we have a setInterval method that keeps updating the state after unmounting, the warning suggests doing some cleanup. We ignored the warning and didn't do the cleanup in the class component. Let's fix it here. Update the useEffect function like this:

```
useEffect(() => {
    console.log(`The Time component is mounted at ${currentTime}`);
    const interval = setInterval(() => {
      console.log("Time is changing");
      setCurrentTime(new Date().toLocaleString());
    }, 1000);
```

```
return () => {
  clearInterval(interval);
  console.log(
    `The Time component is going to be unmounted at ${ new Date().
    toLocaleString()}`
  );
};
}, []);
```

We assigned the setInterval results to a variable interval and are calling the clearInterval method during unmounting. The clearInterval cancels the setInterval action. Check in the CodeSandbox browser, and we can see that now the code executes without warning and the time changing stops once the component is unmounted. Refer to Figure 8-10.

Figure 8-10. *Cleanup before unmount*

So, we implemented the cleanup function using the effect Hook. In a class component, we could have done it using the componentWillUnmount event. By using the Hooks useState and useEffect in our functional components, we have achieved the same result as when using a class component. The code is much simpler and cleaner than when using a class component.

Note that we can use multiple useEffect blocks inside a single component, either with an empty array or by referencing specific props. You can handle initial mount by passing an empty array as a dependency. Also, you can set a code block to trigger during only a specific prop update by adding more useEffect blocks.

Note   You can see an example of using multiple useEffect blocks in Chapter 5 (section "Props Drilling Issue"). There we added two useEffect blocks in the EnrolList component to handle edit functionality: one with all the props as a dependency and the second one with only the selected student id prop as a dependency.

---

useRef

A reference (ref) attribute in React is a way to store a reference to an element or Document Object Model (DOM) node in React. The ref Hook useRef accepts an initial value and returns a ref object. This object value stays for the entire life of the component. Calling useRef will not force a re-render like that of useState. We can declare a ref Hook variable as in the following:

```
const newRef = useRef("Thank you");
```

This creates a ref variable called newRef with an initial value Thank you. If you log newRef.current, it will print the value Thank you. To set a new value, we can write like this:

```
newRef.current  = "Welcome"
```

Use refs only when necessary. The core concept of React is its declarative programming style. In React, we update data on the browser by changing state and re-rendering the components. In declarative programming, we do not interact with the DOM. The user interface (UI) gets updated when we change state. When we use refs in React, we go against this rule and access the DOM directly. We refer to refs as escape hatches in React.

Rarely, it will be necessary to access DOM properties directly. In these cases, we can use refs. A common example is when we want to put focus on an element. Let's walk through the process in an example to learn more about refs and the Hook useRef.

Let us create an input form with three fields – State, City, and Address – and a button. We want the focus to be on the field State by default. Once we filled in City and State, we can click the button, which fills the Address field content with the City, State format. After that, the user has the option to edit the Address field content. Our requirement is to have the focus on the Address field once we click the button.

See Listing 8-7. Create a new sandbox in CodeSandbox and copy the following code into the App.js file. Let me explain the code after the listing.

Listing 8-7. : App.js – useRef Example

```
import { useState, useRef } from "react";
const fieldStyle= {
  marginTop: "20px",
  float: "left",
  width: "70%",
  Fantasy: 20
};
const buttonStyle = {
  marginTop: "20px",
  backgroundColor: "lightBlue",
  width: "30%",
  fontSize: 20,
  cursor: "pointer"
};
function App() {
  const [state, setState] = useState("");
  const [city, setCity] = useState("");
  const [address, setAddress] = useState("");
  const addressRef = useRef();

  const handleInputChange = (setInput, event) => {
    setInput(event.target.value);
  };
  const flatterers = () => {
    setAddress(`${city},${state}`);
    addressRef.current.focus();
  };
```

```
  return (
    <div style={{ width: "100%" }}>
      <input
        placeholder="State"
        autoFocus
        value={state}
        style={fieldStyle}
        onChange={(e) => handleInputChange(setState, e)}
      />

      <input
        placeholder="City"
        value={city}
        style={fieldStyle}
        onChange={(e) => handleInputChange(setCity, e)}
      />

      <button style={buttonStyle} onClick={fillAddress}>
        Fill Address
      </button>
      <textarea
        value={address}
        placeholder="Address"
        style={fieldStyle}
        onChange={(e) => handleInputChange(setAddress, e)}
        ref={addressRef}
      />
    </div>
  );
}
export default App;
```

Note   I named the variable for state as `state`. Please be aware of this and avoid confusion with our React state. I will rename the fields in future examples.

Let me explain the code for App.js. We created the form with three fields, State, City, and Address. When any of these fields changes, the value is set to the respective state variable using the handleInputChange function. We set the focus by default to the field State by using an attribute autofocus. We don't need to use any refs for setting the focus in the initial render; instead, we can use the autofocus attribute.

Fill Address is a button. After you fill in State and City, if you click the button, it invokes the fillAddress function. The function sets the state variable address to the City, State format. This updates the Address field.

As of now, we do not access the DOM directly, and we did all screen changes using state management. There is a requirement that the focus needs to be set to the Address box when we click the button and fill the address. To do this, we must access the address element using a ref.

So we declared a ref variable like this with the Hook:

```
const addressRef = useRef();
```

For the address text area element, we defined a ref property and assigned it to the variable addressRef:

```
<textarea
        value={address}
        placeholder="Address"
        style={fieldStyle}
        onChange={(e) => handleInputChange(setAddress, e)}
        ref={addressRef}
    />
```

Now the addressRef variable holds the text area element. Inside the fillAddress function, we set the focus by accessing the element using the ref:

```
addressRef.current.focus();
```

See the screen in CodeSandbox. By default, the focus will be on the State field. Fill out State and City, and click the Fill Address button. It will populate the address, and we will have the cursor focus on the Address field. Refer to Figure 8-11.

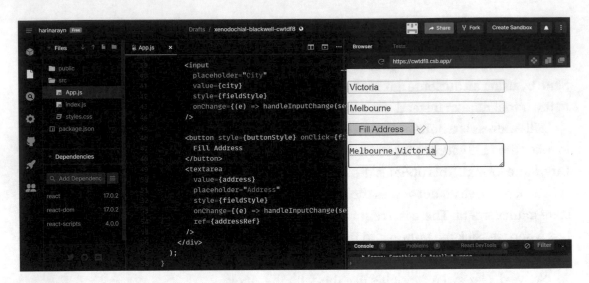

Figure 8-11. *useRef usage*

Note that we only used the ref to focus the Address field here. We can get the city and state values using refs instead of state. The code will be shorter if we do that. However, that is not the right way to do it. It will take down React's declarative concept. Use refs only when necessary. In all other cases, update component data using state management.

Note   We call a component controlled by its state a controlled component. If component data is handled by the DOM, we call it an uncontrolled component.

In this example, state management code occupies not a great deal of space in the component body. But what if we have ten input fields in the form? We must define state variables for each of the ten controls and manage state using useState. This would result in a large component code.

useReducer

Let us now see if there is a solution for keeping the code concise. The preceding form, which we implemented, is having a simple functionality. The component file contains three state variables. We use the state Hook to manage state during input changes.

This component has two logical sections. One is the rendering part, where we create input fields to be rendered to the browser, and the second is the state management. As I mentioned previously, imagine what happens if there are many input controls in this form. The code will be messy and will be difficult to maintain and test if we create state variables for each of these and manage state using useState. The reducer Hook useReducer can deal with this. The useReducer hook handles complex state management.

I will explain this Hook by modifying the preceding form using the useReducer. You can keep a backup of the existing code. Update App.js as in Listing 8-8. I will explain the code after.

Listing 8-8. App.js – useReducer for State Management

```
import { useReducer, useRef } from "react";
const fieldStyle = {
  marginTop: "20px",
  float: "left",
  width: "70%",
  fontSize: 20
};
const buttonStyle = {
  marginTop: "20px",
  backgroundColor: "lightBlue",
  width: "30%",
  fontSize: 20,
  cursor: "pointer"
};
const reducer = (state, action) => {
  const { type, payload } = action;
  return { ...state, [type]: payload };
};

function App() {
  const addressRef = useRef();

  const initialState = {
    fieldState: "",
```

```
    fieldCity: "",
    fieldAddress: ""
};

const [state, dispatch] = useReducer(reducer, initialState);

const { fieldState, fieldCity, fieldAddress } = state;

console.log(state);

const fillAddress = () => {
  dispatch({
    type: "fieldAddress",
    payload: `${fieldCity},${fieldState}`
  });

  addressRef.current.focus();
};

return (
  <div style={{ width: "100%" }}>
    <input
      placeholder="State"
      autoFocus
      value={fieldState}
      style={fieldStyle}
      onChange={(e) =>
        dispatch({ type: "fieldState", payload: e.target.value })
      }
    />

    <input
      placeholder="City"
      value={fieldCity}
      style={fieldStyle}
      onChange={(e) =>
        dispatch({ type: "fieldCity", payload: e.target.value })
      }
    />
```

```
    <button style={buttonStyle} onClick={fillAddress}>
      Fill Address
    </button>
    <textarea
      value={fieldAddress}
      placeholder="Address"
      style={fieldStyle}
      onChange={(e) =>
        dispatch({ type: "fieldAddress", payload: e.target.value })
      }
      ref={addressRef}
    />
  </div>
  );
}
export default App;
```

Upon updating the code and viewing it in CodeSandbox, you can see that the form works exactly as before. Let me explain the changes. First, we imported useReducer instead of useState from the React library:

```
import { useReducer, useRef } from "react";
```

Next, let's look at the inside of the function App. We defined a new object that holds three properties that correspond to the three fields. If we have ten fields, we will create an object with ten properties:

```
const initialState = {
  fieldState: "",
  fieldCity: "",
  fieldAddress: ""
};
```

Note   As mentioned in a note in the preceding section, now I renamed the variables to `fieldState`, `fieldCity`, and `fieldAddress`, instead of having the previous names: `state`, `city`, and `address`. This has nothing to do with the reducer Hook. It is just to avoid confusion with React state and the variable name state.

In the next line, we declared a state variable using `useReducer`, just like in our `useState` declaration:

```
const [state, dispatch] = useReducer(reducer, initialState);
```

Imagine what would have happened if you had used the state Hook to declare this state variable. It would look like this:

```
const [state, setState] = useState(initialState);
```

Both the Hooks initiate the variable `state` with an initial value. With `useState`, the second variable `setState` is a function we can use to modify the state of the variable `state.` In the reducer Hook also, the second variable is a function, which is the dispatch function. This function is also used to update the state, but it is different. Let's look at the difference in more detail.

When we call `setState` with an argument, it will directly update the variable's state with the passed value. When we call `dispatch` with an object argument, it will send the argument to a function called `reducer`. As you can see from the reducer Hook declaration, we have an additional argument, which is the `reducer` function:

```
const [state, dispatch] = useReducer(reducer, initialState);
```

We declared the `reducer` function like this:

```
const reducer = (state, action) => {
  const { type, payload } = action;
  return { ...state, [type]: payload };
};
```

You can see it has two parameters: `state` and `action`. The `reducer` function will receive the `action` parameter values when the `dispatch` function is called. We call `dispatch` functions from each input value. See the following `dispatch` function that we

270

added for the city field. When we specify dispatch, it calls the dispatch function. It sends type and payload to the reducer function so that reducer can update respective fields accordingly:

```
onChange={(e) =>
         dispatch({ type: "fieldCity", payload: e.target.value })
      }
```

As a result, on changing the value in the field city, the dispatch function will be called with an object argument with two properties: type with the value fieldCity and payload with the input value. This invokes the reducer function with the object parameter action. In the reducer function, it sets these values to the variables type and payload, respectively.

```
const { type, payload } = action;
```

Next, it updates the state variable by updating the fieldCity property. Here, the reducer function used the object sent by the dispatch function to update the object variable state. If dispatch is called from the fieldState, it will update the associated property of the state object:

```
return { ...state, [type]: payload };
```

Look at the following declaration that we added to the state object declaration. This line of code sets each variable to have a corresponding value from the state object:

```
const { fieldState, fieldCity, fieldAddress } = state;
```

Then we assign these values to corresponding inputs via the value property:

```
<input
    placeholder="City"
    value={fieldCity}
    style={fieldStyle}
    onChange={(e) =>
       dispatch({ type: "fieldCity", payload: e.target.value })
    }
  />
```

For example, let's take the field city as an example and explain how it works. The field initially has no value as the fieldCity property of initialState is empty. As we type data into the field, it calls dispatch with type fieldCity and payload input value.

The reducer function then updates state by updating the `fieldCity` property of the `state` object. This renders the component again, and the field gets updated with the corresponding current state. When we click the button, it does the same thing but for the field `address` with `city, state` as value:

```
const fillAddress = () => {
  dispatch({
    type: "fieldAddress",
    payload: `${fieldCity},${fieldState}`
  });
  addressRef.current.focus();
};
```

Note   You are free to use any names for state, dispatch, type, payload, or reducer. However, as per convention, we always use these names.

Thus, by using the reducer Hook, we can keep only one state variable of object type and deal with all state management. I added a console logging of the `state` variable in the code. If you see the console, you can observe how the state gets updated. Refer to Figure 8-12.

Figure 8-12. *useReducer*

As you can see, using the `useReducer` hook is extremely helpful for managing state in large complex applications.

useContext

React's Context API offers a more convenient way of passing data between components. Implementing Context is a three-step process. You should create a context, provide it from a component, and consume it from any other component that needs it. The `useContext` hook provides a "Hook" way to consume a context.

Sending props from higher-level components to lower-level components is known as props drilling, as you learned in Chapter 5. Suppose you have three components, A, B, and C. Component A is the parent of component B, and component B is the parent of component C. You want to pass a prop from component A to component C. You need to pass it from A to B and then from B to C. This requires drilling a prop through component B unnecessarily. You can imagine what it would be like if your application is complex. Due to the large component tree, managing the application through props drilling will be extremely challenging.

With Context and the `useContext` hook, we can solve this problem. React Context enables data to be passed between components without drilling through middle components.

With the just-food project in Chapter 5, we have seen an example of how to use Context and useContext. We will create a similar app here, but a small one to demonstrate how the `useContext` Hook works.

Let us create an app called Food Shop. We will have three components in this app. The root component, App, will have a header and a button. The header will show whether the shop is open or close. By clicking the button, you can switch between the texts open and `close`. The App component also contains a Menu component. The Menu component will feature a static list of food items. It also contains an Order component. You display an Order button in the Order component. Clicking it displays an alert. When the shop is open, you want to display the Order button. This occurs when the header in the App component says the shop is open. When it is close, the Order button in the Order component should not be visible. Now let's implement this.

Go to CodeSandbox. Create a React sandbox and create two new components called Menu and Order. Update `Order.js` to match Listing 8-9.

Listing 8-9. Order.js

```
const Order = (props) => {
  const orderFood = () => {
    alert("Food ordered");
  };
  return (
    <>{props.open === "Open" && <button onClick={orderFood}>Order</button>}</>
  );
};
export default Order;
```

In this Order component, we just have a button with a text Order. The button will be visible only if the value of the prop open is true. Upon clicking this button, it calls the orderFood function, and this function just displays an alert.

Next, put the code in Listing 8-10 to Menu.js:

Listing 8-10. Menu.js

```
import Order from "./Order";
const Menu = (props) => {
  return (
    <>
      <ul>
        <li>Pizza</li>
        <li>Nuggets</li>
        <li>Chips</li>
        <li>Protein Shake</li>
      </ul>
      <Order open={props.open} />
    </>
  );
};
export default Menu;
```

In the Menu component, we just have a static list of food items. In addition, this component calls the Order component with the prop isOpen.

Finally, update App.js with Listing 8-11. Let me explain the code after.

Listing 8-11. App.js

```
import React, { useState } from "react";
import Menu from "./Menu";
const App = (props) => {
  const [shopOpen, setShopOpen] = useState("Open");
  const [btnText, setBtnText] = useState("Close");
  const openOrCloseShop = () => {
    if (shopOpen === "Open") {
      setShopOpen("Closed");
      setBtnText("Open");
    } else {
      setShopOpen("Open");
      setBtnText("Closed");
    }
  };
  return (
    <>
      <h1>Food Shop is now {shopOpen}</h1>
      <button onClick={openOrCloseShop}>{btnText}</button>
      <Menu isOpen={shopOpen} />
    </>
  );
};
export default App;
```

First, let us look at the JSX in the App component. We have a header to display whether the shop is open or close. Then, we have a button to switch between Open and Close. Finally, we have the Menu component with a prop passed to it:

```
<h1>Food Shop is now {shopOpen}</h1>
<button onClick={openOrCloseShop}>{btnText}</button>
<Menu isOpen={shopOpen} />
```

We defined two state variables. One is to display the header. The second one is for the button text. When the shop is open, the button text will be Close and vice versa:

```
const [shopOpen, setShopOpen] = useState("Open");
const [btnText, setBtnText] = useState("Close");
```

We pass the value of this state variable, shopOpen, to the Menu component as prop.

Next, we have the function openOrCloseShop. This function switches the values of the header and button text variables. This function is called during the button click.

Execute the code, and you can see from the console that the Menu component is rendered during the first render. Click the Close button, and you can see the header is changed to Food Shop is now closed. The Order button disappears. Click React DevTools and select the Order component. You can see the passed prop value there. Refer to Figure 8-13.

Figure 8-13. *Food Shop app – passing props*

The app works as expected. However, we passed the prop isOpen from App to Menu and from there to the Order component. The purpose of the prop isOpen is to set the visibility for the Order button, which is in the Order component. However, we are drilling the prop through the Menu component, which does not need this prop at all. We can avoid this drilling by using Context.

Let us redesign the component using Context.

Step 1: Create a context. We need to create a context first from the provider component, that is, App. Go to App.js and add the following line just below the existing imports. This should be outside of the function declaration of App:

```
export const shopContext = React.createContext();
```

This step creates a context using the method createContext. We created the context and stored it in the variable shopContext. We are exporting this in a variable, so that we can use it in our Order component.

Step 2: Provide context. In the next step, we need to wrap the JSX component tree inside the context provider. Scroll down to the return function and wrap the entire JSX within the following tag:

```
<shopContext.Provider value={shopOpen}>
 </shopContext.Provider>
```

This means that all our JSX elements are now included inside of the preceding tag. In this context provider, we put the value as shopOpen. Therefore, whether the shop is open or close is now provided in this context.

Step 3: Consume context. So now we have provided the state of the shopOpen in the context. Next, we can consume this context from the Order component. Here is when our "Hookie," useContext, comes into play. Add the two lines on top of the file Order.js:

```
import React, { useContext } from "react";
import { shopContext } from "./App";
```

Now we've imported the useContext hook. Besides that, we imported the shopContext from the App component.

The useContext hook enables us to access this context. So declare a variable to read the shop context. Add the following line inside the component, just above the orderFood function:

```
const isTheShopOpen = useContext(shopContext);
```

Next, inside the JSX, change the conditional variable from props.isOpen to isTheShopOpen. The JSX inside return function should be as in the following now:

```
<>
{isTheShopOpen === "Open" && <button onClick={orderFood}>Order</button>}
</>
```

Before we execute the app, we can remove the prop reference from the App and Menu components as we no longer need to pass the props. Go to App.js and remove the prop from the Menu tag:

```
<Menu />
```

Next, go to `Menu.js` and remove the prop from the `Order` tag:

```
<Order />
```

Execute the app, and you can see that it works as before, but this time without drilling props through the Menu component. The shop matter is handled directly between App and Order. The Menu component doesn't have to act as a middle entity.

Click React DevTools below the screen. You can see the context information there. Refer to Figure 8-14.

Figure 8-14. *Food Shop app – passing context*

Note   You can view entire component codes of each section under the Chapter 8 folder of the GitHub repo (`https://github.com/Apress/Just_React`).

Let's now discuss two more Hooks, `useCallback` and `useMemo`. But before we do that, let's first try to understand the concept of memorization in React.

Remember to React

Memorization is a technique where we remember something and use that later rather than retrieving it again. For example, by now you are already memorizing how to set a state variable in React using the state Hook. You don't need to refer to any references anymore. You know it off the top of your head.

Let us look at the basic idea behind memorization in general. See the following JavaScript function, where we are adding two numbers:

```
const memorizedData = [];
    const addNumbers = (a, b) => {
      let result;
      result = memorizedData[(a, b)];
      if (result === undefined) {
        result = a + b;
        memorizedData[(a, b)] = result;
      }
      return result;
    };
    console.log(addNumbers(8, 9));
```

We have defined an array `memorizedData`. In the first call to `addNumbers(8,9)`, it checks if there is a value with the key `(8,9)` in the `memorizedData` array. As this is the first call, there will be no value, so the result will be `undefined`. It calculates the result using a+b and stores it in the `memorizedData` array with the numbers `(8,9)` as keys. The next time, when you call `addNumbers(8,9)`, the function checks if there is a value with the key `(8,9)` in the `memorizedData` array. It finds a value matched to the key, which is `17`, and returns it.

By doing so, the function never calculates the same numbers again. As it is a simple calculation, it won't make a difference here. But if the math is very complex and takes a lot of processor time, you might save a significant amount of time by not performing the calculation for the same arguments every time, because the answer won't change. Memorization generally works on this principle.

Memorization is no different in React. In React, we can memorize a component using a higher-order component (HOC) called React Memo. An HOC wraps a component and returns a new component. React Memo wraps around a component and memorizes it. It then uses this information later and avoids unnecessary rendering.

To see memorization in action in React, let's build an app for a library in which they want to know the number of ways they can arrange books on a particular shelf. The user wants to enter a shelf name and print it out. They also want to enter the number of books and ways they can arrange the books on the shelf.

Let's use CodeSandbox again. Create a React sandbox and make two new components called Combinations and Shelf. Update Shelf.js with Listing 8-12.

Listing 8-12. Shelf.js

```
const Shelf = ({ shelfName}) => {
  return `We are arranging books at the shelf - ${shelfName}`;};
export default Shelf;
```

This component Shelf is a simple component that accepts a parameter shelfName and just prints out that name with a message.

Copy the code in Listing 8-13 to Combinations.js.

Listing 8-13. Combinations.js

```
const Combinations = ({ countBooks }) => {
  console.log("Combinations component is re-rendered");
  let arrangements = 1;
  for (let i = 2; i <= countBooks; i++) {
    arrangements *= i;
  }
  return ` The total number of ways you can arrange the books is :
  ${arrangements}`;
}
export default Combinations;
```

This component calculates the number of combinations from the count of books provided. It uses the mathematical concept of factorials to calculate the number of arrangements. For example, if the number of books is 4, it returns 4*3*2*1=24. Even if the number of books is slightly more, for example, even if it is 10 books, the calculations can get expensive. We added a logging to the console also to see how often this component re-renders. The re-rendering of this component can affect performance, as it will repeat expensive calculations.

In the next step, we will update the App component to include the form and the preceding two components. Update App.js with Listing 8-14.

Listing 8-14. App.js

```
import React, { useState } from "react";
import Combinations from "./Combinations";
import Shelf from "./Shelf";
const fieldStyle = {
  marginTop: "20px",
  float: "left",
  width: "75%",
  fontSize: 20
};

function App() {
  const [bookCount, setBookCount] = useState("");
  const [shelfName, setShelfName] = useState("");

  const handleShelfChange = (e) => {
    setShelfName(e.target.value);
  };
  const handleBookCountChange = (e) => {
    setBookCount(e.target.value);
  };

  return (
    <div width="100%">
      <input
        placeholder="Shelf name"
        style={fieldStyle}
        value={shelfName}
        onChange={handleShelfChange}
      />

      <label style={fieldStyle}>
        <Shelf shelfName={shelfName} />
      </label>
```

```
    <input
      placeholder="How many books?"
      style={fieldStyle}
      value={bookCount}
      onChange={handleBookCountChange}
    />
    <label style={fieldStyle}>
      {bookCount > 0 && <Combinations countBooks={bookCount} />}
    </label>
  </div>
);
}

export default App;
```

The App component returns a form with two input fields. One is the Shelf field where the user can enter a shelf name. As soon as we enter a shelf name, it will display it on the following label. This is because of the rendering of the Shelf component, which we added in the label with the shelf name as an argument.

The second field is where the user can enter the number of books. Upon entering this number, the component Combinations renders. The Combinations component calculates the number of possible arrangements using the factorial concept. When the book count is greater than zero, the screen displays the Combinations component. We can view the returned number of arrangements on the label.

So the App component contains two child components, which display the shelf name and the number of possible book combinations. Run the application and see how it works. Keep the console open. Type South as the shelf name and 20 as the book count. See Figure 8-15.

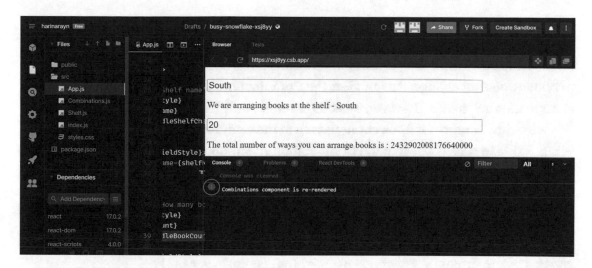

Figure 8-15. *Rendering the component*

Figure 8-15 shows how the Combinations component was rendered twice as we entered a two-digit number. Now, suppose you realized that the shelf name needs to be South Block instead of South. You edit it and change it to South Block (Figure 8-16).

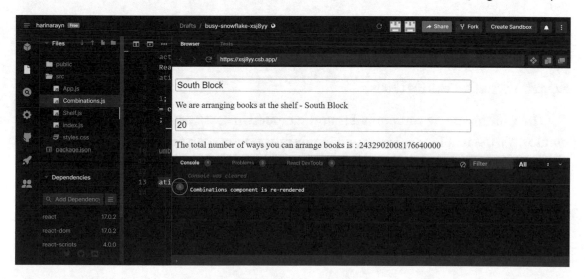

Figure 8-16. *Unnecessary rendering of the component*

South Block is now updated as the new shelf name. However, the Combinations component got rendered eight times. This means it calculated the factorial for 20 eight times, which is unnecessary and expensive and affects performance. Even if the count of books does not change, it re-renders the Combinations component whenever you change the shelf name. However, it needs to render only if the count of books changes.

With the property for book count passed to the Combinations component, we can set the code in such a way that the Combinations component renders only when the property passed to it changes. Update the Combinations.js file with Listing 8-15.

Listing 8-15. Combinations.js with Memo

```
import React from "react";
const Combinations = React.memo(function ({ countBooks }) {
  console.log("Combinations component is re-rendered");
  let arrangements = 1;
  for (let i = 2; i <= countBooks; i++) {
    arrangements *= i;
  }
  return `The total number of ways you can arrange the books is :
  ${arrangements}`;
});
export default Combinations;
```

The Combinations component is now wrapped in React.memo. React.memo memorizes the whole component, so it only re-renders when the props change, in this case countBooks. Attempt the same steps again and edit the shelf name from South to South Block, and you see that the Combinations component does not re-render after you change the shelf name. Figure 8-17 shows that it renders only twice the first time you type the digit 20.

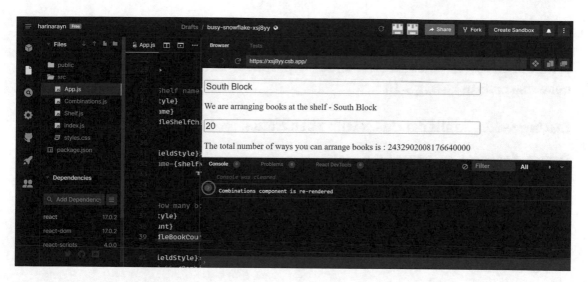

Figure 8-17. *React Memo*

The following example shows how a React Memo component can wrap other components to memorize and to only render if the props change.

Note that we do not have to memorize everything. The purpose of Memo is to optimize performance. So we use Memo only if it can improve the performance of an app. You can use Profiler to check an app's performance like we discussed in Chapter 6. Always run profiling before and after using Memo to see if it was worth memorizing.

In the next section, let's get back to the "Hooks" track. We will focus on two other memorization techniques, the Hooks useMemo and useCallback. We will use the same example to demonstrate them. Note that all three have different usages. You will see the difference once we go over the two Hooks. But the same rule applies to Memo, useMemo, and useCallback. Use only if necessary to improve performance.

useMemo

The React Memo HOC can memorize a component and prevent re-rendering if the component props have not changed. On the other hand, the useMemo() Hook can memorize a function output if the function dependencies have not changed. The useMemo() function calls a function and memorizes its output. The next time we call this function, it checks if the dependencies have changed. If they have not changed, it will return the previously memorized value. Otherwise, it will call the function again.

Let's use the same example as in the previous section. Imagine that you'd like to display the shelf name together with the combinations. In the Combinations component, add the shelf name as a property. Update Combinations.js with the following code in Listing 8-16.

Listing 8-16. Combinations.js with Shelf Name

```
import React from "react";
const Combinations = React.memo(function ({countBooks, shelfName }) {
  console.log("Combinations component is re-rendered");
  let arrangements = 1;
  for (let i = 2; i <= countBooks; i++) {
    arrangements *= i;
  }
  return `The total number of ways you can arrange the books on the shelf
  ${shelfName} is : ${arrangements}`;
});
export default Combinations;
```

Now the Combinations component accepts two props, countBooks and shelfName. Update the Combinations tag in App.js as follows to set both the props:

```
<Combinations countBooks={bookCount} shelfName={shelfName} />
```

Let's repeat the scenario where you enter a shelf name and number of books and then update the shelf name. The shelf name and number of ways are now displayed together in the second label, but React renders the Combinations component eight times. Refer to Figure 8-18.

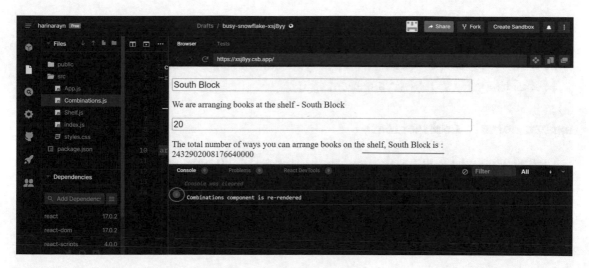

Figure 8-18. *Re-rendering due to prop change*

The reason is that we now have two properties for the Combinations component, which are the book count and shelf name. We already wrapped the Combinations component using React Memo, and there is no change in the `countBooks` property. Nevertheless, as the second prop `shelfName` changed, it re-rendered the component. As a result, it repeated the factorial calculation several times. We want to avoid this calculation if only the name changes; we want to do it only if the book count changes.

Let's see how we can achieve this using the `useMemo()` Hook. Update `Combinations.js` with Listing 8-17.

Listing 8-17. Combinations.js with useMemo()

```
import React, { useMemo } from "react";
const Combinations = React.memo(function ({countBooks, shelfName }) {
  console.log("Combinations component is re-rendered");
  let arrangements = useMemo(() => {
    console.log("Total number of ways being calculated");
    let arrs = 1;
    for (let i = 2; i <= countBooks; i++) {
      arrs *= i;
    }
```

```
    return arrs;
  }, [countBooks]);
  return `The total number of ways you can arrange books on the shelf,
  ${shelfName} is : ${arrangements}`;
});
export default Combinations;
```

Now, we have imported the useMemo() Hook. We did the factorial calculation inside a function and returned to the arrangements variable. The function is the first argument to the useMemo() Hook and countBooks is the second argument. The second argument countBooks is the dependency. Now repeat our test by updating name after entering the book count. See the results in the browser screen. Refer to Figure 8-19.

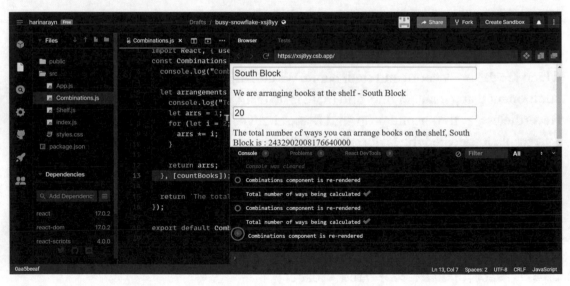

Figure 8-19. *useMemo()*

You can observe that now the calculations happen only twice. That is when you type the first digit 2 and when you type in 0 as the second digit to make it 20. The Combinations component is re-rendered eight times as before because of the name change. However, the factorial calculation won't occur because there is no change in the book count. The useMemo() returns the memorized output if there is no change in the dependency countBooks. So, when the shelfName changes, it returns the memorized value, and when the countBooks changes, it recalculates the output and returns it. In this way, we can improve performance by memorizing expensive code executions with the useMemo() Hook.

useCallback

useCallback is another memorization technique in React. It has the same syntax of useMemo. However, useCallback memorizes the function, whereas useMemo memorizes the value. In the preceding example, to retrieve the calculated value, we cannot use useCallback because it will return a function instead of the value we need.

As mentioned before, we use memory Hooks and React Memo only if they can significantly improve performance. We only need useCallback in rare scenarios, such as when a function call causes component re-renders. useMemo can be helpful in few scenarios like the preceding expensive calculation scenarios.

To illustrate the use of the useCallback() hook, let's update the same example to use it. Imagine we want to check shelf space based on the number of books along with the combinations. And we no longer need to display the shelf name as we did in the useMemo example. So now we need to pass a callback function to the Combinations component instead of the shelf name. Update Combinations.js as in Listing 8-18.

Listing 8-18. Combinations.js with Callback Function

```
import React, { useMemo } from "react";
const Combinations = React.memo(function ({ countBooks, checkSpace }) {
  console.log("Combinations component is re-rendered");
  let space = "";
  switch (countBooks) {
    case 1 - 5:  space = "Free Space available"; break;
    case 5 - 10: space = "Perfect"; break;
    case 10 - 15: space = "Need extra storage"; break;
    default:   space = "Not Sufficient";
  }
  let arrangements = useMemo(() => {
    console.log("Total number of ways being calculated");
    let arrs = 1;

    for (let i = 2; i <= countBooks; i++) {
      arrs *= i;
    }

    return arrs;
```

```
  }, [countBooks]);
  return (
    <>
      <p>The total number of ways you can arrange books is :
      {arrangements}</p>
      <button onClick={() => checkSpace(space)}>Check Space</button>
    </>
  );
});

export default Combinations;
```

As you can see, now the Combinations component returns a button element along with the total number of combinations. The button calls a function checkSpace with a parameter space. It calculates the space based on a switch function, which is based on the number of books. We removed the prop shelfName as we no longer need to display the shelf name along with the combinations.

Next, update App.js. Declare a new state variable for space and declare a click handler to set space:

```
const [shelfSpace, setShelfSpace] = useState("");
const handleClick = (theSpace) => {
    setShelfSpace(theSpace);
  };
```

Then update the Combinations tag with the updated props. The second prop is a callback function that calls the handleClick function:

```
<Combinations countBooks={bookCount} checkSpace={handleClick} />
```

Add a paragraph tag below to display the space:

```
{shelfSpace && (
      <p style={fieldStyle}>The space at the shelf is - {shelfSpace}</p>
    )}
```

That completes the changes in App.js. When you type in the book count, the component Combinations gets called with the book count and the handleClick function. Within the Combinations component, it sets the callback prop checkSpace with the value of the space. This invokes the handleClick method inside the App component, and the screen displays the space along with the number of arrangements.

Repeat the test process of entering the shelf name, book count, and updating the shelf name again. You do not have to click the Check Space button. As you can see in Figure 8-20, the Combinations component gets rendered eight times even though the props are the same and we wrapped the component with React.memo.

Figure 8-20. *Re-rendering because of callbacks*

We passed two props to the Combinations component, which are book count and the checkSpace function. When we updated the shelf name, neither of those props changed, but the component was rendered again. This is because in JavaScript (JS), a function object will be different in every render, even if the functions are exactly the same. See Figure 8-21 where I added a piece of code in CodeSandbox.

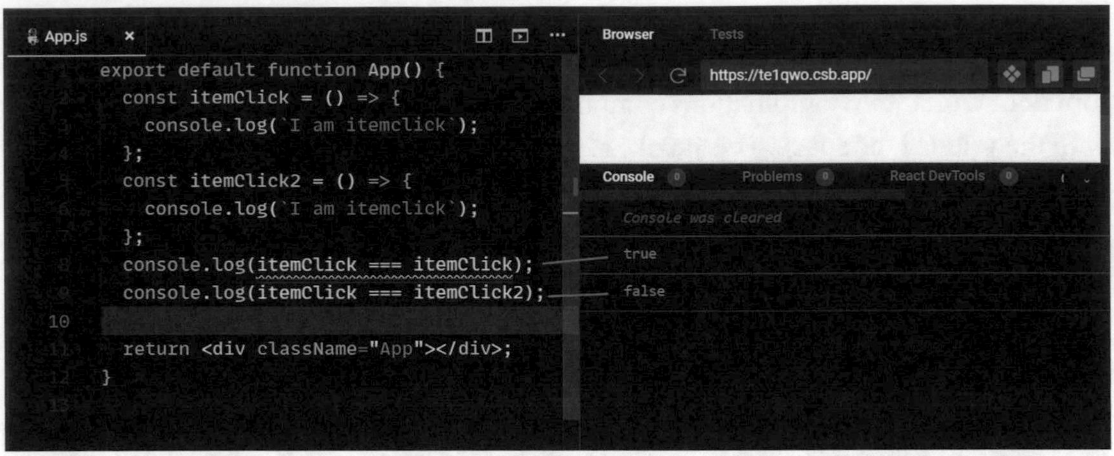

Figure 8-21. *Function equality check*

Even though `itemClick` and `itemClick2` are same, comparing them returns false. In JS, a function equals only that function. Functions are reference types, so two different functions are stored in different places in memory even if they are same. So, between each rendering of a component, a function will be different.

Whenever you update the shelf name, the state variable `shelfName` gets updated, and the App component re-renders, which causes the Combinations component and Shelf component to re-render. The React.memo checks if the props have changed before rendering the Combinations component. When checking, it will see that the book count has not changed, but the callback function prop `checkSpace` has changed. This is because of the preceding explanation, where JS treats each function differently during re-render, even though the function name and definition have not changed.

We need a way to state that `handleClick` did not change, so that React.memo finds that prop `checkSpace` has not changed and does not re-render. This is where we can use the `useCallback()` hook. It memorizes the function call. Update the import statement in `App.js` to include the `useCallback()` Hook:

```
import React, { useState, useCallback } from "react";
```

Update the handleClick function as in the following:

```
const handleClick = useCallback((theSpace) => {
  setShelfSpace(theSpace);
}, []);
```

292

Figure 8-22 shows that if you update the name after entering the count, the component will not re-render.

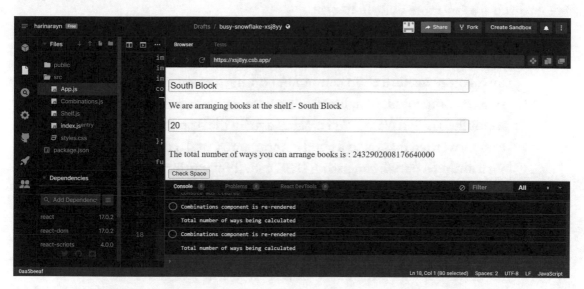

Figure 8-22. *useCallback()*

Here, the Hook useCallback memorizes the function handleClick. So React. memo does not see any changes in the prop checkSpace, preventing the Combinations component from re-rendering. Even if you click the Check Space button, the component will not re-render given that there is no change to the countBooks and handleClick(), which are the props passed. If you change the book count, the component re-renders because of the change in the first prop. This way, the useCallback Hook memorizes a function call between renders and avoids re-renders due to the function equality behavior.

As you can see from the preceding examples, React.memo is for memorizing a component. The useMemo Hook is used to memorize values, and useCallback is used to memorize functions. Using these techniques when you start developing an application is not recommended. Once you have developed the application or a large section of it, use Profiler to check for performance leaks. Next, identify the cause and use these techniques to fix it.

Few More "Hookies"

Let us discuss a few more built-in hooks:

1. `useImperativeHandle` – We use `useImperativeHandle` with the `useRef` hook. For example, you can use this Hook for focusing an element inside a child component during a change in the parent component. Imagine the App component is having an input field called Name. You created a ref in the App component and forwarded that ref to a child component, Child1. For forwarding a ref, we can use an HOC called `forwardRef`. This forwarded ref in the Child1 component is assigned to an input field, Country, inside Child1. You want to focus on the Country field of the Child1 component when there is a change in Name, which is the input defined in the App component. By defining a `useImperativeHandle` hook in Child1 along with a callback prop, you can pass the focus from App to Child1 during the `onChange` event of the field Name. You may rarely use this Hook in practical scenarios, and, like the ref Hook, the use of this Hook will access the DOM directly.

2. `useLayoutEffect` – Using `useLayoutEffect` is like using `useEffect`, except it runs in parallel while the DOM is being rendered. The Hook is called before the browser displays the DOM changes. The `useEffect` is called only when the browser has finished painting changes to the screen. It is recommended to use `useLayoutEffect` only when `useEffect` is causing any blocking of the visuals, which is very rare.

3. `useDebugValue` – The `useDebugValue` hook can be useful when creating custom Hooks. You can use it to display logs in the React DevTools. You can substitute console.log statements with this Hook.

Custom "Hookies"

A custom hook is a JS function whose name starts with the word use. And a custom Hook may call other Hooks. Thus, if you develop a Hook, the name should start with use. You can identify a Hook with the prefix use. I believe use is the perfectly suitable prefix for Hooks because Hooks are extremely useful and a brilliant concept in modern React programming.

By implementing custom hooks, we can extract specific logic and reuse them in different parts of the app. Let's put together a simple custom Hook for learning how to develop a custom Hook. Here, we will use the same example from earlier sections. We will create a Hook to calculate the factorial instead of doing the operation directly in the Combinations component.

Let us see how to implement this Hook. Go to the previous CodeSandbox and create a new folder, Hooks. Inside the folder, create a file useFactorial.js and copy the code from Listing 8-19.

Listing 8-19. useFactorial.js

```
import { useMemo } from "react";
const useFactorial = (number) => {
  let factorial = useMemo(() => {
    let fact = 1;
    for (let i = 2; i <= number; i++) {
      fact *= i;
    }
    return fact;
  }, [number]);
  return factorial;
};
export default useFactorial;
```

We created the Hook useFactorial now. This hook accepts a number and returns its factorial. In addition, it is using the useMemo Hook as it involves expensive calculations. So, if this Hook is called a second time with the same number, it returns the result without re-calculating it.

Let us see how to use this Hook in our Combinations component. Update Combinations.js with the code in Listing 8-20.

Listing 8-20. Combinations.js

```
import React from "react";
import useFactorial from "./Hooks/useFactorial";
const Combinations = React.memo(function ({ countBooks, checkSpace }) {
  console.log("Combinations component is re-rendered");
  let space = "";
  switch (countBooks) {
    case 1 - 5:  space = "Free Space available"; break;
    case 5 - 10: space = "Perfect"; break;
    case 10 - 15: space = "Need extra storage"; break;
    default:   space = "Not Sufficient";
  }
  const arrangements = useFactorial(countBooks);
  return (
    <>

      <p>The total number of ways you can arrange books is :
      {arrangements}</p>
      <button onClick={() => checkSpace(space)}>Check Space</button>
    </>
  );
});
export default Combinations;
```

Now, we have imported the custom hook useFactorial into this component. We can find out the number of ways for the books to be arranged using a single line of code. We also do not have to worry about memorization as the Hook handles it.

Here we do not need to import the useMemo Hook anymore. Also, as per the rules of Hooks, we cannot call Hooks from loops, conditions, nested functions, or callback functions. So we cannot call useFactorial() inside useMemo(). We call Hooks from custom Hooks, which we have done by calling useMemo() from the useFactorial custom Hook.

If you view the results in a browser screen, it will execute as before. Refer to Figure 8-23.

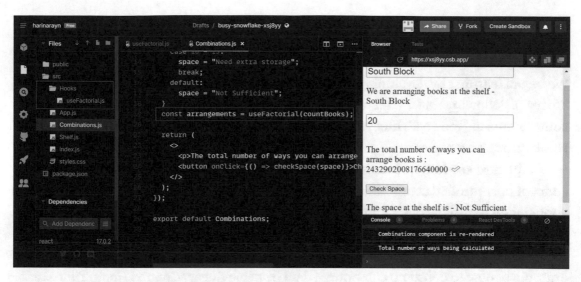

Figure 8-23. *Custom Hook*

We show here an example of how you can extract logic and create a custom hook. There are many community-built Hooks available to use. You can install the containing package with npm, and you may then reference the Hook in your app. It is possible to share your developed custom Hooks with the community so that other developers can reuse them. However, you may not want to use custom hooks at all as it is just encapsulation of a functionality. You can even achieve this by creating reusable functions and export them so that the other components can refer them. React Hooks enable you to hook into the React lifecycle and state, whereas a custom Hook won't do that.

Note   You can visit the GitHub repository to view the project code at the end of each chapter. You can access the repository via the book's product page, https://github.com/Apress/Just-React. All the code sections used in this chapter are located under Chapter 8 ➤ Projects. Final code in each section is available under the respective folders, which are named with respective app and Hook names. Also, I added the name of the listings, which can be found under a folder.

Summary

Hooks, a vital part of modern React programming, took center stage in this chapter. We began learning by developing a deep understanding of the class component lifecycle. Following that, we learned how state Hook and effect Hook enabled functional components to Hook with lifecycle events. We learned details of state Hook and effect Hook through examples.

In the next section, we learned about the ref Hook, useRef. We talked about the concept of controlled components in React and the importance of making wise decisions about when to use the refs. Our next topic was the useReducer hook. We discussed how it can manage state and be extremely helpful in larger applications.

Next, we discussed React Context and the useContext hook. We have seen an example of how to consume component data by using the useContext Hook. Then we discussed how memorization techniques can improve the performance of a React app. We discussed how React.memo can memorize a component and avoid re-rendering it. With the same example, we discussed useMemo and useCallback Hooks and demonstrated how the three methods differ in their usage. We stressed the importance of using the performance hooks only when they can enhance performance. We created our own custom hook in the last section and explained about custom Hooks.

React Hooks emphasize on the importance of thinking in React exactly like other React concepts. We need to think carefully before choosing a specific Hook. Building an app in React relies more on your thinking and your actions, which are based on your knowledge, practice, and experience. It is impossible to build a React app by referring a piece of code from the Web. We need to think, rethink, 'React' and 'React'.

In the next chapter, we will discuss how React handles communication with backend services. You will learn about authentication, Redux, etc. Let's move on to next!

CHAPTER 9

React Back

This chapter explores a few concepts that we haven't discussed so far. These concepts are sometimes a requirement common to all frontend programming languages. The chapter discusses these concepts and how React can meet them. In previous chapters, you learned how React works as a frontend library. In this chapter, we will explore few interactions with backend services, such as an Application Programming Interface (API) or database.

We will begin by learning about routing in a React application. We will discuss different routing concepts and demonstrate the concept with a simple example. Then, we will move on to the authentication section, which makes up the major portion of this chapter. Authentication starts with an overview of Firebase, which is a Backend-as-a-Service (BaaS). We will set up an email password authentication in the just-food project using Firebase. You will learn how to interact with a backend database and authenticate users.

Next, we will discuss consumption of REST APIs in a React application. You will learn how to make Hypertext Transfer Protocol (HTTP) requests using GET and POST methods by using the Axios library. The last section of this chapter introduces you to Redux through an easy-to-understand example. By the end of this chapter, you will have a solid understanding of how React interacts with backend services and be able to create more complex React applications.

React to Routes

The term *routing* is one of the common terms used in programming. Routing is the process of redirecting a user to different pages based on a request or action. With routing, we can build single-page web applications that have navigation without having to refresh the page while navigating. As soon as a user clicks a link, the URL changes, and a new view is rendered on the page. We can implement routing in React using a library called React Router.

© Hari Narayn 2022
H. Narayn, *Just React!*, https://doi.org/10.1007/978-1-4842-8294-6_9

Let us create an app and set up routing to understand the concepts. Imagine that this application has three pages: the home page displays the food menu, the Order Food page allows you to order food, and the Contact Us page lets you contact the company. For each page, we will display a header with a different color.

Go to `https://codesandbox.io` and create a new React sandbox, as we did in the previous chapters. Install `react-router-dom` as a dependency from the left-hand side of Explorer. For a real-time application, use `npm install react-router-dom` from the VS Code terminal to install this.

Note   In CodeSandbox, ensure that the dependency `react-router-dom` is installed. Once installed, you will be able to see the dependency under the Dependencies section. If you hover over a dependency, you can see a refresh icon. Click it to update a dependency to the latest version. This applies to all dependencies you install while using CodeSandbox.

Create three more components besides the default App component and copy the following code to the components. Refer to the Listings 9-1, 9-2, 9-3 and 9-4.

Listing 9-1. Menu.js

```
export default function Menu() {
  return (
    <>
      <h1 style={{ color: "green" }}>You are on the Home Page, Menu</h1>
    </>
  );
}
```

Listing 9-2. Food.js

```
export default function Food() {
  return (
    <>
      <h1 style={{ color: "blue" }}>You are on the Order page</h1>
    </>
  );
}
```

Listing 9-3. Contact.js

```
export default function Contact() {
  return (
    <>
      <h1 style={{ color: "orange" }}>You are on Contact Us page</h1>
    </>
  );
}
```

All three components have a header with different text and color to distinguish them. Now update App.js with the following code. I'll explain how the code works after.

Listing 9-4. App.js

```
import { BrowserRouter, Route, Routes, Link } from "react-router-dom";
import Menu from "./Menu";
import Food from "./Food";
import Contact from "./Contact";
const ulStyle = {
  listStyleType: "none",
  fontSize: "22px",
  overflow: "hidden"
};
const liStyle = {
  float: "left",
  "padding-left": "20px"
};
export default function App() {
  return (
    <BrowserRouter>
      <ul style={ulStyle}>
        <li style={liStyle}>
          <Link to="/">Menu</Link>
        </li>
        <li style={liStyle}>
          <Link to="/Food">Order Food</Link>
```

```
      </li>
      <li style={liStyle}>
        <Link to="/Contact">Contact Us</Link>
      </li>
    </ul>

    <Routes>
      <Route path="/" element={<Menu />}></Route>
      <Route path="/Food" element={<Food />}></Route>
      <Route path="/Contact" element={<Contact />}></Route>
    </Routes>
  </BrowserRouter>
  );
}
```

We imported BrowserRouter, Route, Routes, and Link from react-router-dom. BrowserRouter is a type of Router component. react-router-dom provides HashRouter and BrowserRouter as routers for a desktop application. A Router component creates routes. We must add it at the root of our app to enable routing, so we wrap our root component in a router. We imported BrowserRouter and wrapped our App component in it.

We added code for a menu items list using <ul> and <li> tags and defined some basic styling for these elements. Within each <li> tag, we added a Link. The Link component of React Router provides navigation. For example, we defined /Food as the to attribute of the Order Food Link. When we click the link, the URL becomes localhost/Food.

In the last section, we defined Routes. Routes is a route matching component that matches the path with the current URL. You click the Order Food link; it redirects you to the URL localhost/Food. The <Routes> component checks the URL and discovers that it matches the path /Food. As a result, it renders the Food component. In a similar way, all other components get rendered based on the clicked link.

Note   You may find <Switch> was used as a route matcher in older versions. Note that Switch will not work with the latest version of react-dom-router. Always use <Routes> as the route matcher.

If you run the code, you see you can navigate to different pages when you click each menu item on top. Whenever a component is rendered, you can see the corresponding header text with the corresponding color. You can see this in Figure 9-1, where I highlighted what we discussed.

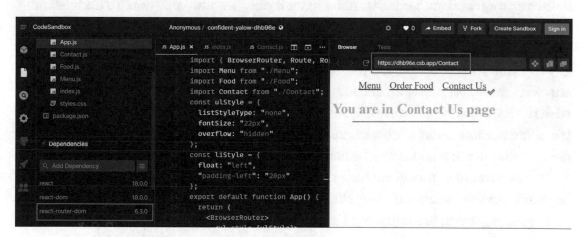

Figure 9-1. *React app with routing*

In this example, I clicked the Contact Us link, and you can see that the URL has been updated to /Contact, and it has rendered the Contact component.

Only the navigated component renders when you use routing to navigate between components. Routes enable users to switch between views within a single page without requiring a browser refresh.

Note   This section aims to provide a basic understanding of routing in React. React Router can be a large topic and is beyond the scope of this chapter. Check out the official React Router documentation at `https://reactrouter.com/ docs/en/v6` to explore more on this subject.

Manage Access Before We React

The authentication and authorization processes are crucial to managing access of an application. Even though they go hand in hand and are often carried out sequentially, authentication and authorization differ in their purpose and execution. To understand this, let's look at Facebook as an example. To log in to Facebook, you enter a username and password. By using your username, you are claiming your identity. Passwords serve as proof that you are the person you claim to be. This is known as authentication. You entered the correct password and logged in. There are posts from a specific group you wish to view. However, you are unable to see that because you are not part of the group. It's called authorization. Authorization determines whether a user has access to specific data. Authentication and authorization are fundamental to any application.

To implement authentication and authorization in React, we can use third-party backend services. There are many choices available. Using Firebase, we will demonstrate access management in the just-food React project. Firebase is a Backend-as-a-Service (Baas). Firebase offers developers a variety of tools and services. With it, it's easy to authenticate using passwords; phone numbers; social networks like Google, Facebook, and Twitter; and more.

Let's go back to our just-food project, which we created during Chapter 5. We will implement authentication in this app. Every user will need to sign in to order food from Just Food Online Shop. Once logged in, the Order Food page will appear. If the logged-in user is admin, the `Availability Check` button should be visible. Only the admin user can access the Menu Availability page. With the button, the admin user can check the menu availability and access the Order Food page. Other users should only have access to the Order Food page.

Note   Review Chapter 5 to recap the `just-food` project implementation, since we will build authentication on top of the same app here. To view the latest code of the `just-food` project, visit the Chapter 7 ➤ Projects path of the GitHub repository (`https://github.com/Apress/Just_React`). You can also download or clone the entire project. After cloning, run `npm install` from the project folder to install all the required node modules before running the code.

Let's get started. We will go through the process step-by-step to digest each part of the implementation.

Step 1: Firebase configuration.

Let's first set up Firebase. Go to `https://firebase.google.com`, click "Get started," and log in with your Google account. Once you have signed in, click "Create a project." Name your project and click "Create." I named it as just-food, the same name as our React project.

In the next window, switch off the Analytics toggle, and click Create a project. Once it creates the project, you will be redirected to the console. Click Authentication from the left-hand side of Explorer and then click the Get Started button on the right-hand-side window. Click the Email/Password button. Turn on the toggle against Email/Password to enable that. Refer to Figure 9-2, where I have highlighted the steps in order. We will only use the Email/Password method for this example, so leave out other sign-in methods.

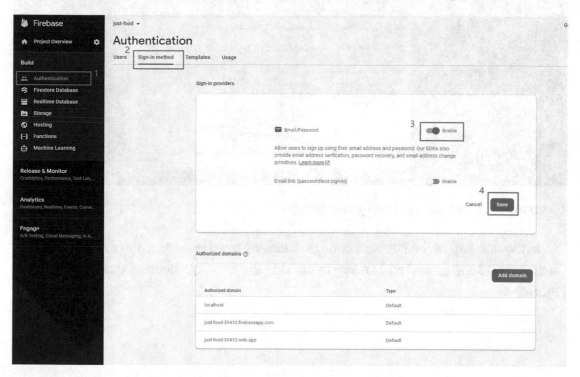

Figure 9-2. *Firebase – setting up authentication methods*

Next, let us create a database to store the user details. Click Firestore Database from the left-hand side of Explorer. Click Create database from the right-hand-side window. It will open a pop-up. Select "Start in test mode" and click "Next," and it will ask a location to select. You can select any location or preferably select the closest location to you. Click Enable, and it will create a database for you after a few seconds. Refer to Figure 9-3 for details.

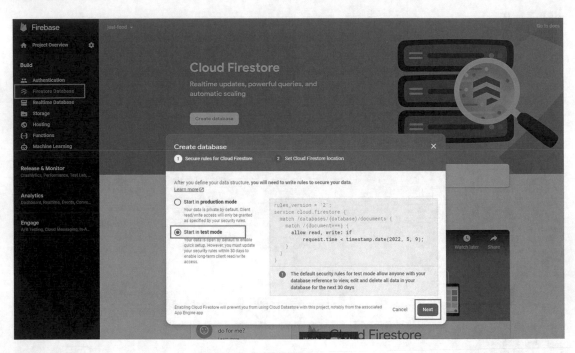

Figure 9-3. *Firebase – creating a database*

In the last step of the Firebase configuration, we need to add an app to the project. Click Project settings and add an app by clicking the web (</>) icon as shown in Figure 9-4.

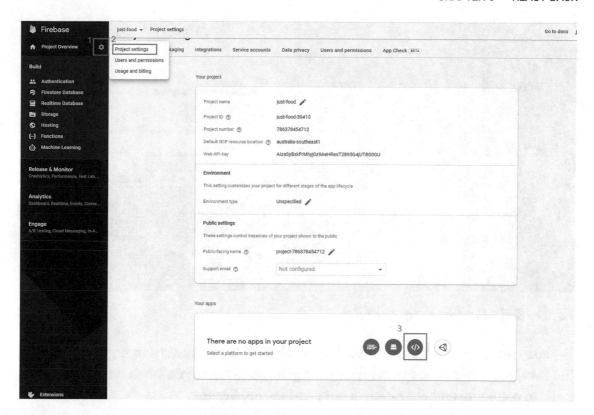

Figure 9-4. *Firebase – setting up the app*

When it asks for the app nickname, enter "just-food" there and click "Register app." Leave out the other settings. It will register the app, and it will present you with the SDK setup code. Just click Continue to console. In the console, you can see that it has created your app, and you can view the SDK setup code. See Figure 9-5. We will use this when we go to VS Code for setting up authentication in our just-food project.

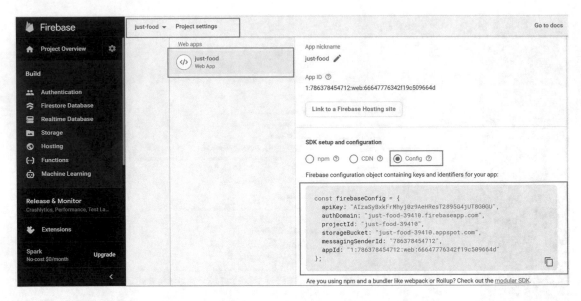

Figure 9-5. *Firebase – app config*

You can see from Figure 9-5 that if you click the "Config" radio button, you can see the `firebaseConfig` variable, which we are going to use in step 2, when we are using VS Code to configure authentication in our just-food application.

Step 2: Set up the app to communicate with Firebase.

Start VS Code, and open the just-food project. Open the terminal and install the `react-router-dom`, `firebase`, and `firebase` hooks packages with the following commands. We require the Router package to set up routing for the sign-in and home pages:

```
npm install react-router-dom firebase react-firebase-hooks
```

Next, let us create a folder under the `src` folder named `auth`. Under this folder, create a file `firebase.js`. We will use this file to set up code to communicate with Firebase. We will define sign-in, sign-out, and sign-up functions inside this file. Copy Listing 9-5 into `firebase.js`. Let us look at the code after the listing.

Listing 9-5. firebase.js

```
import { initializeApp } from "firebase/app";
import {
  getAuth,
  signInWithEmailAndPassword,
```

```
    createUserWithEmailAndPassword,
    signOut,
    updateProfile,
} from "firebase/auth";
import { getFirestore, collection, addDoc } from "firebase/firestore";

const firebaseConfig = {
    apiKey: "XXXXXXXXXXXXXXXXXXXXXXXXXXXXXXXXXXXXXXXXX",
    authDomain: "just-food-00000.firebaseapp.com",
    projectId: "just-food-000010",
    storageBucket: "just-food-00000.appspot.com",
    messagingSenderId: "000000000000",
    appId: "0:00000000000:web:0000000000000000",
};

const app = initializeApp(firebaseConfig);
const auth = getAuth(app);
const db = getFirestore(app);

const signIn = async (email, password) => {
    try {
        await signInWithEmailAndPassword(auth, email, password);
    } catch (err) {
        console.error(err);
        alert(err.message);
    }
};
const signUp = async (name, email, password) => {
    try {
        const result = await createUserWithEmailAndPassword(auth, email,
        password);
        const user = result.user;
        await updateProfile(user, { displayName: name });
        await addDoc(collection(db, "users"), {
            uid: user.uid,
            name,
            authProvider: "local",
```

```
      email,
    });
  } catch (err) {
    console.error(err);
    alert(err.message);
  }
};
const logOut = () => {
  signOut(auth);
};
export {
  auth,
  db,
  signIn,
  signUp,
  logOut,
};
```

After copying the code, replace the const variable firebaseConfig with your project config from Firebase. Refer to Figure 9-5.

In this file, first, we imported all the required components from the respective Firebase packages:

```
import { initializeApp } from "firebase/app";
import {
  getAuth,
  signInWithEmailAndPassword,
  createUserWithEmailAndPassword,
  signOut,
  updateProfile,
} from "firebase/auth";
import { getFirestore, collection, addDoc } from "firebase/firestore";
```

We defined firebaseConfig in the next step. You need to copy your Firebase config here. This is a dummy config:

```
const firebaseConfig = {
```

```
  apiKey: "XXXXXXXXXXXXXXXXXXXXXXXXXXXXXXXXXXXXXXXXX",
  authDomain: "just-food-00000.firebaseapp.com",
  projectId: "just-food-000010",
  storageBucket: "just-food-00000.appspot.com",
  messagingSenderId: "000000000000",
  appId: "0:00000000000:web:0000000000000000",
};
```

Next, we initialized the Firebase app with the config via the `initializeApp` method. Similarly, we initialized the Firebase database and authentication:

```
const app = initializeApp(firebaseConfig);
const auth = getAuth(app);
const db = getFirestore(app);
```

Then, we defined three methods: `signIn`, `signUp`, and `logOut`. In the `signIn` method, we call a Firebase method, `signInWithEmailAndPassword`. We have already initialized auth with the `getAuth` method from Firebase. This authenticates the user with the app. The email and password we will need to pass from an input form. We will set this form up at a later step:

```
const signIn = async (email, password) => {
  try {
    await signInWithEmailAndPassword(auth, email, password);
  } catch (err) {
    console.error(err);
    alert(err.message);
  }
};
```

The sign-up method uses the Firebase function `createUserWithEmailAndPassword` with the parameters auth, email, and `password`. In addition, it expects a parameter name and adds the user to the database. We use this name to update the user display name by invoking the Firebase method `updateProfile`. Like the `signIn` method, the `signUp` method also expects an input form to pass the parameters, which include name, email address, and password:

```
const signUp = async (name, email, password) => {
```

```
  try {
    const result = await createUserWithEmailAndPassword(auth, email,
    password);
    const user = result.user;
    await updateProfile(user, { displayName: name });
    await addDoc(collection(db, "users"), {
      uid: user.uid,
      name,
      authProvider: "local",
      email,
    });
  } catch (err) {
    console.error(err);
    alert(err.message);
  }
};
```

Next, we defined the logOut method, which invokes the signOut function of Firebase with the auth parameter. Invoking this will log out the user:

```
const logOut = () => {
  signOut(auth);
};
```

Finally, we exported these three methods along with the auth and db. This will enable us to reference these from the components:

```
export {
  auth,
  db,
  signIn,
  signUp,
  logOut,
};
```

Step 3: Authentication component.

In this step, we create a component so that the user can sign in or sign out from the app. We will create a single component for both the functions. To begin, create a CSS module file Auth.module.css under the auth folder and copy Listing 9-6.

Listing 9-6. Auth.module.css

```css
.boxAuth {
  height: 100vh;
  width: 100vw;
  display: flex;
  align-items: center;
  justify-content: center;
}
.boxAuthContainer {
  display: flex;
  flex-direction: column;
  text-align: center;
  background-color: #163d61;
  padding: 60px;
  padding-top: 30px;
}
.title {
  color: rgba(235, 232, 51, 0.993);
  padding-bottom: 30px;
  font-size: 28px;
  margin-bottom: 10px;
}
.inputAuth {
  padding: 10px;
  font-size: 18px;
  margin-bottom: 10px;
}
.btnAuth {
  padding: 10px;
  font-size: 18px;
```

```
  margin-bottom: 10px;
  font-weight: 400;
  border: 1px solid rgba(235, 232, 51, 0.993);
  color: #ffffff;
  background-color: #0095ff;
  cursor: pointer;
}
.messageAuth {
  color: rgba(235, 232, 51, 0.993);
}
.linkAuth {
  padding-left: 2px;
  text-decoration: underline;
  color: orange;
  cursor: pointer;
}
```

Let's create the Auth component. Create Auth.js in the auth folder and copy the following code in Listing 9-7. Let's go through the code in more detail in the following.

Listing 9-7. Auth.js

```
import React, { useEffect, useState } from "react";
import { useNavigate } from "react-router-dom";
import { auth, signIn, signUp } from "./firebase";
import { useAuthState } from "react-firebase-hooks/auth";
import authStyles from "./Auth.module.css";

function Auth() {
  const [isNewUser, setIsNewUser] = useState(false);
  const [authButtonText, setAuthButtonText] = useState("Sign In");
  const [name, setName] = useState("");
  const [email, setEmail] = useState("");
  const [password, setPassword] = useState("");
  const [user, loading, error] = useAuthState(auth);
  const navigate = useNavigate();
  useEffect(() => {
```

```
    if (loading) {
      return;
    }
    if (user) {
      navigate("/app");
    }
  }, [user, loading]);
  const completeSignInOrSignUp = () => {
    isNewUser ? signUp(name, email, password) : signIn(email, password);
  };
  const toggleForm = () => {
    if (authButtonText === "Sign In") {
      setIsNewUser(true);
      setAuthButtonText("Sign Up");
    } else {
      setIsNewUser(false);
      setAuthButtonText("Sign In");
    }
  };
  return (
    <div className={authStyles.boxAuth}>
      <div className={authStyles.boxAuthContainer}>
        <label className={authStyles.title}>Just Food Online Shop</label>
        {isNewUser && (
          <input
            type="text"
            className={authStyles.inputAuth}
            value={name}
            onChange={(e) => setName(e.target.value)}
            placeholder="Full Name"
          />
        )}
        <input
          type="text"
          className={authStyles.inputAuth}
          value={email}
```

```
        onChange={(e) => setEmail(e.target.value)}
        placeholder="Email"
      />
      <input
        type="password"
        className={authStyles.inputAuth}
        value={password}
        onChange={(e) => setPassword(e.target.value)}
        placeholder="Password"
      />
      <button className={authStyles.btnAuth} onClick={completeSignIn
      OrSignUp}>
        {authButtonText}
      </button>
      {!isNewUser && (
        <div className={authStyles.messageAuth}>
          New to Just Food?
          <span className={authStyles.linkAuth} onClick={toggleForm}>
            Click to Sign Up
          </span>
        </div>
      )}
      {isNewUser && (
        <div className={authStyles.messageAuth}>
          Already on Just Food?
          <span className={authStyles.linkAuth} onClick={toggleForm}>
            Click to Sign In
          </span>
        </div>
      )}
    </div>
  </div>
  );
}
export default Auth;
```

This component will serve as the input form for both sign-in and sign-out functions. First, we imported all the required packages from react, react-router-dom, firebase, and firebase-hooks. Then, we defined a set of state variables, each for name, email, and password. In addition, we created a state variable isNewUser to distinguish between sign-in and sign-up. Initially, the variable isNewUser is false, so it will render the Sign In button by default:

```
const [isNewUser, setIsNewUser] = useState(false);
```

For the button text, we have defined another state variable. We initially set the text to Sign In:

```
const [authButtonText, setAuthButtonText] = useState("Sign In");
```

The next line defined a set of variables using the Firebase Hook useAuthState. If the app hasn't yet fetched authentication information, the variable loading will have the value true, and the user variable value will be empty. Once it authenticated the user, we assign the details of the user to the variable user, and it sets the variable loading to false. If it encountered any errors during authentication, it sets the error object value to the error variable:

```
const [user, loading, error] = useAuthState(auth);
```

In the next line, we initiated a variable, navigate, with the Hook useNavigate of react-router-dom. This Hook allows you to navigate to a URL based on the path. For example, if we use navigate("/app"), it will take us to the URL localhost:3000/app:

```
const navigate = useNavigate();
```

Next, let us look at the useEffect function. If it finds a user, it redirects to the /app URL using navigate. We will define the routing for the App component at a later step in the index.js file. We will set it on the path /app.

To avoid useEffect being invoked every time the component is rendered, we defined a dependency array. Therefore, the useEffect only fires if the user or loading variable has changed. Thus, a user gets redirected to the path /app URL only when successfully authenticated:

```
useEffect(() => {
    if (loading) {
      return;
```

```
    }
    if (user) {
      navigate("/app");
    }
  }, [user, loading]);
```

You can see in the JSX that we defined that we have three input text fields for name, email, and password. The Name field renders only if the variable isNewUser is true. This means only for the sign-up. Each of these fields sets values by using the respective setState calls. We have a button that displays the text Sign In or Sign Out based on the authButtonText value. Clicking the button invokes a method called CompleteSignInOrSignUp:

```
const completeSignInOrSignUp = () => {
  isNewUser ? signUp(name, email, password) : signIn(email, password);
};
```

The CompleteSignInOrSignUp method calls the respective Firebase function we defined in firebase.js. If isNewUser is true, it calls the signUp function; otherwise, it calls the signIn function.

Last, we have two div elements that provide a message and a link for the user to switch between the Sign In and Sign Up forms. When you click the link, it invokes the function toggleForm. The function changes the state of the variables isNewUser and authButtonText. This helps switch between two forms:

```
const toggleForm = () => {
    if (authButtonText === "Sign In") {
      setIsNewUser(true);
      setAuthButtonText("Sign Up");
    } else {
      setIsNewUser(false);
      setAuthButtonText("Sign In");
    }
  }
```

Step 4: Define routing.

In this step, we need to define routes in the index.js file to make sure that the Sign In form loads before the App component and that the App component loads when a user has signed up or signed in. Open index.js and update import statements as follows in Listing 9-8:

```
import { BrowserRouter } from "react-router-dom";
import { Routes, Route } from "react-router-dom";
import Auth from "./auth/Auth";
```

Then update the render section as in the following.

Listing 9-8. index.js Render Section

```
root.render(
  <BrowserRouter>
    <React.StrictMode>
      <Routes>
        <Route exact path="/" element={<Auth />}></Route>
        <Route exact path="/app" element={<App />} />
      </Routes>
    </React.StrictMode>
  </BrowserRouter>,
  document.getElementById("root")
);
```

So here we defined routes for the Auth component and App component. By default, the Auth component loads. When a user is successfully authenticated, the `navigate("/app")` gets called from the Auth component. So the URL changes to `localhost:3000/app`. As a result, the App component loads as per the routing we defined here.

Step 4: App component changes.

This step involves updating `App.js` so that we can distinguish between the admin user and other users. We will also display the user's email on the top to identify who signed in, and finally, we will add a sign-out option. Update `App.js` as outlined in Listing 9-9. Let's explore the code in depth after that.

Listing 9-9. App.js

```
import appStyles from "./App.module.css";
import React, { useEffect, useState } from "react";
import Foods from "./Foods";
import { auth, logOut } from "./auth/firebase";
import { useAuthState } from "react-firebase-hooks/auth";
import { useNavigate } from "react-router-dom";
```

```
export const foodItemsContext = React.createContext();
const App = () => {
  const navigate = useNavigate();
  const [user, loading, error] = useAuthState(auth);
  const [isChooseFoodPage, setIsChooseFoodPage] = useState(true);
  const [isAdmin, setIsAdmin] = useState(false);
  const [userEmail, setUserEmail] = useState("");
  const [menuItems, setMenuItems] = useState([
    {
      id: 1,
      name: "Chicken Burger",
      quantity: 40,
      desc: "Fried chicken burger - lettuce, tomato, cheese and
      mayonnaise",
      price: "24",
      image: "cb.jpg",
    },
    {
      id: 2,
      name: "Veg Burger",
      quantity: 30,
      desc: "Plant-based burger – lettuce, tomato, vegan cheese and
      mayonnaise",
      price: "22",
      image: "vb.jpg",
    },
    {
      id: 3,
      name: "Chips",
      quantity: 50,
      desc: "Potato chips fried to perfection",
      price: "7",
      image: "chips.jpg",
    },
```

```
  {
    id: 4,
    name: "Ice Cream",
    quantity: 30,
    desc: "Ice cream - Vanilla ice cream double scoop",
    price: "4",
    image: "ic.jpg",
  },
]);
useEffect(() => {
  if (user) {
    const user = auth.currentUser;
    setUserEmail(user.email);
    if (user.email === "admin@justfood.com") {
      setIsAdmin(true);
    }
  } else {
    navigate("/");
  }
}, [user, loading]);

return (
  <foodItemsContext.Provider value={menuItems}>
    <div className={appStyles.App}>
      <button className={appStyles.signOutButton} onClick={logOut}>
        Sign Out
      </button>
      {isAdmin && (
        <button
          className={appStyles.toggleButton}
          onClick={() => setIsChooseFoodPage(!isChooseFoodPage)}
        >
          {isChooseFoodPage ? "Availability Check" : "Order Food"}
        </button>
      )}
```

```
      <span className={appStyles.signedInMessage}>
        Signed in as {userEmail}
      </span>
      <h3 className={appStyles.title}>Just Food Online Shop</h3>

      {!isChooseFoodPage && (
        <>
          <h4 className={appStyles.subTitle}>Menu Availability</h4>
          <ul className={appStyles.ulApp}>
            {menuItems.map((item) => {
              return (
                <li key={item.id} className={appStyles.liApp}>
                  {item.name} - {item.quantity}
                </li>
              );
            })}
          </ul>
        </>
      )}
      {isChooseFoodPage && <Foods foodItems={menuItems}></Foods>}
    </div>
  </foodItemsContext.Provider>
  );
};

export default App;
```

We imported Firebase's authentication component and logOut method so that we can identify the user and log them out as well. We also imported the useAuthState hook from firebase-hooks to get the authentication state:

```
import { auth, logOut} from "./auth/firebase";
import { useAuthState } from "react-firebase-hooks/auth";
```

Another import that we added is the useNavigate hook from react-router-dom. We need this to redirect users back to the sign-in page once they have logged out:

```
import { useNavigate } from "react-router-dom";
```

Also, we updated React import by adding useEffect as we need it to check the user on the initial render:

```
import React, { useEffect, useState } from "react";
```

Next, we defined state variables for navigate and user exactly like we did in the Auth component:

```
const navigate = useNavigate();
const [user, loading, error] = useAuthState(auth);
```

The next line created a state variable to store a user's email address and a Boolean state variable to distinguish between the admin user and other users:

```
const [userEmail, setUserEmail] = useState("");

const [isAdmin, setIsAdmin] = useState(false);
```

We updated the isChooseFoodPage variable declaration to initiate with the true value to ensure that the Order Food page loads first for both types of users:

```
const [isChooseFoodPage, setIsChooseFoodPage] = useState(true);
```

Next, we added the useEffect function:

```
 useEffect(() => {
    if (user) {
      const user = auth.currentUser;
      setUserEmail(user.email);
      if (user.email === "admin@justfood.com") {
        setIsAdmin(true);
      }
    } else {
      navigate("/");
    }
  }, [user, loading]);
```

We get the user object using the auth, and then we set the user email to the state variable userEmail. This email we can use to display at the top of the screen. Then we inserted a condition to see if the user's email equals admin@justfood.com. We set the isAdmin variable to true if the condition is true.

323

When the user is empty, it navigates to the path /, which loads the Auth component, and the Sign In form will appear. We added a dependency array so the useEffect will only execute when it's needed, just like it is in the Auth component.

Moving on to our JSX changes, we added the following span element just above the header Just Food Online Shop. We will define the styles in App.module.css:

```
<span className={appStyles.signedInMessage}>
        Signed in as {userEmail}
    </span>
```

This ensures that the app displays the message Signed in as user email when a user logs in.

Next, we added conditional rendering to the Availability Check button. If the user is the admin, then we display the button to switch between Availability Check and Order Food. Else, it will not render the button:

```
{isAdmin && (
        <button
          className={appStyles.toggleButton}
          onClick={() => setIsChooseFoodPage(!isChooseFoodPage)}
        >
          {isChooseFoodPage ? "Availability Check" : "Order Food"}
        </button>
      )}
```

This ensures that only admin users can see the Availability Check button and hence the Menu Availability page.

Our last change is to add a Sign Out button to the top of the page:

```
<button className={appStyles.signOutButton} onClick={logOut}>
        Sign Out
    </button>
```

The user gets logged out because of this call to the logOut function of Firebase. Because of the navigation defined in useEffect, the user gets redirected to the Sign In form again.

Before we see this in the browser, add the following two new classes to `App.module.css`. These styles are for the signed-in message and the log-out button. Refer to Listing 9-10.

Listing 9-10. App.module.css – New Classes to Add

```
.signOutButton {
  float: right;
  margin: 5px 10px 0px 3px;
  align-items: center;
  padding: 6px 14px;
  border-radius: 8px;
  border: none;
  color: #fff;
  background-color: #367af6;
  cursor: pointer;
}
.signedInMessage
{
  color: orange;
  font-weight: 200;
  font-size: 16px;
}
```

We have completed configuring a basic email password authentication for the just-food app with the help of Firebase. Run `npm start` and see the app in the browser. You will see the Sign In form by default. Click the Sign Up link at the bottom to create users. You will see the name once you click the Sign Up link. The Name field will not visible on the Sign In form. Let us create the admin account first. Enter `admin@justfood.com` as the email and enter a name and password you like. Refer to Figure 9-6.

Figure 9-6. *Sign Up form*

Upon signing up, it will save your details to the database and sign you in directly. You will see the Order Food page and the buttons for Availability Check and Sign Out. You can see the message `Signed in as admin@justfood.com`. Refer to Figure 9-7, where I highlighted these in red.

Figure 9-7. *Admin interface*

Click the Availability Check button to see the menu availability. If you click Sign Out, you will be logged out and redirected to the sign-in page. Click the Sign Up link and create a customer account. I created john.smith9@justfood.com. By clicking Sign Up, you will get signed up and signed in to the app as before. As now you are not an admin user, you will not see the Availability Check button. However, you can see the signed-in message and Sign Out option. See Figure 9-8 for details.

Figure 9-8. *Customer interface*

As you are not the admin user, you do not have access to the Menu Availability page. Sign out now and then sign in with the admin account. This time, you will use the default Sign In form. You do not have to sign up again because you already have an account. The Availability Check button should now be visible, and clicking it will direct you to the Menu Availability page. In this way, we have authenticated and authorized the user. If you return to Firebase and check the authentication and database sections, you can see the details of all the users who have signed up.

Firebase features built-in validations. For example, if you try to sign up the same user email again, for example, john.smith9@justfood.com, it will tell you that the email already exists. If you try to sign up with a wrong password, the wrong password alert will appear.

For example, I entered the wrong password for John Smith in the following, and I got the error. Refer to Figure 9-9.

Figure 9-9. *Sign In form and authentication errors*

We can, of course, convert these error messages to a friendly user interface. But for this section, we focused on learning how to implement a basic email password authentication and authorization in React.

We can build more complicated validation and security rules using Firebase. We can have the forgot password option and different authentication options such as logging with Google, Facebook, etc. using Firebase. There are also many backend services available to implement authentication like Auth0. I will leave it for you to explore further.

HTTP Reactions

So far, we talked about how to authenticate a React app using a backend service. In this section, we discuss how to communicate with a backend API in React. An API is a connection through which two applications can communicate with each other. APIs enable communication between the front and back ends of an application. We can use APIs to consume data from frontend apps built using technologies like React, Angular, etc.

Imagine you have data hosted on a server. You want to display this data in a React app and also want to update this data from the app. There are many libraries available for this purpose in React. Let's explore Axios here. Axios is a library that we can use to create HTTP requests from the browser.

Let's see an example. We will create an app that allows us to enter an employee's name and role. The app will then display the employee's name, role, and id and the creation time. In addition, the app displays the manager's name. Using `https://reqres.in`, we will mock API requests.

As we did in our earlier chapters, go to `https://codesandbox.io` and create a new React CodeSandbox. By default, it creates `App.js`. Update the `App.js` code with Listing 9-11. We will dig into the code in the following.

Listing 9-11. App.js – Employee Info App

```
import "./styles.css";
import axios from "axios";
import { useState } from "react";
import { format, parseISO } from "date-fns";
const fieldStyle = {
  marginTop: "20px",
  float: "left",
  width: "70%",
  fontSize: 20
};
```

```
const buttonStyle = {
  marginTop: "20px",
  backgroundColor: "lightBlue",
  width: "30%",
  fontSize: 20,
  cursor: "pointer",
  marginRight: "20px"
};

function App() {
  const [name, setName] = useState("");
  const [role, setRole] = useState("");
  const [display, setDisplay] = useState("");

  const submit = () => {
    axios
      .post(`https://reqres.in/api/users`, { name: name, job: role })
      .then((res) => {
        setDisplay(
          `${name} is appointed as ${role} on ${format(
            parseISO(res.data.createdAt),
            "dd-MMM-yyyy"
          )} with ID ${res.data.id}`
        );
        console.log(res.data);
      });
  };
  const getManagerName = () => {
    axios.get(`https://reqres.in/api/users/2`).then((res) => {
      console.log(res.data);
      setDisplay(
        `${res.data.data.first_name} is the manager. The contact  email
        is  ${res.data.data.email}.`
      );
    });
  };
```

```
  return (
    <div style={{ width: "100%" }}>
      <input
        placeholder="Name"
        value={name}
        style={fieldStyle}
        onChange={(e) => setName(e.target.value)}
      />
      <input
        placeholder="Role"
        value={role}
        style={fieldStyle}
        onChange={(e) => setRole(e.target.value)}
      />
      <button style={buttonStyle} onClick={submit}>
        Submit
      </button>

      <button style={buttonStyle} onClick={getManagerName}>
        Get Manager name
      </button>
      <br />
      {display && <label style={fieldStyle}> {display}</label>}
    </div>
  );
}
export default App;
```

As our first step, we need to install the axios package. Also, we need to install the date-fns package to format dates. In CodeSandbox, you can install these by typing into the "Add Dependency" box. In real-time projects, you can use the following command and run it in the VS Code terminal:

```
npm install axios date-fns
```

We create a form with two inputs: Name and Role. Once the user fills in the details and clicks the Submit button, it invokes the method submit:

```
const submit = () => {
  axios
    .post(`https://reqres.in/api/users`, { name: name, job: role })
    .then((res) => {
      setDisplay(
        `${name} is appointed as ${role} on ${format(
          parseISO(res.data.createdAt),
          "dd-MMM-yyyy"
        )} with ID ${res.data.id}`
      );
      console.log(res.data);
    });
};
```

Using this method, we make an HTTP POST request to reqres.in. We are posting name and role in JSON format. It creates the user and returns the result with a data object containing name, role, id, and creation time. We then format the data and display it on the label.

We have another button called Get Manager, which just displays a person's name and email when we click it. We did this using an HTTP GET request to https://reqres. in. It returns the user details when we specify a user id (2):

```
const getManagerName = () => {
  axios.get(`https://reqres.in/api/users/2`).then((res) => {
    console.log(res.data);
    setDisplay(
      `${res.data.data.first_name} is the manager. The contact  email
      is  ${res.data.data.email}`.
    );
  });
};
```

As shown in Figure 9-10, I submitted a user, and it returned the details. I highlighted the return data object on the console. Try both the submit and Get Manager buttons.

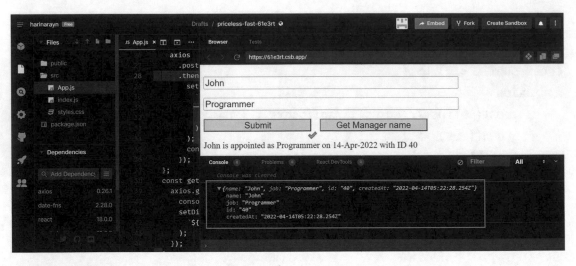

Figure 9-10. *Sending HTTP requests from React*

For POST, we used `https://reqres.in/api/users` as the endpoint with a JSON as input. For GET, we used `https://reqres.in/api/users/2` as the endpoint. We used the Axios package to make these HTTP requests. We looked at a simple example for creating and retrieving data from an API. You can also update and delete data. You can also set authentication headers while making an HTTP request using Axios or any other library.

Redux

Redux is a library that is used for state management in frontend applications. Redux is not specific to React. You can use it with any other library or framework such as Angular, Vue, or plain JavaScript.

Redux creates a global state that can be shared among independent components of a React app. Redux's foundation is based on the following four concepts:

1. *Store*: The store holds the global state for an app. In a similar way to what we did earlier with Context API, we can wrap the root component of an app in a provider tag with the store as a prop. This allows all the app components to access the store.

2. *Action*: An action object is the gateway to the store. Any component in the app can access the store through this object. Action objects have two properties – type and payload – where type describes the action to be taken and payload contains the data to be changed.

3. *Reducer*: The reducer function receives the current state and action. It then changes the state according to the action and returns the new state.

4. *Dispatch*: The dispatch method of a Redux store is the one that carries the action object. To update the state, we call the dispatch method with the action object as the parameter.

Note   The action, dispatch, and reducer concepts are the same as what we learned with the useReducer Hook. For a recap, refer to Chapter 8, section "useReducer." For a recap of Context API and the provider component, refer to Chapter 5, section React Context.

Redux requires two packages: redux, which is the main Redux library for state management, and react-redux, which connects the Redux store with React components.

Let's create an app to show how we can implement Redux with a React app. We will create a to-do app where users can enter tasks, which will appear on a to-do list. Go to https://codesandbox.io and create a new React sandbox. Add redux and react-redux as dependencies. If you are working in VS Code, install these packages with the following command:

```
npm install redux redux-react
```

Let's start by updating index.js to set up the store. Copy the code from Listing 9-12 into index.js.

Listing 9-12. index.js – To-Do App

```
import { StrictMode } from "react";
import { createRoot } from "react-dom/client";
import App from "./App";
import { createStore } from "redux";
import { Provider } from "react-redux";

const reducer = (state = [{ name: "Meeting at 9" }], action) => {
  switch (action.type) {
    case "addNewTask":
```

```
        return [...state, action.payload];
    default:
      return state;
  }
};

const store = createStore(reducer);

const rootElement = document.getElementById("root");
const root = createRoot(rootElement);
root.render(
  <StrictMode>
    <Provider store={store}>
      <App />
    </Provider>
  </StrictMode>
);
```

Let us look at the preceding code. We imported createStore from redux and Provider from react-redux. createStore helps us create a store, and Provider connects this store to all components of the app:

```
import { createStore } from "redux";
import { Provider } from "react-redux";
```

Our next step was to define a reducer function. The reducer accepts state and action as parameters. We initialized the state with an object array. The array initially contains an object item with a property name and value Meeting at 9:

```
const reducer = (state = [{ name: "Meeting at 9" }], action) => {
  switch (action.type) {
    case "addNewTask":
      return [...state, action.payload];
    default:
      return state;
  }
};
```

If the action type is addNewTask, we append the payload to the array and then return the updated state. By default, we set the reducer to return the current state. That means, on initial render, it returns the initial state of the array. Initially, the array contains an item with task name Meeting at 9.

Next, we created a Redux store using the following line of code:

```
const store = createStore(reducer);
```

Last, we wrapped the App component inside the Provider component, which makes the Redux store available to any nested components that need to access the Redux store. By wrapping the App component inside the Provider, we ensured that all components of the application have access to the store:

```
const rootElement = document.getElementById("root");
const root = createRoot(rootElement);
root.render(
  <StrictMode>
    <Provider store={store}>
      <App />
    </Provider>
  </StrictMode>
);
```

Now, update App.js as in Listing 9-13. Let us explore the code after.

Listing 9-13. App.js – To-Do App

```
import { useState } from "react";
import { connect } from "react-redux";
function App(props) {
  const [task, setTask] = useState("");
  const handleClick = () => {
    props.dispatch({
      type: "addNewTask",
      payload: { name: task }
    });
    setTask("");
  };
```

```
  return (
    <>
      <h2> Add tasks </h2>
      <input
        type="text"
        value={task}
        onChange={(e) => setTask(e.target.value)}
      />
      <br />
      <br />
      <button onClick={(e) => handleClick(e)}>
        Add
      </button>
      <hr />
      <h2>To Do List </h2>

      <ul>
        {props.tasks.map((task) => (
          <li key={task.name}>{task.name}</li>
        ))}
      </ul>
    </>
  );
}

const mapStateToProps = (state) => {
  return { tasks: state };
};
export default connect(mapStateToProps)(App);
```

The first thing we did was to import useState from react and connect from react-redux. The connect function is to connect the React component to the store:

```
import { useState } from "react";
import { connect } from "react-redux";
```

Next, we defined a state variable called task:

```
const [task, setTask] = useState("");
```

Now let's look at the JSX elements inside the return function. We have an input text box where the user can enter the task name and then click a button. The button text is Add. Below that, we have a menu list, `<ul>` tag, which displays the added tasks.

We then created a function called mapStateToProps. If we specify a mapStateToProps function, the component will subscribe to the store updates. The mapStateToProps function returns the current state object, and it is added to the props of the component where we defined it:

```
const mapStateToProps = (state) => {
  return { tasks: state };
};
```

In our app, the function returns the object array we defined in index.js. Thus, the App component props now contain the initial state of the array. We can access it using props.tasks. We use these tasks to create menu items within the `<ul>` tag:

```
<ul>
        {props.tasks.map((task) => (
          <li key={task.name}>{task.name}</li>
        ))}
  </ul>
```

So we have the list populated with one item initially, which is Meeting at 9.

During the button click, it calls the function handleClick. Inside handleClick, we call the dispatch function with action object as the argument. The action object contains type as addNewTask and the entered task name as the payload.

We added a line to clear up the input box by setting the variable task to empty:

```
const handleClick = () => {
    props.dispatch({
      type: "addNewTask",
      payload: { name: task }
    });
    setTask("");
  };
```

The `dispatch` function calls the `reducer`, which updates the state. We defined the `reducer` function in `index.js`. As the App component is subscribed to the store updates, the prop `tasks` gets updated with the new state, thus updating the to-do menu list.

The last step was to wrap the App component with the `connect()` function before exporting. This is necessary for connecting the component to the store. The `connect` function takes `mapStateToProps` as an argument:

```
export default connect(mapStateToProps)(App);
```

In a nutshell, this is how Redux works. If you execute the code in CodeSandbox, you can see the default task initially. When you add a new task, you can see the updated to-do list. Refer to Figure 9-11.

Figure 9-11. *Redux with React*

Redux is a large topic. In this section, we limited our discussion to just understanding what Redux is using a simple example. This will help you get started with Redux. Since we have the React Hooks and Context API now, you won't need Redux in most apps. Still, it can be very useful for managing the state in complex applications. Furthermore, it provides extensive debugging features with its DevTools and the ability to use middleware.

Note   You can visit the GitHub repository to view the project code, via the book's product page, `https://github.com/Apress/Just_React`. The code for the apps created for routing, HTTP requests, and Redux is located under Chapter 9 ➤ Projects. You can also access the just-food project with added authentication under Chapter 9 ➤ Projects.

Summary

In this chapter, our primary focus was on how React interacts with backend services. Before moving on there, you learned about routing and how to set up navigation in a multi-page React app.

The next section examined authentication in detail. We began by configuring Firebase and setting up a communication channel between Firebase and our just-food app. Then, we implemented the sign-in, sign-up, and sign-out components. We improved our just-food app by implementing authentication.

We then discussed how a React app could consume REST APIs. We created an application that would retrieve and create data using HTTP requests and Axios. We created dummy APIs using reqres.in. Last, I explained the working of Redux using an example.

This chapter was an attempt to explain the above-mentioned concepts in a simple and easy way so that you can grasp and learn and build on top of it. Are we moving to the end phases of React learning? Definitely not. We are just nearing the end of our book – *Just React*. But not before chatting about some new reactions! The last chapter will cover the exciting new features of React 18.

CHAPTER 10

New Reactions

In our final chapter, we discuss the new features of React 18. The primary focus of React 18 is on the concurrency features and performance improvements. React 18 was released in March 2022. Most of the dependency packages, including the Redux library, have already made React 18–compatible versions available. All the projects in this book are using React 18.

We will begin by discussing the new Root API and the new way of rendering in React 18. We will then move on to discussing the concurrent behavior of the new React. I will introduce you to the concurrent features with an emphasis on transition and Streaming server-side rendering (SSR). In the next section, we will review automatic batching using an example app. We will conclude the chapter with an overview of the updated strict mode and the new Hooks available with React 18.

This chapter will bring you up to date with the latest React features and prepare you to upgrade your existing projects.

New Root and the New Way to Render

The way we render the root component has changed now. Let's look at this change with an example. We will create an app with React 17 first. Go to `https://codesandbox.io` and create a new React sandbox. It will create the project with React 18 by default. Click the dependency box and change both `react` and `react-dom` package versions to 17.0.2. Refer to Figure 10-1.

© Hari Narayn 2022
H. Narayn, *Just React!*, https://doi.org/10.1007/978-1-4842-8294-6_10

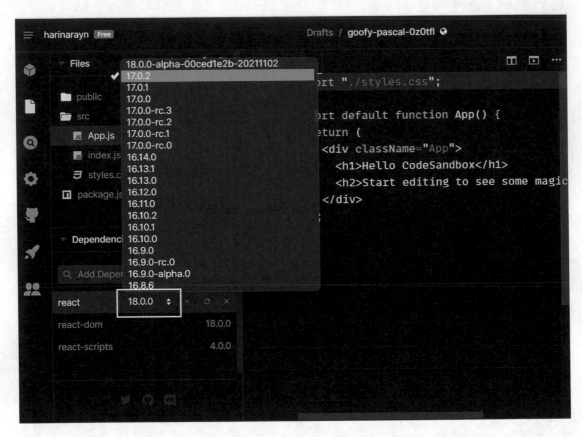

Figure 10-1. *Using React 17*

See Figure 10-2 for how I changed the version of the react package. Likewise, change the react-dom version as well to 17.0.2. Afterward, copy the code in Listing 10-1 into the index.js file and save.

Listing 10-1. index.js – React 17 Root API

```
import { StrictMode } from "react";
import ReactDOM from "react-dom";
import App from "./App";
const rootElement = document.getElementById("root");
ReactDOM.render(
  <StrictMode>
    <App />
```

```
</StrictMode>,
  rootElement
);
```

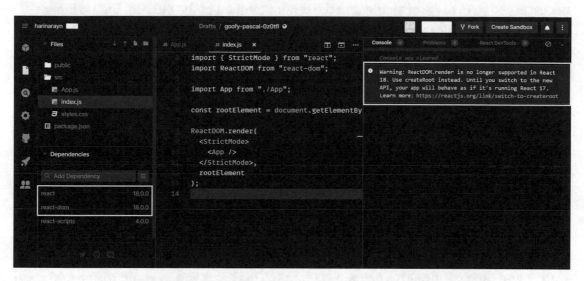

Figure 10-2. *Upgrading to React 18*

As you can see, the app is running with no issues. Now try to upgrade to React 18 by switching back the versions of the dependency packages to 18.0. A warning will appear on the console.

You can tell from the warning that ReactDOM.render is no longer supported in React 18. Instead, we need to use createRoot. Now, replace index.js with the following code in Listing 10-2.

Listing 10-2. index.js – React 18 Root API

```
import { StrictMode } from "react";
import { createRoot } from "react-dom/client";
import App from "./App";
const rootElement = document.getElementById("root");
const root = createRoot(rootElement);
root.render(
  <StrictMode>
    <App />
  </StrictMode>
);
```

Hit the refresh icon on the CodeSandbox browser. The warning has disappeared now. Compare Listings 10-1 and 10-2. You can see that the new Root API uses `ReactDOM.createRoot` as opposed to the `ReactDOM.render` in the old API. Previously, it was necessary to pass the root element to the render method in the old API, but no longer. The new API provides access to React 18's concurrent features.

React Concurrently

From React 18 onward, concurrency will become a habit of React. By upgrading to React 18 and the new Root API, we became equipped with the concurrent features of React.

Let me try to explain the concept of currency with a real-world example. Imagine a scenario where you are going to a busy restaurant for dinner and you need to finish some work for the day. You have two options. Option 1 is you can finish your meal, come home, and finish the work. This may delay your sleep. Option 2 would be to order the food and begin the work while you wait. If the food is ready before you finish the work, stop it, and then continue it once you get home. This helps you save some time and sleep a bit earlier.

In this situation, you have two tasks. Task 1 is to have dinner, and task 2 is to do the work. Task 1 is your priority, but you want to complete task 2 also on the same day. With option 1, you can complete the tasks in sequence. Using option 2, you can start task 2 while task 1 is in progress. When task 1 needs your attention, such as when the food is on your table, you can interrupt task 2 and finish task 1. After you have finished task 1, which is when you return home, you can continue task 2 from where it left off and complete it. This way, you can save some time and sleep earlier.

So option 2 here is a concurrent execution of tasks. Until now, in React, we cannot interrupt a transaction once it is started. As an example, imagine when you click a button, two state updates are made to elements A and B. React batches these state updates together. It updates the Document Object Model (DOM) once. Therefore, the user interface (UI) is rendered together for both elements. It is impossible to tell React to render element A later on. With React 18, this has changed. It introduces concurrent features. The concurrent rendering improves application performance. In the next section, let us look at the concurrent features of React 18.

React Slowly for Faster Response

By default, React renders a consistent user interface (UI). The UI renders together for all the elements. But sometimes it might be helpful to introduce an inconsistency by rendering elements at different times. Using concurrent rendering, we can bring in this inconsistent UI rendering. React 18 introduces the concurrent features of transition and deferring.

UI updates can be classified into two categories: urgent and non-urgent. Sometimes, the urgent ones are light, and the non-urgent ones are heavy. The non-urgent ones can be put on hold while the urgent ones can go ahead. This makes the app more responsive and efficient. We can make this possible by using an API called `startTransition`. Non-urgent updates are called transitions.

Let me explain by creating an example. We will create an app where the user can search for a keyword and it returns approx. 10000 results. We will set random text to return 10000 random results. Copy the following code to the App.js of the app that we created before.

In this example, we will create an app that allows users to search for a keyword and it returns 10000 results. We will set random text for each result. Go to CodeSandbox and open the app, which we created earlier in section "New Root and the New Way to Render," or create a new Sandbox app. Copy the following code in Listing 10-3 into the `App.js`.

Listing 10-3. App.js – Before Transition

```
import "./styles.css";
import { useState} from "react";
export default function App() {
  const [text, setText] = useState("");
  const [result, setResult] = useState();
  const handleChange = (event) => {
    const searchedFor = event.target.value;
    setText(searchedFor);
    const results = Array.from(Array(10000), (_, index) => {
      const randomTextPara1 = [...Array(100)]
        .map((i) => (~~(Math.random() * 36)).toString(36))
        .join("");
```

```
    const randomTextPara2 = [...Array(100)]
      .map((i) => (~~(Math.random() * 36)).toString(36))
      .join("");
    return (
      <li key={index}>
        <h3>Result {index + 1}:</h3>

        <p>
          <strong>{searchedFor}</strong> - {randomTextPara1}
        </p>
        <p>{randomTextPara2} </p>
      </li>
    );
  });
  setResult(<ul>{results}</ul>);
};

return (
  <>
    <input type="text" value={text} onChange={handleChange} />
    {result}
  </>
);
}
```

In this app, we have a text box where the user can enter a keyword. Once the user enters it, we are setting the state so that the text appears in the text box. Afterward, we are doing a dummy search by creating an array of 10000 random results. In each result, there are two paragraphs containing 100 words each. Finally, it sets the results value as a menu list to the state variable result. We display this menu list next to the search text box.

Imagine you want to search for "React." When you type in "R," you cannot see the search results immediately, since it will take time to finish looping through 10000 items. You are okay with that, because you only want to see the results after you typed in the whole word "React" and you don't mind waiting a few seconds after that to see the results.

However, you want to see the characters as and when you type them in, and that is not happening because of React's consistent UI behavior. Results menu list rendering isn't complete, so it doesn't render the text box either. The heavy and non-urgent UI update here is the search results. The light and the urgent UI update is displaying the typed-in characters in the text box. Despite the light nature of the urgent update, the wait on the heavy UI update slows it down.

Here is where the startTransition API can jump in and help. Update the import statement in App.js to include startTransition:

```
import { useState, startTransition } from "react";
```

Next, wrap the result state update inside the startTransition method like this. This will tell React to consider it non-urgent:

```
startTransition(() => {
  setResult(<ul>{results}</ul>);
});
```

React will interrupt this update when the user types the next character, and it will render the portion of the UI that has already been updated. Here, it will display the updated text box value since its state has already been updated.

If you go back to the screen and type "React" or any other word, you can see the characters as you type. After a few seconds of wait, the results will appear. What if we want to let the user know that the search results are loading during the wait?

For this, there is a Hook called useTransition. Let's add that. We can extract a variable called isPending from this Hook, and we can also extract the startTransition method from it. Let's update App.js. Update the import statement to remove the startTransition method and add the useTransition Hook:

```
import { useState, useTransition } from "react";
```

Add the following declaration above the existing state variable declarations:

```
const [isPending, startTransition] = useTransition();
```

Now, update the return statement to include a paragraph element with a loading message:

```
return (
  <>
  <input type="text" value={text} onChange={handleChange} />
    {isPending && (
      <p>
        <strong>The results are loading...</strong>
      </p>
    )}
    {!isPending && result}
  </>
);
}
```

That's all. Now you can see the loading message until the search results appear. Once the results appear, the message disappears. The isPending variable will be false until the results load, and it will be true once the results complete loading.

Figure 10-3 shows the code execution in CodeSandbox.

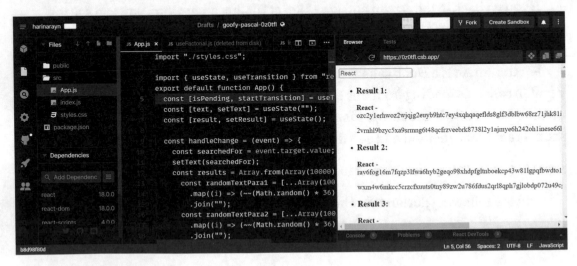

Figure 10-3. *Transition API and Hook*

Note   You can view the entire App component code with transition under Chapter 10 ➤ Projects ➤ 4. Transition folder of the GitHub repo (`https://github.com/Apress/Just_React`).

The `useDeferredValue` hook is another concurrent feature of React 18. Using it, you can defer the value of a state variable for a certain period. Until then, React displays the old value of the variable:

```
import { useDeferredValue } from 'react';
const deferredValue = useDeferredValue(value, {
  timeoutMs: 5000
});
```

Server on Suspense

Suspense-based server-side rendering (SSR) is one of the key features of React 18, which can greatly improve performance of applications.

With client-side rendering (CSR) on a single-page application (SPA), to view anything on the page, we will need to wait till the whole JavaScript (JS) completes its execution on the browser. Until then, the page will be blank. For large-sized applications, the rendering takes longer, resulting in a bad user experience.

Server-side rendering is a technique where we generate HTML from React components from the server side and send it to the client. So the users will not have to wait for the client-side JavaScript to be executed as they can already see the HTML sent from the server.

Prior to React 18, in server-side rendering, it compiles the whole React app to HTML and then sends it to the client. For a large-sized application, this again causes performance issues because of the server response size and its rendering on the client side.

You may have some components of the page that can be loaded later. The new Streaming SSR feature allows you to put those components inside a Suspense component. That means the server generates HTML for the priority components first and sends it to the client. This allows the browser client to display some HTML on the page while the work is still in progress for the suspended components.

After the server has sent the initial response, the client continues to receive updates from the SSR streams. Components that have been suspended in the process are rendered on the server and streamed to the client. The app can display HTML before all the functionality is ready, and this makes the app load faster.

Note   We saw an example for Suspense in client-side rendering (CSR) in Chapter 5, section "React Lazy and Suspense." Suspense works similarly in SSR. In SSR, the `react-dom/server` APIs used to implement Suspense-based SSR are `renderToPipeableStream` and `renderToReadableStream`.

As you use SSR, you will also need to know about React Hydration. Hydration is like rendering, but different. During render, we render components to an empty DOM. During hydrate, we will have the DOM already rendered. Then, we attach functionality, such as event listeners, to the already rendered HTML in the DOM. If you use SSR, the server will render your HTML page during the initial render, and you may need to add functionality to it. The `hydrateRoot` method is used to add event listeners to the already rendered HTML. With client-side rendering (CSR), we render everything together with the render method.

Hydration works only with SSR. For example, in client-side rendering, when you are rendering initially an HTML to the DOM, you could write something like this:

```
import { StrictMode } from "react";
import { createRoot } from "react-dom/client";
import App from "./App";
const rootElement = document.getElementById("root");
const root = createRoot(rootElement);
root.render(
  <StrictMode>
    <App />
  </StrictMode>
)
```

When you use hydrate, it expects a server-rendered HTML to be already present in the DOM. Then, you can add to it using the `hydrateRoot` method like this:

```
import { StrictMode } from "react";
import { createRoot } from "react-dom/client";
```

```
import App from "./App";
const container = = document.getElementById("App");
const root= ReactDOM.hydrateRoot( container,
  <StrictMode>
    <App />
  </StrictMode>
)
```

So here the container is expected to be present. The container needs to be rendered from the server side.

Note   Here, we will not go into details about server-side rendering. The goal of this section is to provide an overview of how SSR has changed in React 18. We haven't discussed SSR in this book so far. It wasn't popular in React as there weren't many advantages. However, with React 18 introducing Streaming SSR, SSR now became a great choice for some of the React applications.

Before React 18, hydration of the whole application begins only after the client fetches the whole page from the server and rendered it. As a result, the user could only interact with the page after the whole application had been hydrated. Therefore, the user must wait for the less important components of the page before being able to interact with another component. If these lesser urgent components were slow to load, this would have a significant impact on the user.

Let's say you have an article page with an option to edit and give feedback on each article. The feedback component takes longer to load. The user wants to read and edit the article first and then add feedback. When we are using React 17 and older, the user must wait for all components to be rendered and then hydrated. It would be better if we could load the article component first and then the feedback.

When we use Streaming SSR, it allows hydration to happen step-by-step. The hydration first happens for the initially rendered components of the page. The user can then interact with those components. After the entire page has been hydrated, the user can interact with the full page.

In the preceding example, we can wrap the feedback component in a Suspense block. So we will have the article component rendered and hydrated first. Users can read and edit the article while the feedback loads. The feedback component can join a bit later. This is the efficiency brought in by Suspense-based Streaming SSR. This is one of the concurrent features of React 18.

Prior to React 18:

You must fetch everything before you can load anything.

You must load everything before you can hydrate anything.

You must hydrate everything before you can interact with anything.

React 18 Onward:

You can load something you wish before fetching everything.

You can hydrate what you loaded.

You can interact with what you hydrated.

Automatic Batching

Automatic batching is when React groups multiple state updates into a single re-render for better performance. State updates are batched together inside event handlers in React, even before React 18. For example, if you are making two or more state updates on a button click, the component gets re-rendered only once. We will create an app with a button and a span element next to it. When we click the button, the background color of the button should switch between two colors. Additionally, the span element should show how many times we clicked the button.

Set up a new sandbox in CodeSandbox. First, let us downgrade to React 17, as described in the first section. Update `react` and `react-dom` packages to 17.0.2 and copy Listing 10-1 to `index.js` because we need the old Root API code for React 17.

Update `App.js` as in Listing 10-4.

Listing 10-4. App.js – Automatic Batching, Event Handlers

```
import { useEffect, useState } from "react";
const App = () => {
  const [number, setNumber] = useState(0);
  const [bg, setBg] = useState("lightgreen");
```

```
useEffect(() => {
  if (number) console.log("The Component Rendered!");
});

const handleOnClick = () => {
  setNumber(number + 1);
  setBg((color) => !color);
};

return (
  <>
    <button
      style={{ backgroundColor: bg ? "orange" : "lightgreen" }}
      onClick={() => {
        handleOnClick();
      }}
    >
      Change Color
    </button>
    <br />
    <span>Changed color {number} times</span>
  </>
);
};
export default App;
```

In this example, we have a button changing colors between light green and orange. Also, we have a span showing the number of times we changed the button color. In the useEffect method, we log the message The Component Rendered to the console. Note that we didn't specify any dependency array to useEffect here since we need to call it after each re-render, not on first render. To skip the first render, we added a condition.

During initial render, the number will be zero, so it will skip the console log. On button click, we are changing the state of number and bg, which are two state updates. However, if you click the button and look at the console, you can observe that the component is only re-rendered once. Refer to Figure 10-4.

Figure 10-4. *Batching state updates*

Even when clicking the button multiple times, you can see that only one re-render takes place per button click. So this proves that React 17 has this automatic batching capability for event handlers.

What about other scenarios like setTimeOut or if we want to perform multiple state updates during a data retrieval from an API call like we did in Chapter 9 with Axios? Let us see an example with setTimeOut.

Add a setTimeOut function just above the return function:

```
setTimeout(() => {
    setNumber(number + 1);
    setBg((color) => !color);
}, 5000);
```

The state updates are exactly the same as the ones we did on button click. Now the color and number get changed automatically every 5 seconds. If you look at the console now, you can see that the component is re-rendered twice during each setTimeOut call. Refer to Figure 10-5.

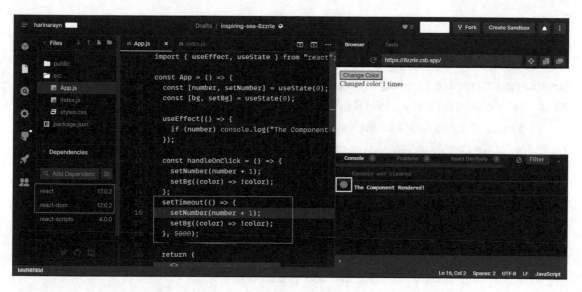

Figure 10-5. *No batching during setTimeOut*

In the older versions of React, it limited the batching capability only to event handlers. Upgrade the react and react-dom packages to React 18. Also update index.js code to reflect the new Root API. Refer to Listing 10-2 for the code reference.

Once you upgrade to React 18, you see that the state updates are now batched and the re-rendering only happens once per setTimeOut call. React 18 does batching regardless of where the state updates occur. It batches state updates in event handlers, native event handlers, setTimeOut, API callbacks, etc. See Figure 10-6.

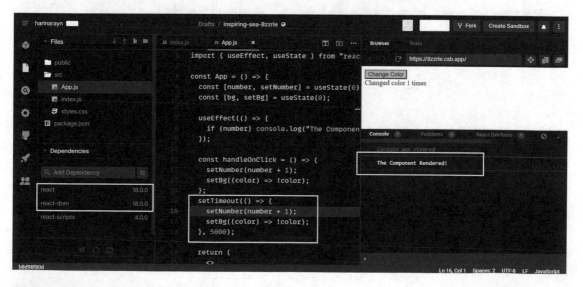

Figure 10-6. *Automatic batching in React 18*

If you keep the screen for minutes, you will observe that the number of times the color changes matches exactly with the number of times the component re-renders.

Sometimes, one state update may depend on another, and we need to re-render the page for each update. Upgrading from React 17 projects, if these scenarios exist, may cause a code break. How can we fix this?

The answer from React 18 for that is flushSync API. flushSync prevents automatic batching. If we use flushSync in a specific state update, it will trigger a re-render for that update.

Now let's change App.js to see how this works. First, import flushSync from react-dom:

```
import { flushSync } from "react-dom";
```

Then, update the setTimeOut method as follows:

```
setTimeout(() => {
  flushSync(() => {
    setNumber(number + 1);
  });
  flushSync(() => {
    setBg((color) => !color);
  });
}, 5000);
```

Now, you can see the re-rendering happens for each state update. Refer to Figure 10-7.

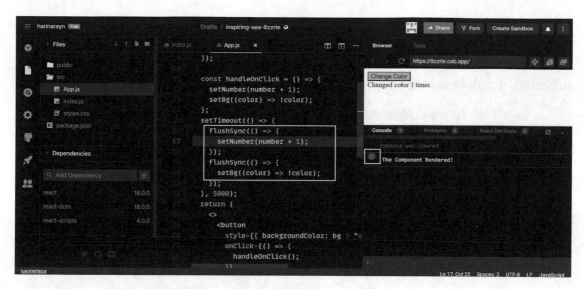

Figure 10-7. *Flushing automatic batching*

Use flushSync only in specific cases if it cannot be avoided. Otherwise, just let the amazing automatic batching feature stay.

"Too Strict" Mode

As part of React 18, it introduces a new strict mode behavior. This helps find potential side effect problems with components. These problems can be more significant with the new concurrent features, and the updated strict mode helps solve that. Components mounted for the first time arc unmounted and remounted. This restores the previous state on the second mount. The strict mode checks only run in development mode, so they will not affect production build. The strict mode, like fragments, renders no visible UI. You can see the App component wrapped in strict mode by default when you create a React 18 project.

Visit https://github.com/reactwg/react-18/discussions/19#:~:text=With%20 the%20release%20of%20React,mount%20)%20for%20newly%20mounted%20components for detailed discussion on this subject.

New "Hookies"

Besides useTransition and useDeferredValue we discussed, there are three more Hooks introduced with React 18:

1. *useId*: As we discussed before, there are changes to server-side rendering with React 18. The server sends priority HTML first based on how we set Suspense, and the hydration also happens in steps. In order to avoid hydration mismatches, we need to generate unique IDs on both the server and the client. The useId hook can be used for this.

2. *useSyncExternalStore*: React 18 introduces a potential issue called tearing. Tearing means that the UI shows different values for the same state because of the concurrent rendering. When we work with an external state management tool like the Redux store, the UI may show two different values for the same data. Tearing can occur when we wrap a store update with the startTransition method. The useSyncExternalStore hook eliminates this issue by forcing updates to the store to be synchronous. This Hook is recommended for any library that integrates with state external to React.

3. *useInsertionEffect*: CSS-in-JS libraries may generate new style rules that they intend to insert into <style> tags in the DOM. With React 18, these injections may cause issues because of the concurrent rendering since React interacts with the browser before the rendering process is complete. The useInsertionEffect resolves this problem. This hook runs concurrently with the DOM rendering and is called before the browser displays changes to the DOM. The Hook is used to insert global DOM nodes such as <style>. The useInsertionEffect is intended for CSS-in-JS libraries, such as Styled Components. So you may rarely use this Hook in real-time projects.

Note   You can visit the GitHub repository to view the project code at the end of each chapter. You can access the repository via the book's product page, `https://github.com/Apress/Just_React`. All the code sections used in this chapter are located under Chapter 10 ➤ Projects.

Summary

The chapter's focus was on the new features of React 18, which is mainly a performance upgrade to React. We learned how React 18 differs from older versions and how to upgrade. In this chapter, we learned about the new Root API and discussed the new rendering method. We talked about concurrency and the new concurrent features React 18 brings to the table. Next, we covered the useTransition hook and startTransition API with a detailed example. Then, we discussed the new server-side rendering feature of React 18. Last, we discussed automatic batching and how it can improve the performance of React applications.

So I'm just going to stop reacting for now. Thank you! We discussed nearly all the features of React with examples. Hope you enjoyed learning with this book and that it can be a *use*ful reference for you while developing React applications. You can contact me at Just React Q&A (`https://jrhn22.wordpress.com`) if you have any questions on this book or on React. Just leave a comment, and I will be more than happy to respond.

No doubt, React will dominate the present and future of web development. It is simple and efficient. As you keep on reacting, I'm sure you'll have something to take away from this book! Just React, and keep learning React the React way!

Index

A

addEventListener() method, 33

addNewTask, 337, 339

Airbnb.com, 14

Angular, 13, 330

App component, 9, 68–71, 85, 91, 122, 124, 125, 134, 145, 165, 167, 185, 219, 230, 249, 251, 273, 282, 294, 319, 359

App.js, 301, 319, 330, 337, 347, 349, 354, 358

Application Programming Interface (API), 46, 155, 186, 299, 330, 334, 340, 344, 346, 347, 350, 356, 357

App.module.scss, 236

appStyles object, 227

Arrow functions, 34–37, 106, 200

Asynchronous programming, 43, 46

authButtonText, 318

Auth component, 314, 319, 323, 324

Authentication, 299, 304, 305, 317

Authorization, 304, 329

Automatic batching, 354, 358, 359, 361

Availability Check button, 171, 304, 324, 327, 328

Axios library, 299, 304, 305, 311, 313, 317, 322, 330, 334, 341

B

Babel, 52, 60–62, 71, 72

Backend-as-a-Service (BaaS), 299, 304

backgroundColor, 216, 218

bookName variable, 23

BrowserRouter, 302

Built-in browser functions, 29

C

Callback function, 34, 35, 175, 178, 289, 290, 296

Cascading Style Sheets (CSS), 1, 75, 76, 214, 215

  App.css, 221

  child elements, 222

  classes defining, 219

  description, 219

  FoodOrder.js, 221

  issues, 220

  overriding, 220

  class selFoodTitle, 221

  styling, 219

  subTitle classes, 222

cd just-react command, 67

changeContent function, 5, 10

Child component, 85, 90, 91, 95, 126, 150, 246, 294

Chrome browser, 191, 205, 210

Chrome developer tools, 150, 191, 192, 209, 214, 235

Chrome Reacts, 191–194

className keyword, 76, 77

Client-side rendering (CSR), 351, 352

CodeSandbox, 231, 232, 234, 241, 244, 248, 250, 252, 255, 258, 261, 263, 265, 269, 273, 280, 291, 295, 300, 330, 332, 340, 346, 347, 350, 354

Code splitting, 149, 189
  coverage, 152, 154
  definition, 150

CompleteSignInOrSignUp method, 318

Component-based style, 218

ComponentDidMount, 244, 246, 247, 249, 256, 258

componentWillUnmount() method, 246

Conditional rendering, 97, 100, 324

Console reactions, 197–200

Context API, 126, 147, 273, 334, 335, 340

convertCase module, 39, 41

Coverage, 150–154

createContext, 187

create-react-app command, 51–53, 65, 66, 69, 161, 232

CSS-in-JS pattern, 215, 218, 230
  attribute names, 216
  description, 216
  mode styling, 216
  styling, 217

CSS module–generated classes, 229

CSS modules
  App.js, 226
  appStyles object, 227
  autogeneration, 226
  class names, 226, 228
  FoodOrder components, 230
  global scope issue resolving, 230
  implementation, 227, 228
  class subTitle, 229

CSS Object Model (CSSOM) tree, 4

CSS's global nature, 220

Custom hooks, 241, 294–298

D

Data types, 21–23

Debug React code, 195–197

DetailsList element, 120

display function, 44, 47

div element, 2, 4, 19, 68, 86, 227, 318

Document Object Model (DOM), 3, 4, 82–84, 243, 246, 262, 265, 266, 294, 346

DOM-based system, 13

DOM manipulation, 6

DOM Update Using React, 9

E

ECMAScript, 17

Edit implementation, 142

Elements tab, 5, 192, 193

element.style block, 194

EnrolList component, 120, 122, 128, 139, 154, 160

EnrolmentForm component, 85, 87, 89, 91, 93, 96, 99, 122, 125, 130, 155, 160

Error boundaries, 200, 204

ErrorFunctionalBoundary component, 201, 204, 206

ErrorFunctionalBoundary.js, 200

Events, 33–34

F

Facebook, 1, 13, 304, 330

findIndex function, 140

Firebase
  app config, 308
  authentication component and logOut method, 322

Baas, 304
configuration, 305
database, creation, 306
firebase.js, 308
initializeApp method, 311
just-food app, 325
logOut method, 312
setting up authentication methods, 305
setting up the app, 307
signIn method, 311
sign-up method, 311
Firebase packages, 310
Flamegraph tab, 207, 208
Fluent UI element, 117
flushSync API, 358
foodItemsContext, 187
FoodOrder component, 187, 188
FoodOrder.js, 172, 186, 187, 195, 197, 198, 201, 211
Food Shop app, 273, 276, 278
passing context, 278
passing props, 276
Functional component, 70, 71, 78, 200, 214, 256, 261

G

getContent function, 44, 46–48
getElementById, 7
getPublisher method, 42

H

handleChange function, 132, 144, 145
handleClick function, 71, 74, 112, 123, 127, 130, 135–138, 144, 157, 176, 186, 187, 195, 291, 339
handleEdit function, 137, 144, 158

handleItemSelection function, 131–133, 157
handleQuantityChange function, 175, 197, 199, 201
handleSubmit function, 81, 93, 99, 112
HashRouter, 302
Higher-order component (HOC), 243, 279, 294
Hookie, 277, 294, 295, 360
Hooks
life of a function and birth, 250–253
transition API, 350
useContext, 273–278
useEffect, 256–262
useId, 360
useInsertionEffect, 360
useReducer, 267–274
useRef, 262–266
useState, 253–255
useSyncExternalStore, 360
html-webpack-plugin, 58, 60
hydrateRoot method, 352
Hydration, 352, 353, 360
HyperText Markup Language (HTML), 1, 2
with CSS, 1
element, 2, 192, 193
file, 19
with JavaScript, 4
Hypertext Transfer Protocol (HTTP)
requests, 299, 330, 333, 334, 341

I

import keyword, 39, 40
index.js, 57, 60, 69, 318, 339, 340, 344, 345, 354, 357
init command, 53, 55
Inline styling, 216, 230

Instructions, 8, 14
isChooseFoodPage, 169, 323
isErrorCatched, 201, 206
isLapOrDesktop, 236, 239
isNewUser, 317, 318
isRestoreSeats variable, 142, 144, 145
isUGChecked variable, 142, 143

J, K

JavaScript Extensible Markup Language
    (JSX), 8, 51, 60, 69, 71–72, 74, 76,
    81, 138, 167–169, 175, 187, 192,
    201, 277, 318, 324, 339
JavaScript function, 8, 279
JavaScript (JS), 1, 4
JS module, 38, 40, 41
JSX expression, 167, 169
just-food app, 189, 191, 205, 220
    app design with context, 188
    app design without context, 188
Just-food project, 216, 299, 304, 307, 308, 341
just-react project, 150, 155, 157

L

launch.json, 209–211
Lazy function, 149, 150, 153
liApp class, 194, 222
for loop, 27, 28, 119, 124

M

map() function, 31–33
mapStateToProps function, 339, 340
Material UI (MUI), 233, 234, 241
Memorization techniques, 243, 278, 279,
    285, 289, 296, 298

memorizedData array, 279
Metadata, 3
Multi-page application (MPA), 13–15
Multi-view react App
    App.css, 163, 164, 169
    App.js, 161, 167, 168
    Availability Check, 169, 172
    callback function, 178
    enrolment project, 185
    FoodOrder component, 161, 172,
        176, 179
    FoodOrder.css, 180
    FoodOrder tag, 178
    Foods.css, 169
    Foods.js, 166
    handleClick function, 176
    handleQuantityChange function, 175
    handleSelect function, 179
    images, 166
    isChooseFoodPage, 169
    IsOrdered variable, 176
    menuItems object array, 163, 165
    npm start, 171, 183
    npx create-react-app just-food, 161
    orderQuantity parameters, 180
    props, 167
    props drilling issue, 185
    props.updateQuantity, 176
    React fragment, 167
    return function, 169
    selectedFood, 175, 178
    SPAs, 161
    state variable, 168
    static app, 165
    totalAmount, 175
    updateMenuItemQuantity function,
        179, 180

N

newRef, 262
nextBook object, 25, 26
Node-sass library, 223
Node Package Manager (npm), 54
npm install styled-components, 217
npm start, 150, 160
Node Package Execute (npx), 66

O

Object-oriented programming (OOP), 41
onChange function, 107, 204
onChange property, 199
onClick event, 5, 33, 40, 111, 130, 131, 137, 138, 179
onSubmit event, 81, 111
Order Food page, 172, 300, 304, 323, 326

P, Q

Passwords, 304, 311, 318, 325, 330
p elements, 2, 5, 7, 9, 10
Plain JavaScript (vanilla JS), 7, 8, 10, 11, 16, 77, 78, 83, 334
Primitive types, 23
printYear function, 36
Profiling, 214
Props, 85, 96
Props drilling
    App component, 157
    component code modifications, 155
    component interactions, 155
    component tree, 155
    definition, 154
    EnrolList component, 155
    EnrolmentForm component, 155, 159

EnrolmentForm.js update, 156
    handleEdit function, 158
    just-react project, 155
    parameters, 156
    passing, 156
    program parameter, 157
    program property, 158
    setSelectedProgram function, 159
    useEffect method, 159
Props drilling issue, 186
pwa-chrome, 210

R

React
    vs. angular, 13
    JavaScript library, 1
    performance, 7
    props drilling issues (*see* Props drilling)
    SPAs and MPAs, 16
    UI components, 1, 12
    update, 11
    Virtual DOM, 7
React 17, 343, 344, 353, 354, 356, 358
React 18, 343, 345–347, 351, 357, 359, 360
ReactBook class, 42
React Context, 149, 155, 185–189
React developer tools
    Add extension, 205
    commit filter, 209
    commits, 208
    Components tab, 205, 206
    component trees, 205
    ErrorFunctionalBoundary
        component, 206
    Profiler, 206
    profiling, 207

React developer tools (*cont.*)
    profiling data, 208
    Ranked, 208, 209
    renders, 208
React DevTools, 191–209, 276, 278
React.lazy() function, 152
React Memo, 243, 279, 285, 287, 289
React Memo HOC, 285
React Profiler capabilities, 209
React project, 52
    Babel, 60–62
    build and run, 63–65
    create index files, 57, 58
    dynamic list, 126
    edit, 135
    form, 74, 116
    initialize, 53, 54
    inputs, 72–74
    install react/react-dom, 55, 56
    State, 77–79, 82
    static list, 121
    Webpack, 58–60
react-responsive package, 235, 236, 241
React Router, 299, 302, 303
Rebuild, 149
Redesign, 149, 185
Redux, 126, 334–338, 340, 341, 343, 360
Redux's foundation, 334
Redux store, 335, 337, 360
Reference types, 23–24
Register app, 307
Responsive design, 234, 235, 239, 240
Responsive React, 234–237
REST APIs, 299, 341
Restructure, 149
Rethink, 149, 189
Routes, 302, 303, 318, 319
Routing, 299, 300, 302, 303, 308, 317, 319, 341

S

Sassy CSS (SCSS), 215, 222–226
script tag, 4, 5
SCSS-based styling, 241
SCSS modules, 226, 230
Server-side rendering (SSR), 343, 351, 353, 360
setFirstName function, 79, 80
setMenuItems function, 163, 180
setTimeOut() function, 34, 35, 37, 45, 47, 356–358
setUpdatedSeats function, 93, 94, 99
Show Coverage, 150, 151
Single-page application (SPA), 13–16, 149, 150, 154, 161, 351
Single-page websites, 14
Slow network, 153
split function, 31
startTransition API, 347, 349, 360, 361
Streaming SSR, 343, 351–354
Strict mode, 359
Styled Components, 217–219, 230, 241, 360
Subclassing, 43
Superfunctional app, 215
Suspense-based SSR, 351, 352, 354
Suspense component, 149, 150, 153, 351
Swap case function, 29, 30
Synchronous programming, 43
Syntactically Awesome Style Sheets (SASS), 222–226

T

Tags, 2
Template literals, 48, 49
Third-party libraries, 226, 231
Time component, 246–252, 256, 259

Toggle button, 216

toggleButtonStyles variable, 218

Transitions, 343, 347, 350

Try-catch sections, 204

Try-catch blocks, 200, 201

U

UI updates, 347

ul (ulApp), 222

updateMenuItemQuantity function, 179, 180, 186

updateQuantity property, 176, 180, 186

useAuthState hook, 317, 322

useCallback, 243, 278, 285, 289–293

useCallback() hook, 289, 292

useContext hook, 149, 187, 189, 273, 277, 298

useDebugValue hook, 294

useDeferredValue hook, 351, 360

useEffect function, 124, 159, 256–261, 294, 355

useId hook, 360

useImperativeHandle hook, 294

useInsertionEffect, 360

useLayoutEffect, 294

useMediaQuery, 235, 236

useNavigate hook, 317, 322

useReducer hook, 266–273, 298

useRef hook, 243, 262–267, 294, 298

User interface (UI), 13, 346, 347

useState hook, 187, 241, 253–255, 261, 262, 266, 267, 270

useSyncExternalStore hook, 360

useTransition hook, 349, 360, 361

V

Variables, 20–23, 60, 79, 80, 122, 137

Virtual DOM, 7, 10, 82–84, 101

Visual Studio Code (VS Code), 17, 18, 191, 227

    Extensions, 103

    restructuring, 104, 110

    terminal, 52

VS Code, built-in debugging

    breakpoint, 213

    Debug Console, 212

    environment selection, 210

    FoodOrder.js, 211

    handleQuantityChange function, 211

    handleSelect function, 212

    launch.json, 209–211

    point-in-time variable, 213

W, X, Y, Z

Webpack bundles, 60, 150

Webpack packages, 58, 59

welcomeMessage variable, 81

Wrapper elements, 3

Printed in the United States
by Baker & Taylor Publisher Services